THE FIRST

XI

WINNING ORGANISATIONS IN AUSTRALIA

THE FIRST

XI

WINNING ORGANISATIONS IN AUSTRALIA

GRAHAM HUBBARD, DELYTH SAMUEL,
SIMON HEAP AND GRAEME COCKS

WILEY

John Wiley & Sons Australia, Ltd

First published 2002 by
John Wiley & Sons Australia, Ltd
33 Park Road, Milton, Qld 4064

Offices also in Sydney and Melbourne

Typeset in 12.5/14pt Vittate

© G. & J. Hubbard Services P/L, Delyth Samuel, ERU Consulting and Productive Workplaces P/L.

National Library of Australia
Cataloguing-in-Publication data

The first XI : winning organisations in Australia.
Bibliography.
Includes index.
ISBN 1 74031 065 9.
1. Organizational effectiveness. 2. Success in business - Australia. 3. Management - Australia. I. Hubbard, Graham. II. Title : First 11. III. Title : First eleven.
658.400994

Cover design by Rob Cowpe

Reprinted October 2003

Acknowledgement
Extracts from *Built to Last: Successful Habits of Visionary Companies* by J. Collins & J. Porras, published by Century Business Books. Reprinted by permission of The Random House Group Ltd.

Printed in Australia by McPherson's Printing Group
10 9 8 7 6 5 4 3 2

Disclaimer
The material in this publication is of the nature of general comment only, and neither purports nor intends to be advice. Readers should not act on the basis of any matter in this publication without considering (and if appropriate, taking) professional advice with due regard to their own particular circumstances. The authors and publisher expressly disclaim all and any liability to any person, whether a purchaser of this publication or not, in respect of anything and of the consequences of anything done or omitted to be done by any such person in reliance, whether whole or partial, upon the whole or any part of the contents of this publication.

Contents

Acknowledgements

This project would not have been possible without the support of many people, all of whom played important roles in putting the pieces of this jigsaw puzzle together. We thank them all.

To Mt Eliza Business School for providing research funding and time to develop this project.

For assistance with our research and findings: Murray Ainsworth, Gail Avard, Robert Belleville, Carole Christopherson, Ray Cotsell, Lynette Francis, John Harvey, Terry Heap, Lan Huong, Andrew Hubbard, Judy Hubbard, Michael Hubbard, Shahebaz Khan, Josephine Maio, Gerry Moriarty, Bruce McKern, Paul Mills, Judith Mitchell, Margaret Nash, Leeanne O'Connor, Gary Pemberton, Jerry Porras, Janette Quinn, Adam Steen and Mark Suares.

To all those respondents who answered the initial questionnaires and to our MBA and executive students who assisted us with our search for possible winning organisations.

To our interviewees and their organisations for providing their time and assistance: Michael Angwin, Margaret Armstrong, Fiona Balfour, Roger Bamber, Tom Barlow, Robin Batterham, Gail Burke, Robert Burns, Matthew Butlin, Peter Callender, David Clarke, Roger Corbett, Barry Cusack, Bev Davis, Douglas Davis, Andrew Downe, Tim Duncan, Kim Edwards, Paul Edwards, David Forsyth, Peter Hanley, Peter Hughes, Mark Johnson, John Jeffrey, Hayden Kelly, Narendra Kumar, Megan Lane, Stuart Lee, Michael Lin, Andrew Lockwood, Ian MacDonald, Peter McKinnon, Garth McKenzie, Sandra McPhee, Roland Matrenza, Nick Minogue, Nicholas Moore, Allan Moss, Alan Oster, Ross Pinney, Bob Prowse, Gary Reid, Michael Rocca, Bill Scales, Richard Sheppard, Michael Sharpe, Greg Smith, John Stanhope, Peter Stansfeld, John Staite, Les Strong, Brian Thomas, Phil Young.

For assistance with publication: Vanessa Battersby, Lesley Beaumont, Anna Clemann, Benjamin Cocks, Josie Gibson, Ronnie Gramazio, Brenda Harkness, Jennifer Hodge, Wendy Morell and Anthony Stone.

Foreword

Australia has been through a period of unprecedented change over the last 20 years. Decision-makers in organisations of all types and sizes have been exposed to a barrage of management fads and concepts, yet the principles of good organisational practice seem to keep recurring.

In 1999, Mt Eliza Business School decided to fund a ground-breaking three-year research project into 'winning' Australian organisational practice, seeking answers to the questions, 'Who are the best organisations over the long term in Australia and what are their practices?' We saw this work as valuable not only to Australian business but also to provide rigour for our own thinking, learning and teaching about how organisations do succeed in Australia. Of all the practices organisations and executives might focus on, which ones distinguish the best?

The research is based on the *Built to Last* methodology, an internationally acclaimed piece of research, but it also takes account of the unique aspects of the Australian business and social environment. Based on analysis of organisations which have existed for at least 20 years, it seeks timeless principles of 'winning' rather than the hype related to any current fads or fashions.

The unique findings of this thought-provoking research justify the investment which the School has made. The nine principles which the research team has identified, the sub-factors behind each of the principles and the 'myths' of current practice which are exploded will provide rich food for thought for all thinking senior executives. Virtually none of the management fads are recognised in these principles as being important.

This is not a simple follow-the-dots recipe. 'Winning' is hard work. It is complex. It takes time. But it is rewarding. Australia needs more leaders and organisations which are prepared to learn from others, seek alignment and execute effectively if this country is to take advantage of the international opportunities, while coping with the increasing threats of international competitors.

Importantly, the research focuses deliberately on 'organisations', not just businesses. Government organisations and not-for-profits need good organisational practices just as much as commercially-focused businesses.

The book highlights the fundamental drivers of sustainable winning organisations so that the lessons learned from them can be evaluated and adapted by others. The research also highlights how limited our competitive and international experience is as a country. The speed with which the Australian economic environment has changed is laid out clearly. A framework for thinking about the 'strategic cycle' of development for an organisation will put into context many of the difficulties which Australian organisations experience as they venture overseas, as they must in an internationalising world.

Every thinking board member, CEO, senior manager, would-be manager, consultant and business student should read this book. It is a book to be kept close by, for frequent reference over time. It is a book that will stimulate earnest conversation, reflection and action by leadership teams throughout the country. It is a book that can help Australian management and organisations to raise their standards. It is a book that will become part of the heritage of this country's management scholarship. It is a research-based book that is highly readable. It is a book that reflects the best of what Mt Eliza Business School offers in its development programs for individuals and organisations. We are proud of this work. I commend it to you.

John Harvey
Chief Executive Officer
Mt Eliza Business School

Preface

The genesis of this project was in 1992 when Graham Hubbard accepted a visiting professorship position at the University of Minnesota. Frustrated with the inability of both MBAs and executives in Australia to be able to classify or determine which organisations were performing well, he began researching how organisations actually measured 'performance'.

Over the next three years, through three empirical research projects in the US and then back in Australia, Graham concluded that 'performance' was little understood, even within organisations. Yet, for a strategist, organisational performance is the key result area. Organisational performance simply must be understood if we are to highlight 'high-performing' organisations and try to understand what makes them tick.

In 1994, *Built to Last* was published. Following the 1982 publication of *In Search of Excellence,* this book focused Graham's mind. Reinforced by a client company which was also galvanised by *Built to Last*'s findings, Graham wanted to conduct a 'built to last' for Australia to answer two burning questions:

- Which were the high-performing organisations in Australia?
- What were the organisational practices that set them apart?

The opportunity to pursue the idea did not come until 1999, when Graham moved to Mt Eliza Business School and got support from the School to begin this project. The research team was then developed. Delyth and Simon joined the project on graduating from the MBA program. Delyth's background in technology, innovation and international competitiveness and Simon's in marketing and consulting complemented Graham's expertise in strategic management and accounting. Graeme, with 20 years' practical experience in technology, executive roles, operations and change management, joined Mt Eliza Business School and the project shortly afterwards. The team was deliberately structured to include people from a variety of backgrounds, with wide experience and strong opinions, yet who were team players.

We believe this project goes a long way towards providing answers to the two questions. We have identified nine principles of organisational life that lead to 'winning'. We believe these principles, if applied properly to most organisations, would see an enormous improvement in the quality of organisational outcomes in Australia. Indeed, further, we believe that we know what is needed to be a winner. But how difficult it is to apply it!

We do not believe, however, that the 11 organisations identified here, the 'First XI', are the only 'winning organisations' in Australia. Indeed, we feel major sectors of Australian organisational life – all except the public-listed sector – are under-represented. But at least we have made a start and found, tested and highlighted some organisations grown in Australia which have succeeded over long periods.

We hope the principles and the specific examples from the winning organisations identified here will provide leadership teams and individual leaders with the inspiration and a practical framework for improving their organisational practice, and consequently their organisational performance.

But we warn readers – this book is not about easy fixes. The ideas here are complex. They take time to develop, to implement and to realise. Becoming a winning organisation is not something that happens in 12 months, or even in several years. It takes time. It is difficult. But it can be done. And it can be done by any organisation, wherever it begins its life, and whatever industry it is in. There is hope! Do you want to commit yourself to pursue 'winning'?

We believe that the principles of 'winning' are pretty timeless! There are differences between our findings and those of *In Search of Excellence* and *Built to Last*, but the similarities are much greater than the differences. And virtually none of the fads are important or recognised in these principles.

It is timely that this book captures the fundamental drivers of sustainable winning organisations, so that the lessons learned from them can be evaluated and adapted by others. In this way, we hope that more organisations in Australia will be successful so our people, communities and society will prosper and share in the wealth and knowledge that follows success. The message we bring is that the existence of winners does not mean there must be losers.

Graham Hubbard (ghubbard@mteliza.com.au)
Delyth Samuel (d.samuel@muprivate.edu.au)
Simon Heap (simon@simonheap.com)
Graeme Cocks (gcocks@mteliza.com.au)
October 2002

About the authors

Graham Hubbard

Graham Hubbard is Professor of Strategic Management at Mt Eliza Business School where he teaches on local and international MBA programs and undertakes and supervises research in the area of strategic management. He is the author or co-author of 11 books mainly in the area of strategy, concentrating particularly on strategy in the Australian context. Graham consults widely and has written many case studies, mainly on Australian organisations. He has also taught at University of Minnesota and Cranfield University overseas and Melbourne, Monash, Adelaide, RMIT, Deakin, and Swinburne in Australia.

Delyth Samuel

Delyth Samuel is a strategist focusing on competitive business strategy, innovation and technology management. With a PhD in textile technology (Leeds, UK), she also recently completed her MBA from Mt Eliza Business School (Melbourne). Her business career includes key roles in textile manufacturing and research and development programs and project management, encompassing the entire value chain from production through processing for one of Australia's premier export commodities. More recently she has undertaken strategy and research consultancy assignments with leading organisations in the corporate and public sectors.

Simon Heap

Simon Heap is an Australian Business Evolutionist. He has been a disciple of 'excellence' from an early age, initially in professional sport through his membership in the Australian national ski team, then later in business. Simon's main focus is the evolution of successful organisations. He is a Director of ERU Consulting Group and advises organisations globally on how to improve their performance. Simon is also engaged by GS-Advisors, a London-based boutique corporate finance consultancy, for which he advises on organisational strategy and value enhancement. Visit Simon at www.simonheap.com

Graeme Cocks

Graeme Cocks is a member of the MBA faculty at Mt Eliza Business School and is a specialist in business integration, project management, corporate restructuring and change management. He has over 20 years of practical experience in executive management and international roles in a range of public interest and commercial enterprises. Graeme's development interests include deployment of business strategy, performance management and strategies to achieve sustainable organisational excellence.

1

'WINNING': A JOURNEY, NOT JUST AN OUTCOME

THE AIMS OF THIS BOOK

Despite the tremendous amount of media coverage of business in Australia, there is little agreement about which are the best organisations in Australia and what practices they have followed to become the best. In these times, when organisations face an increasingly turbulent international world of competition, Australian businesspeople and Australian organisations need to know and understand how to win, and win in the long term, not just how to shine briefly and then fade away.

This book sets out to answer these two questions:

1. What are the 'winning' organisations in Australia?
2. What do they do to be winners?

From this book, you will come to understand what it takes to be a winning organisation in Australia. Hopefully, if more organisations seek out the recipe for winning, we'll have better organisational performance, and better organisations, in Australia. And that would be good for everybody – shareholders, employees, customers, governments, suppliers, managers and local communities. It's not easy, but it *is* possible.

However, the questions are difficult and the answers have taken some time to develop. In this chapter, we explain how we went about addressing these questions. We take you on our three-year journey to find and understand the answers.

As a result of the research we also explode some myths which exist – the common practices which organisations are following which *do not* lead to success.

Then we provide the *framework* we have developed to explain winning in Australia. Lastly, we show that organisations undergo a *strategic cycle* – each stage of which requires different sets of capabilities for success.

BEGINNINGS OF THE PROJECT

This project began in the late 1980s, when several strategists in Australia began to think about what organisations had to do to succeed in Australia and whether and how that was different from other countries.

1. Developing management principles for Australia

In the early 1990s, three key developments provided the foundations for this project (see Figure 1.1). First, during the 1990s a series of authors and groups wrote about the Australian business landscape and also wrote case studies of Australian organisations. These works provided general frameworks for strategic management and some detailed examples of successful role models. The Australian Manufacturing Council produced *The Global Challenge* in 1990 and *Leading the Way* in 1992 to indicate generally how Australian organisations might compete and what the challenges were for them. Lewis, Morkel and Hubbard (1991–98), Viljoen (1991–94) and Hubbard, Taylor and Pocknee (1996) were some who developed early comprehensive Australian strategic management texts for business executives.

During this period, too, Australian organisations were turning to the quality movement to understand and absorb its principles and apply them to organisational processes, in order to contend with international competitors. The Australian Quality Council produced a framework for assessment for the Australian Quality Awards which helped many organisations to improve their processes.

Figure 1.1 – The foundations of the research

Research into management/strategic management practices/challenges in Australia		
Australian Manufacturing Council 1990–94	Strategic Management: Lewis, Morkel & Hubbard 1991–98 Viljoen 1991–94 Hubbard, Pocknee and Taylor 1996	Australian Quality Council 1991 onwards (now Australian Business Excellence Framework)

Research on measuring organisational performance	Which are Australia's high-performing organisations and why?	Research on identifying high performance
Performance Cube Hubbard 1994–96 Balanced Scorecard Kaplan & Norton 1992–96		In Search of Excellence Peters & Waterman 1982 Built to Last Collins & Porras 1994

2. How to measure organisational performance

Second, at this time the balanced scorecard model of measuring organisational performance was developed by Kaplan and Norton. This provided a four-sector method of measuring performance – measuring financial, market, internal efficiency, and long-term growth and innovation performance – rather than simply measuring financial performance. The model was favourably received by managers, who felt it represented what was intuitively important to them in managerial practice.

At about the same time, insights into empirical research conducted in Australia and overseas by Hubbard (1996) led to the development of the 'performance cube' model for assessing the organisational performance of any organisation in any industry at any time. The model provided a way of thinking about how to measure 'success' for all types of organisations, not just those listed on the sharemarket.

3. How to assess winning organisations overseas

Third, in 1994, Collins and Porras published *Built to Last*, which identified 18 high-performing companies (17 from the US plus Sony) and the common factors which Collins and Porras thought were the key to their success. This book excited Australian executives who read it. It seemed to hit a lot of the key issues which managers felt were important but that were too subtle to be picked up in standard management literature.

Built to Last advanced Peters and Waterman's seminal 1982 book *In Search of Excellence*, which also identified a group of excellent American companies and their key management practices. Its methodology was clearly laid out, it appeared to be based on objective evidence and it appeared to be very thorough, with the authors and their large research team having spent six years on the work. A key element that gave the book credibility was that it started with CEOs' opinions of high-performing companies, then used rigorous analysis to test these opinions and to analyse the common factors associated with that group of companies.

ASSESSING WINNING ORGANISATIONS IN AUSTRALIA

These three developments provided the foundations for this project. What was still missing was an Australian equivalent to *Built to Last* or *In Search of Excellence*. Which companies in Australia might qualify for such a list? Were their practices similar or different to those in the US studies? What made it more difficult was that whenever we asked managers which were the best performing companies in Australia, we got three consistent responses:

- They still found it difficult to make the assessment at all. Typical replies were "What do you mean by 'best'?" or "We don't know."
- Their choices were very wide-ranging and subject to considerable dispute with their peers. That is, the organisations chosen by some were regarded by others as poor performers... and there was no easy way to resolve these anecdotal views.
- Many of the companies identified were well-known American examples such as Microsoft, General Electric, McDonald's, Disney, etc., not local organisations.

The questions still remained: how could Australian managers learn from their own role models, facing an Australian environment? Is Australia just the same as overseas? If it is not, how is 'winning' different in Australia? We simply had no well-researched information or even general anecdotal agreement.

The project begins

In 1999, this project formally began at Mt Eliza Business School. Its aims were:

- To identify organisations operating in Australia which were considered to be high performing, or 'winning' over the long term.
- To understand what the common characteristics were for these organisations.

Our research methodology

Our methodology followed that of Collins and Porras where feasible and appropriate. However, in addition, we gathered and analysed a substantial body of literature on 'successful' companies which had been developed using a variety of methodologies. This literature and its findings are summarised in Chapter 12. While

5

these provided some insights, we felt that the Collins and Porras work used a superior methodology and was practical to follow.

Initially, we surveyed CEOs of the 1,000 largest organisations in the country to ask them to identify 'winning' organisations. We believed that they were in the best position to be aware of other organisations and to be able to assess their performance. We also sought the opinions of executives on public senior management courses at Mt Eliza Business School. We were interested in all types of organisations – listed, private, government, non-profit and subsidiaries of overseas organisations.

In seeking nominations, we defined 'winning' as being '*extremely successful over long periods of time*'. We defined 'success' generally as '*using a balanced scorecard approach*'. To qualify for assessment, organisations had to be in existence for at least 20 years and had to have had more than one CEO. This ensured that the organisation would have endured both good and bad economic cycles and minimised the possibility that the success of the organisation might be due simply to the original founder/CEO.

From this survey in 1999–2000, 199 organisations were nominated. We chose the 14 organisations which were most nominated for our initial analysis, as there seemed to be a clear break point between these organisations and the next group.

We first analysed the financial statements and the share price performance (where relevant) of the organisations for the last 20 years to ensure that financial performance both in accounting and sharemarket terms was at least reasonable, taking into account the type of industry. Two of the organisations were eliminated at this stage – though popular, their financials simply did not stand up.

Evidence of success

While we then chose the winning organisations on the basis of their balanced scorecard and performance cube rather than their financial performance, the latter is the only common measure we can use to give you an idea of their performance.

Figure 1.2 shows what would have happened if you had invested $1,000 in the listed organisations and left it there over the period 1982–2001 compared with investing the same amount in the All Ordinaries Accumulation Index. It shows that the investment would have grown to $42,550, while the Accumulation Index would have grown to $14,650, outperforming the index by almost three times!

Figure 1.2 – Sharemarket performance 1980–2001 for the winning organisations

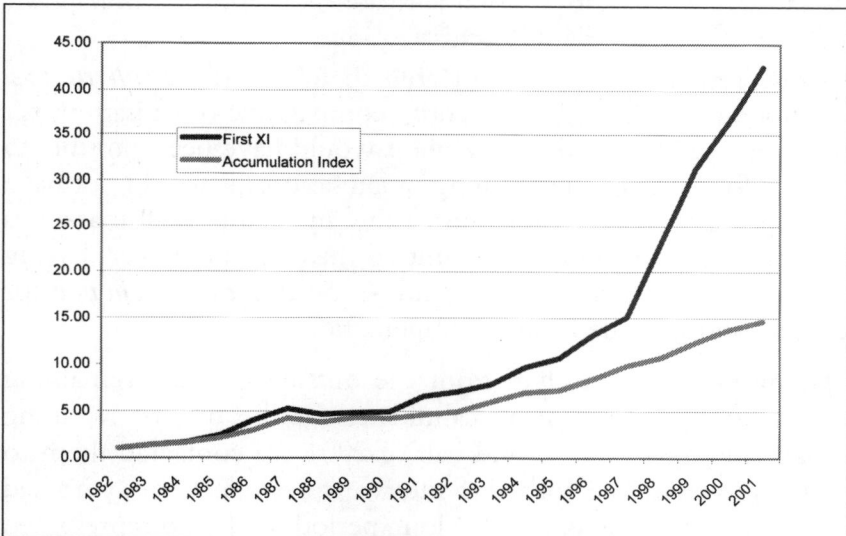

Source: Developed from information supplied by JBWere and the Reserve Bank of Australia

Using a balanced scorecard/performance cube approach to assess performance more widely, we analysed the annual reports of the selected organisations over the 20-year period to get a wider perspective on performance and to try to understand the key factors which had led to that performance. We attempted to understand the organisation's financial and market position, its internal efficiency and effectiveness and its ability to grow and develop, taking account of the type of organisation, its industry and its position. Three of us read every company annual report in detail – over 6,000 pages of reading each – to ensure that we captured all the key issues over the long time span we were covering.

The team which undertook this work was deliberately chosen to have a wide variety of experience and backgrounds. Consequently, getting agreement about both the organisation's performance and the key factors for success was challenging, but the team's diversity was an undoubted strength. At the end of this process, we eliminated another organisation from the sample. While its financial and market positions were very good, the organisation had been in turmoil for some years and it appeared to be 'stuck' in terms of leadership and strategy, while employees were damning in their criticism of its internal processes.

In one respect, we were not able to follow the *Built to Last* methodology. We did not identify comparative organisations for the winning organisations. While it would have been possible to do this for some of the winning organisations, it would not have been possible to do so for quite a few in such a small market as Australia. Consequently, we omitted this step. However, having the findings of *Built to Last* and *In Search of Excellence* for comparison provided some compensation.

Having satisfied ourselves from the outside that the remaining organisations were worthy candidates for the title of 'winning organisations', in the second half of 2001 we contacted them to seek interviews. We wished to interview key executives who had been with the organisation for long periods and who represented a variety of different perspectives from within the organisation. We also sought out books, case studies and other significant analyses of the organisations, particularly those which had a historical or long-term perspective. Interviews generally lasted one hour and were attended by at least two members of the research team, again to ensure that different views were covered, opinions were agreed on and to act as a double check on the information recorded.

Not all the organisations were co-operative at this stage, as several were caught up in major organisation- and industry-changing events such as the airline industry upheaval, the turmoil which followed the events of September 11, 2001, global mergers and CEO changes. So we used our networks to identify other people who could give us insights on the organisation, either from their past employment in or consulting experiences with it.

At no stage in the interview process did we divulge our views of what the key factors were thought to be. All interviews and discussions began with a simple but fundamental question: 'What do you think have been the causes of success for [organisation] in the long term?'

From individual organisation success to generic success factors

Having agreed amongst ourselves on the key factors for success for each organisation, we then met to find – if possible – a common set of generic success factors across the organisations. Some of the team were doubtful at the start that any factors would be 'common', given the great variety of organisations, industries, histories and positions studied. However, over several meetings during the research, we gradually agreed that, as both Collins and Porras and Peters and Waterman found, a common set of factors did exist.

We subsequently checked this set of factors against each organisation to be confident that each factor did apply. We compared the factors to those chosen by Collins and Porras to see the degree of similarity – and the differences. See Chapter 12 for a comparison of our findings with those of Collins and Porras and with other important studies about the elusive nature of 'winning'.

Finally, we also discussed for each organisation – and overall – what factors, if any, were unique to the Australian environment. Did it make any difference that the organisations developed in Australia, or are the factors for success common across countries? Chapter 11 addresses what makes 'winning' different in Australia.

Notes of caution

We strike two notes of caution at this point. First, like Collins and Porras, we do not claim that these are the only 'winning' organisations in Australia. Interestingly, some of these organisations were not well known to us at the start of the research. If we were making our own choices, other organisations might have been included. But this, of course, would have made our findings very subjective. Instead, we took the nominations of the experienced CEOs and senior managers as our base data set.

All the winning organisations are large and all but one are listed on the stock exchange. Size and being listed on the exchange attracts publicity and makes information about organisational performance easier to come by and to assess by outsiders.

However, we are sure that there are other organisations which would qualify as winning organisations. Private companies, not-for-profits, government enterprises and subsidiaries of overseas corporations are notable for their absence. We believe they were not widely nominated because their long-term stories are not well enough known or widely enough understood. Indeed, we hope that one of the outcomes of our work will be further well-researched pursuit and identification of other 'winning organisations' that will show how to be successful in Australia.

Second, we do not claim that these 'winning' organisations have not made mistakes. Indeed, at any time we expect that at least one or two will be facing significant challenges. No organisation is perfect. All organisations, even winning ones, go backwards at some time in their lives.

What we do claim is that the principles for winning organisations will hold true into the future. As such, we believe that an organisation which practises these principles over the long term will be well-placed to succeed, whatever its industry. The organisations identified here, having been winning organisations for a long period, are more likely to be able to recover from setbacks or challenges than new organisations which have never faced adversity or change.

Nevertheless, just because an organisation is identified as a long-term high performer does not guarantee that it will remain so forever. Decline and failure are as much a part of the market system as growth and success. Organisations which forget that, or which grow complacent, eventually reap their just deserts.

WHAT 'WINNING' IS *NOT* ABOUT

During the course of our research, we found that a number of ideas which are widely held to be important for success in the business community simply did not feature in the practices of the winning organisations, in terms of making a difference. We want to explode these myths before we start. They are:

1. 'Winning' is *not* about vision and mission statements

For strategists, this is an extremely disconcerting finding. Most organisations seem to have at least one of these statements, if not more than one of both (different mission and vision statements in different divisions/departments).

Only one of our winning organisations even had one of them at the end of the analysis period. In no case was the mission or vision pointed out to us as an important element of success, or in any explanation of the strategy of the organisation. Yet many firms spend hundreds of hours and thousands of dollars generating these statements that have become perceived as necessary for a 'real' organisation.

Why did they not feature here? First, we are not saying that 'strategy' is not important, only that vision and mission *statements* are not. Second, vision and mission statements are extremely varied in practice. There is little agreement amongst strategists or businesspeople about exactly what should go into each, or even if there should be one or both. No wonder they have little impact! Third, they have become increasingly long and/or bland. As such they are neither memorable nor unique... which is exactly what they were designed to be!

In summary, you may be wasting your time and money developing these statements. Having a clear strategy is important... but it doesn't have to be called a vision or mission.

2. Winning is *not* about Big Hairy Audacious Goals (BHAGs)

Collins and Porras found that BHAGs were one of their key principles for their winning organisations. They said:

> A BHAG should fall well outside the comfort zone. People in the organization should have reason to believe they can pull it off, yet it should require heroic effort and perhaps even a little luck ... A BHAG should be so bold and exciting *in its own right* that it would continue to stimulate progress even if the organization's leaders disappeared... (p. 112)

We did not find a single BHAG in our winning organisations. Some research which looked at appropriate leadership styles for Australian organisations found that Australians want clear guidelines and directions about where they and the organisation are heading. They also want a reason that has social and moral implications – a cause – for why the organisation is moving in that direction. Without this clear view, the study concluded that people will not become committed to and involved with the organisation. The study also found that Australians are innately insecure. Together, these two findings suggest that Australians will not identify with BHAGs, which are too confronting and carry too high a risk of failure.

3. Winning is *not* about great breakthrough ideas

None of our organisations succeeded simply on the basis of a single 'breakthrough' idea. Our winning organisations are in low-tech and mature industries, in the main. While there is a great deal of entrepreneurship in these organisations, none is based on 'one big idea' or 'one big innovation'. Winning is the outcome of a lot of decisions and activities, not one, and not just luck.

4. Winning is *not* about charismatic or high-profile leaders

Our bet is that you will be able to name less than half of the CEOs of our winning organisations. Further, we will be surprised if you can name any person who has been a CEO of some of them, regardless of when that was! (Check Appendix A for lists of all the CEOs.)

Why is this? Despite the personalisation of large organisations over the last 10 to 15 years, publicity has not had a lot to do with 'winning'. Instead it has more to do with activity (e.g. acquisitions, growth, scandals, large losses, changes, or an outspoken leader). Much publicity does not investigate how well the organisation is doing, only that it has done something or said something. All three of the organisations we rejected had extremely high public profiles. We surmised that they were considered to be 'winning' simply because they were changing a lot.

While organisation success or failure is often attributed to the CEO, the reality is that in truly winning organisations there are whole groups of people, coupled with systems and processes, that are difficult, even boring, or impossible to write about in the popular press. Winning organisations are about much more than an individual leader, attractive though charismatic CEOs are to us all.

5. Winning is *not* about profits alone

There is a strong body of business opinion that profits and profitability alone are what counts in the end. We reject this argument. While the winning organisations are profitable (or, in the case of the non-profit, it covers its costs each year), and often highly so, they are not the most profitable organisations, even in the longer term. In a survey by A.T. Kearney (Kavanagh, 2001), none of the winning organisations were in the top 10 for average shareholder return over the previous five years... but all of them were in the top 50. This shows that their financial performance is very good, but not the absolute best. Winning is about more than profits.

The reason for this is that profitability is only one of the measures of organisational performance. In line with the balanced scorecard/ performance cube approach, naturally the winning organisations do well on the financials, but they also have to do well in regard to customers, efficiency, development, employees and key stakeholders. Financial performance is important but it is not the sole way to judge how well an organisation is doing. All-round, long-term performance is what matters.

6. Winning is *not* about formal organisational structure

A great deal of space is devoted in management courses to the correct structure for the organisation. One of the first solutions normally proposed for an organisation in trouble is 'restructure'. One model of strategic success has three elements – strategy, structure and process. Yet neither our findings nor those of Collins and Porras or others conclude that structure is an important element for success.

How can so many people be so wrong? Of course, it helps if you have a good structure that is consistent with, and aligned to, the goals of the organisation. But you can also succeed without it. We found our organisations were constantly restructuring, some virtually every year. There is a useful saying:

> Good people can get around a bad structure. A good structure can't make bad people good.

Structures in winning organisations are being constantly changed to cope with new projects starting and old ones stopping. Promotions, external changes, innovation and new organisational themes were other causes for structural change. Not one organisation mentioned structure as a cause of success. In fact, structure only appeared as a constraint to operation (e.g. as silos that impeded information flows or as bureaucracy, creating barriers that were unnecessary).

So, if you are thinking about structure as part of your change process, or as a way to solve the problems of your organisation or create a winning organisation, we suggest you think again.

7. Winning is *not* about marketing promotion

This is another very uncomfortable conclusion, but this is what the evidence tells us. Ask yourself the question, "If an organisation had poor products and services over the long term, but great marketing promotion, would it succeed?" We doubt it.

Naturally, marketing promotion helps. But it seems that understanding the customer, innovation, alignment and execution matter a lot more. The product has to be right before you put it into a nice package and promote it. As a consequence, organisations can waste a lot of marketing expenditure if the products and services being marketed simply don't deliver. Here is another way in which organisations may need to rethink what they need to do to become winners. Get the products and services right first, then apply good marketing.

8. Winning is *not* about high pay levels

Recently there has been a great increase in the attention given to the incentive role of pay for staff. Intriguingly, we found that the winning organisations were quite inconsistent in regard to their positions on the importance of pay. Some made it clear that they were not high payers, simply trying to be at or around the average. Others, which did aim to get the best people, were often prepared to pay for them, in the belief that the true cost of the best people was actually much lower than it seemed due to their efficiency or innovative skills. What did seem to matter to them was the fixed/variable ratio of pay and the ability to link individual performance to variable compensation.

We found that people were very committed to their organisations, to the 'cause' of the organisation. Staff turnover at all organisations was considered to be low. Consequently, pay was not the determinant of performance it often appears to be.

Of course, it also helps if the organisation is successful! Working for a successful organisation is likely to be more rewarding than working for a losing one.

'WINNING' IN AUSTRALIA: THE KEYS TO SUCCESS

From the 199 organisations nominated by CEOs and senior managers, we analysed 14 in detail and selected 11 as winning organisations. This may seem a small number, but Collins and Porras included only 18 in their original study from the US – a country around 10 times the size of Australia. Collins' (2001) more recent study of underperforming listed companies that have turned themselves around and performed well for at least 15 years – *Good to Great* – was released during our research period. It included only 11 companies, so we feel that our number is in the ballpark, and there is a risk if a very small number is used that the findings will be biased by the specifics of those few organisations.

As a result of the three years of research involved in this specific project, the 11 organisations chosen are shown in Table 1.1.

Table 1.1 – Winning organisations in Australia

Organisation	Services/Operations
Brambles	Diversified industrial services
Harvey Norman	Discount specialist retailer
Lend Lease	Property developer and manager of property
Macquarie Bank	Specialist banking and funds management services
National Australia Bank	Retail bank
Qantas Airways	Airline
Rio Tinto	Diversified resource explorer, miner and developer
Salvation Army	Religious welfare agency
Telstra	Telecommunications
Westfield	Shopping centre developer
Woolworths	Retailer

Appendix A outlines a brief history of each of these organisations. In business terms, it is a very diverse group:

- While 10 of them are well-known listed public companies, one is a church which is known and respected for its welfare agency activities.
- Two of the organisations represent privatisations of government-owned enterprises, an area not generally regarded as a source of well-run organisations.

16

- Two of the organisations are subsidiaries of overseas organisations (Rio Tinto, which was CRA until Rio Tinto re-acquired it in 1995, and the Salvation Army, which represents two geographical branches of the global organisation).
- Most of the products and services are in 'basic' industries, with only Telstra and perhaps Westfield and Qantas benefiting from being in significant growth industries during the period.

All this suggests that it is the organisations themselves, not their industries, which are the underlying causes of their success.

So what are the key elements that this unusual collection of winning organisations does differently? We found nine elements which they shared (see Figure 1.3 for the winning framework).

Figure 1.3 – The winning framework for organisations in Australia

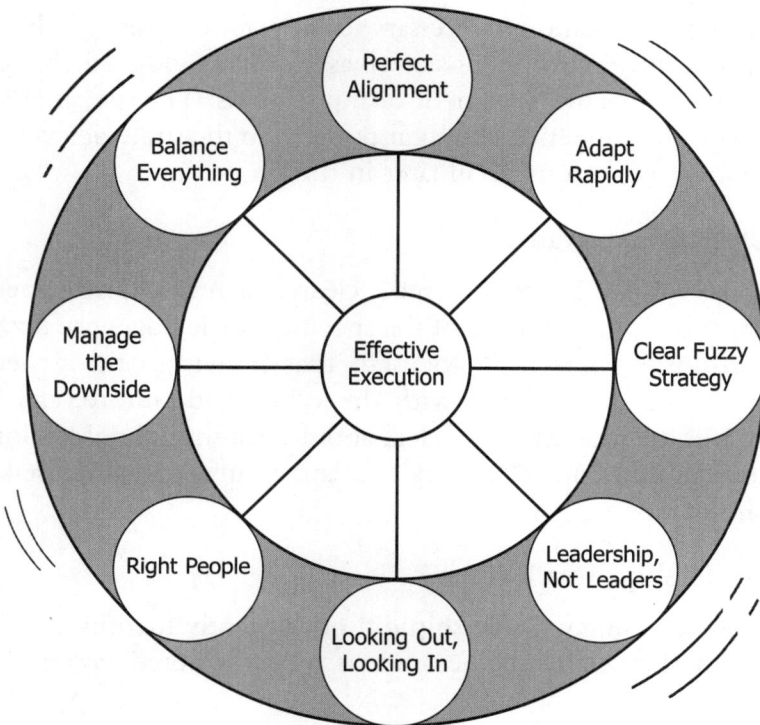

17

1. Effective execution

These organisations do what they say they will. They deliver results – on time and within budget. They are efficient. They are rigorous. They do not cross-subsidise underperforming business units. How simple... but how different.

2. Perfect alignment

In order to get execution, these organisations' systems, procedures, people and leaders are all aligned, almost perfectly. And they are able to deliver the same products and services, consistently, over and over again.

3. Adapt rapidly

However, these organisations do not simply provide the same products and services over and over again. As organisations grow and develop, they must change. They adapt themselves, and do it rapidly. This adaptation is necessary to allow for externally induced changes in the environment as well as internally induced changes from continuous improvement or innovations. The specific type of changes are influenced by their position in the strategic cycle (a concept we explain in detail later in this chapter).

4. Clear fuzzy strategy

Yes, that's right. Strategy is both clear and fuzzy. The general direction is clear, but some of the specifics at the edges are fuzzy. Opportunities (externally focused) that fit within the general direction and, particularly, with the values and culture, can be taken. But the strategy is also clear about what should not be done (perfect alignment) and is quick to adapt to any strategic mistakes that are made.

5. Leadership, not leaders

Perhaps surprisingly, leadership did not instantly identify itself as one of the key elements, because, as we have noted earlier, few leaders of winning organisations are charismatic. But we could not get away from the conclusion that leadership is one of the keys. It is often the decisions of the leaders that start the journey, but it is not a single charismatic leader whose own actions are the cause of the success. While there are plenty of examples here of significant leaders, it is the actions leadership takes as a group to build the organisation, not the personalities of the individual leaders, that are critical.

6. Looking out, looking in

While these organisations are internally aligned and execute to deliver results, they are equally externally focused. They are looking outwards all the time. Customers matter to them. They have networks. They manage relationships outside the organisation. They know their place in the value chain and understand how value is created, not only by them, but by others in the chain. These external activities and orientation are critical to their overall success.

7. Right people, committed and proud

Despite the common mantra 'people are our greatest assets', we did not find that the *best* people are necessarily hired. What is important is to get the *right* people – the people who fit into the particular system with its specific culture and values. We also found that the people invariably have a fierce pride in what their organisation is doing. They feel they are working for a cause, not just holding down a job. They are committed to the goals and culture of the organisation. However, they don't jump up and down and shout this out loud. While they are committed and proud, they are actually quite reluctant to demonstrably show this.

8. Manage the downside

While the organisations grow rapidly and innovate significantly, they all regard themselves as cautious and conservative! This is because, while they take risks, they evaluate the risks well, plan for them and take actions to minimise those risks to themselves, rather than simply reducing the amount of risk.

9. Balance everything

Combining the above eight elements is very difficult. Some seem contradictory. Yet that is exactly what these organisations do. The final element is that they 'balance' everything. It is not either/or. It is both, or all elements, everything together: and, and, and. Achieving this balance is what enables execution to occur – it all comes together, at the right time. And that's what makes them winning organisations.

In the chapters that follow, we take each one of these elements and discuss them in detail, using examples from each of the winning organisations to demonstrate how the framework works.

Figure 1.3 shows how the framework fits together. It shows the central role of effective execution. We see this as both an element of the framework and representing the outcome of the framework. The other elements of the winning organisation 'wheel' are connected together to make the wheel work and steer the organisation toward its goals. There is no 'start' or 'finish' to the wheel. All elements are important.

DIFFERENT ORGANISATIONS, DIFFERENT STAGES: THE JOURNEY OF THE STRATEGIC CYCLE

We have pointed out that the organisations are different in many ways. We have 'captured' them at a particular point in their development, even though we have studied them in detail over the 20-year study period and for longer spans where possible.

This book is about the commonalities amongst the journeys of the organisations. However, the organisations are clearly at quite different stages in their lives and the issues which each faces are quite different at any particular time. For instance, while Macquarie began in investment banking in 1969, the National Australia Bank (NAB) began retail banking in 1858 – 90 years earlier! While Macquarie has only recently begun to enter overseas markets, NAB has owned significant overseas banks for 15 years and has had international operations for much longer.

The degree to which the organisations are 'international' in their operations is another example. Brambles, Lend Lease, Rio Tinto and Westfield have more than 50 per cent of their sales overseas. This leads to quite different issues for the organisation than if it is almost wholly domestic, as Woolworths and Harvey Norman are. Yet, given the size of the Australian market and the general research on the lack of success of diversified organisations, the paths of Brambles and others are likely to be the paths that Woolworths and others will eventually embark on.

What does this 'path' look like? Our study of these organisations, together with knowledge of the developments of other Australian organisations and knowledge of the context of the Australian market size, suggests that there is a 'strategic cycle' that organisations go through, with each stage of the cycle requiring different capabilities, leadership and organisational processes.

Figure 1.4 suggests the key stages in the strategic cycle of the development of an Australian organisation over time. First, the organisation begins by starting its business, usually in one state. This is the *focused – domestic regional* stage of the strategic cycle. For instance, Woolworths and Harvey Norman both began retailing in Sydney. Then, if it is successful, the organisation takes that activity across the country, usually on a state-by-state basis, as the geographical spread in Australia makes this expansion quite difficult, especially given the small market size of the whole country. Woolworths has spread across the country, while Harvey Norman is only just reaching 'national' coverage.

At some point the organisation begins to expand the products and services – and businesses – which it operates. This is called the *related expansion* stage of the cycle. For instance, Telstra was originally set up to provide a phone in every home. Once that task was largely completed in the early 1990s, Telstra began to provide a variety of products and services, including pay-TV. The Salvation Army, too, now offers aged care, youth crisis, marriage enrichment, disaster relief and intellectual disability services and safe houses, amongst other services.

21

Figure 1.4 – The strategic cycle of growing organisations

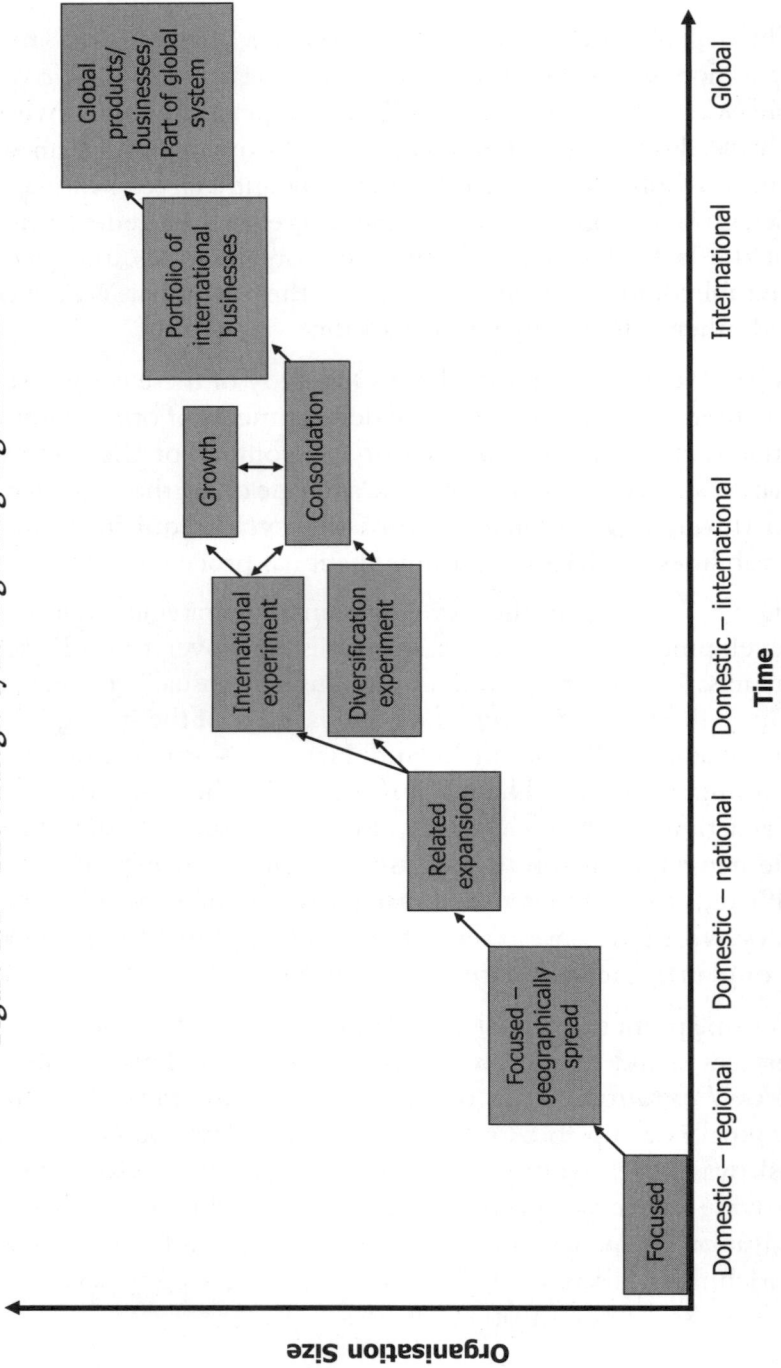

Organisation Size (vertical axis)

Time (horizontal axis)

Domestic – regional | Domestic – national | Domestic – international | International | Global

Focused

Focused – geographically spread

Related expansion

International experiment

Diversification experiment

Growth

Consolidation

Portfolio of international businesses

Global products/ businesses/ Part of global system

Based on the success of this, the organisation then appears to take one of two paths. The more traditional route has been to diversify activities within Australia. In particular, many of the winning organisations diversified significantly during the 1980s. We call this the *diversification experiment* stage of the cycle. Perhaps the classic is Westfield, which went into resources and television ownership. Rio Tinto diversified into biotechnology, Qantas diversified into ownership of leisure resorts, Brambles diversified into environmental waste management.

However, the increasingly popular route is to take the existing products and services which have been successful within Australia and to go 'international' with them. This is the *international experiment* stage. If the initial experiment works, the organisation begins to expand internationally in a *growth* stage. For instance, Telstra has entered a major joint venture with Pacific Century Cyber Works in Asia for primarily mobile phone markets. NAB bought banks in the UK, Ireland and the US. Westfield bought shopping centres in the US. Lend Lease undertook large-scale property developments in the UK and the US. Brambles established pallet joint ventures in Europe.

Regardless of which of these two routes is taken, the risks always seem to be greater than expected, as most organisations at some stage enter a consolidation period, to recover from errors and to learn from experiences before moving forward. This is the *consolidation* stage. NAB has sold out of US banking, Brambles has sold its rail wagon operations in Europe, Lend Lease sold its Australian funds management operations.

Not all the organisations have reached this stage. For instance, Woolworths, Harvey Norman, Macquarie and Telstra have limited or no overseas operations. The Salvation Army is restricted to Australia, as it is part of a global organisation which has its own operations in other countries (this was also the situation that CRA found itself in prior to its re-acquisition by Rio Tinto, its parent).

Even where organisations have retained their activities overseas, the development is quite slow, indicating that it takes a long time

23

to become 'established' in any overseas markets. Indeed, most of the organisations have only been in international markets to any degree since the mid-1980s. (This is even true of Australia's established international players, such as News Corporation, CSR, Foster's and Southcorp.) In reality, our organisations have limited international experience. This is called the *portfolio of international businesses* stage. This is a new area for future development.

Finally, one or two of the organisations have reached the 'global' stage, i.e. they are operating in many countries with largely similar products. This is called the *global products* stage. Lend Lease has recently changed its strategy to reflect this true global focus on its two businesses – real estate development and property funds management. Brambles, through its merger with Guest Keen & Nettlefold plc (GKN), is moving on to that path through the CHEP pallet system business. Rio Tinto has been acting 'global' since it became a dual listed company in 1995. Once again, however, our organisations have very limited experience of this stage of development. No conclusions can yet be drawn, but it seems likely that this stage will prove as difficult as the first stages of internationalisation.

While the principles we outline in this book apply at each stage, the specific capabilities and activities will be quite different at each stage. 'Looking out' when moving from one state to another within Australia has quite a different meaning from 'looking out' when entering the international market or trying to develop a global business. The skills required of leadership will be different. And so on.

Identification of the stage of the strategic cycle for the organisation is important to enable the issues that arise within each element to be identified too. This is particularly vital considering the increasing internationalisation of business and the very limited international experience which most Australian organisations – even the winning organisations – have.

2

EFFECTIVE EXECUTION

Do what you say
Delivering results

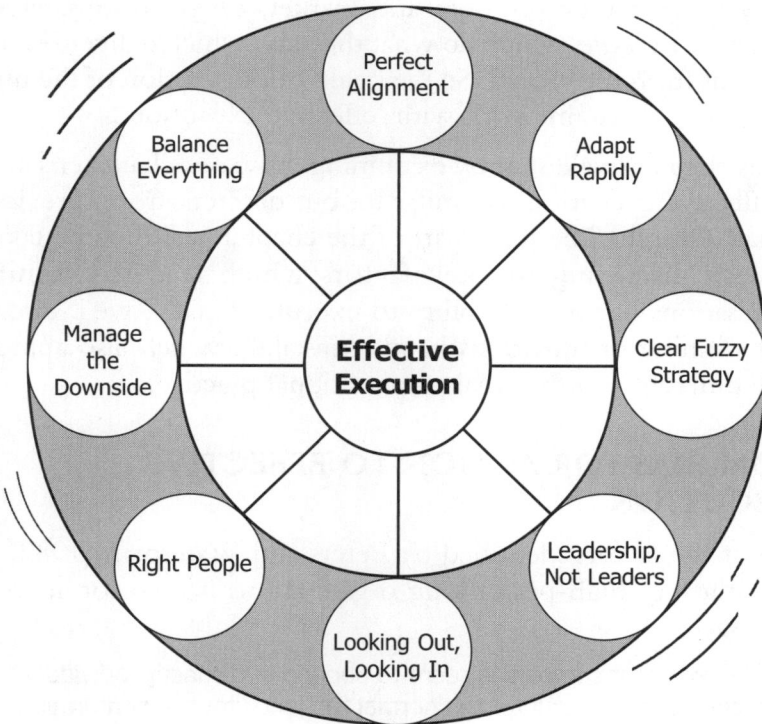

From the framework developed in Chapter 1 (see figure above), you're probably wondering why we would start with execution, when this appears to be one of the last elements, perhaps even the end result of all the other elements.

We asked ourselves the same question. Originally we planned to start this book with leadership. But as we asked ourselves the question, "What really makes these organisations different from others?", we realised that it was the results that occurred, the results which they delivered, that was the difference. We chose these organisations on the basis of their results. And it is effective execution that enables them to deliver these results. That is what makes them different.

In everyday dealings with all types of organisations, one thing stands out fairly consistently. Most organisations disappoint their stakeholders by their failure to deliver what they say, what they promise, what they promote and market. Organisations which *effectively execute*, which do what they say, which deliver results, stand out from the crowd. So we begin our discussion of the nine elements of the framework with 'effective execution'.

In this chapter, we'll start by examining how our characterisation of 'effective execution' is similar to, but different from, previous similar research. The main part of the chapter will then be taken up with discussing the key factors which lead to winning organisations having the ability to execute. Finally, we'll discuss how winning organisations handle mistakes, which also appears to be different from normal organisational practice.

FROM BIAS FOR ACTION TO EFFECTIVE EXECUTION

One of the factors identified by Peters and Waterman (1982) in their study of high-performing organisations is 'bias for action'. They say:

> The excellent companies seem to abound in distinctly individual techniques that counter the normal tendency toward conformity and inertia. Their mechanism comprises a wide range of action devices, especially in the area of management systems, organisational fluidity, and experiments – devices that simplify their systems and foster a restless organisational stance by clarifying which numbers really count or arbitrarily limiting the length of the goal list. (p. 121)

Similarly, Collins and Porras (1994) included 'try a lot of stuff and see what works' as one of their factors:

> ...we were struck by how often they made some of their best moves not by detailed strategic planning, but rather by experimentation, trial and error, opportunism, and – quite literally – accident. (p. 141)

> If you add enough branches to a tree (variation) and intelligently prune the deadwood (selection), then you'll likely evolve into a collection of healthy branches well positioned to prosper in an ever-changing environment. (p. 146)

But our view of these ideas is subtly different. It is not simply about 'action' for action's sake. It is not about 'experimenting' for experimenting's sake. It is about action and experimentation to execute, to do what you say, to deliver results.

The winning organisations say what they are going to do and then do it. And they keep doing it, again and again. This is quite frightening for most organisations, because saying what you are going to do sets an expectation and a target – did you achieve what you said you would? For most organisations, this invites an assessment of failure. For winning organisations, however, it provides the opportunity to demonstrate success. For instance:

- Brambles announced in 1984, when its profit was $33 million, that it wished to add $100 million within five years... which it did.
- Harvey Norman announces each year how many stores it will open in the next year... and it does so.
- Macquarie planned to become the first new entrant to receive a full banking licence when the industry was deregulated and opened more than six months before any other new entrant.
- NAB announced the cost/sales ratio it planned to achieve, which was well below that of its competitors, and achieved it.
- Rio Tinto consistently brings mines into production on time and on budget (see Illustration 2.1).

Illustration 2.1 – Rio Tinto on time and on budget

Throughout CRA/Rio Tinto's annual reports for the period we studied, there were consistent references to its ability to complete projects on time and on budget. These included:

1982	Blair Athol first coal shipment on schedule
1983	Tarong first coal deliveries ahead of schedule, Blair Athol first steaming coal ahead of schedule
1984	Argyle diamond development activity on schedule and within budget
1985	Blair Athol (Phase II) constructed below budget
1986	Argyle diamond mine completed on schedule and within budget
1992	Peak gold mine completed on schedule and within budget
1993	Channar iron ore mine development on schedule
1994	Weipa bauxite dump station on schedule and under budget
1995	Boyne Island aluminium smelter on schedule
1997	Boyne Island completed six months ahead of schedule and on budget
1998	Yandicoogina iron ore mine five months ahead of schedule and under budget.

- Woolworths announced in 1999 the cost savings it expected from its long-term Operation Refresh would be $100 million per annum. In 2000, it announced that it expected savings to increase to $134 million per annum by 2002–03.

A Woolworths' executive summarised Woolworths' approach to delivering results:

> We are successful because we have an execution culture... The job is a repetitive process so we have to do the same job today and tomorrow and tomorrow. We have to do it consistently, but get better each year and find scope for improvement... We are very focused. We have targets and budgets. This is a numbers game.

We understand customer needs. This is a simple business. We are not cutting edge in market research or information technology but we do seem to understand what customers need. We get this by talking to them and passing that information up the chain. This is part of our culture.

To cope with varying demand, we use a lot of casual staff and kids at the checkout, which is where much of the contact between Woolworths and its customers takes place. We have high turnover with this type of staff, but we rely on their interactions with the customer.

There is no magic formula here, nothing that is a unique management tool. Execution is the difference. These organisations do what they say... and they say what they are going to do. Just do it.

'Results' means a balanced scorecard approach

When we talk about results here, we remind you that this does not mean simply profits or return on equity (ROE). Doing what you say and delivering results applies for all stakeholder groups – not only shareholders, but also customers (which is how market share is gained), suppliers, employees and others.

Of course, in business, 'results' which favour one group may well be at the expense of other groups. The 'balanced' nature of winning means though that results must not be seen just from a financial perspective. All stakeholder groups need to benefit. Rio Tinto publishes its 'statement of business practice'– 'The Way We Work' – on the internet to address this issue. This is a much broader statement than a normal vision or mission statement and covers several different stakeholder groups. It includes the following statements – which can be measured – and are:

- deliver superior returns to our shareholders over many years
- long-term and responsible approach to exploring
- making a direct contribution to economic development and employment in those countries where we invest
- work as closely as possible with our hosts, respecting laws and customs, minimising adverse impacts, and ensuring transfer of benefits and enhancements of opportunities
- set ourselves high environmental and community standards

- our commitment to health, safety and the enhancement of the skills and capabilities of our employees is second to none in mining
- make lasting contributions to local communities.

HOW DO WINNING ORGANISATIONS EXECUTE TO DELIVER RESULTS?

So what is it that winning organisations do to facilitate execution and the delivery of results? In addition to the other major elements of the framework, we found seven specific factors which directly contribute to delivering results (see Figure 2.1). They are:

- clear processes
- operational and technical efficiency
- taking personal responsibility
- good management control systems
- rigorously measuring performance
- handling mistakes positively
- no cross-subsidisation of business units.

Figure 2.1 – Achieving effective execution

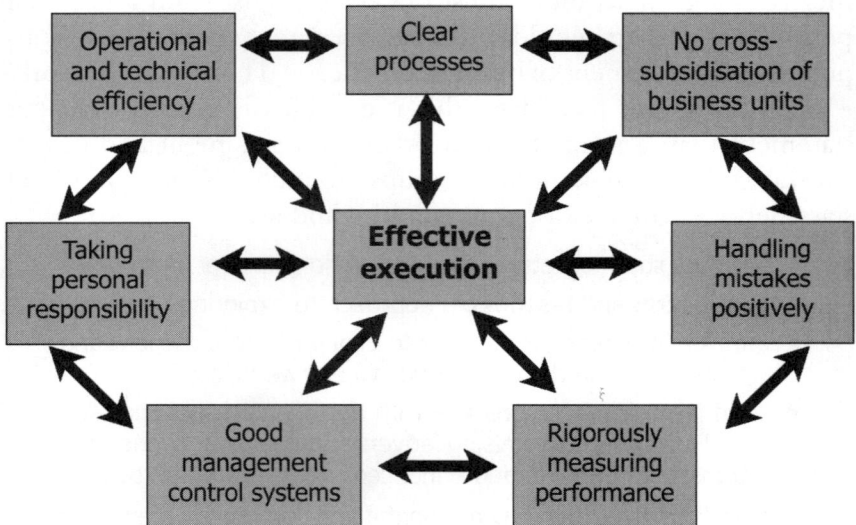

These factors are linked with each other as well as being causal factors for execution. Let's explore how this works.

Clear processes

The first factor in helping execution is having clear processes. Knowing what you are supposed to do – having clear processes – is an important ingredient for delivering outcomes. Having structures that support these processes and delegating the authority and responsibility to carry out the processes – and make decisions quickly in borderline or grey area cases – supports the completion of the organisation's tasks and activities.

But what does a 'clear process' look like? The specifics of 'clear processes' and the associated structures and responsibilities varies greatly from one organisation to another. For instance, the Salvation Army has the most formally structured approach to clear processes amongst the winning organisations. This comes from the 'Army' or military set of values within the organisation. Structure and discipline are considered highly valuable. The Salvation Army has processes for everything, including such issues as entry into new countries, annual staff appointments and church and service reviews. In the case of staff appointments, all staff receive a letter at the end of October telling them where they will be going the following January. Everyone knows what is happening, and when.

Woolworths is similarly highly structured, as it depends on repetitive consistency in transacting many small items to achieve its results. Early in its history Woolworths developed detailed operating manuals which were referred to as the Bibles. They covered every aspect of Woolworths' operations. They were regarded as encyclopaedias of detail and were constantly updated to ensure they reflected best practice.

But 'clear processes' does not mean simply, or always, having highly structured and mechanistic processes. At Harvey Norman, 'clear process' occurs through the decisions about what items to purchase. The buying committee, which meets to decide what product range to purchase, includes representatives of the franchisees/sellers as well as the head office purchasing function. This process overcomes a key problem in most retail organisations where the buyers and sales force are separate and independent. In a regular retail organisation, the buyer is all powerful. Buyers 'know best' and buy what they think the market will want without consulting the sellers. At Harvey Norman, in contrast, the sellers order directly with their suppliers for delivery of the product directly to their franchised premises.

Westfield resolves its issues in the same way each time, in a very informal process. A meeting (ironically named a formal action meeting) is called, at which everyone who is involved and affected by the issue is present. Everyone is able to, and is expected to, have their say. This practice evolved from the early days of the organisation, when Frank Lowy and John Saunders, the joint 50/50 founders of Westfield, used to always meet together to discuss issues before making decisions.

Westfield believes it has a big advantage in having all functions and activities represented and getting all perspectives on the issue, especially when so much of the organisation is vertically integrated and so is 'in house'. At the end of a meeting a decision is made. While the process is 'democratic' during the meeting, if an impasse is reached the CEO(s), will decide. Originally, when an impasse was reached, Lowy and Saunders would step outside to confer. A decision would be made and brought back to the meeting. While the individual meetings are long, the decision–making process is quick compared to the conventional method of a series of cascading meetings with different parties and different perspectives at each meeting.

What is implicit in 'clear processes' is that people accept the process and the outcomes. Whether the process is highly structured or highly democratic, acceptance by those who form part of the process and who must make the process and decisions work is critical. We'll address this more fully in the third section, 'Taking Personal Responsibility'.

Operational and technical efficiency

It is not enough just to have 'clear processes', of course, to get execution. Bureaucracies have clear processes – these organisations need to be efficient too! The second contributor to achieving effective execution is being efficient, in both an operational and a technical sense. Keeping costs down and changing systems over time to meet different circumstances are other aspects of achieving efficiency (see Figure 2.2).

Figure 2.2 – Factors affecting efficiency

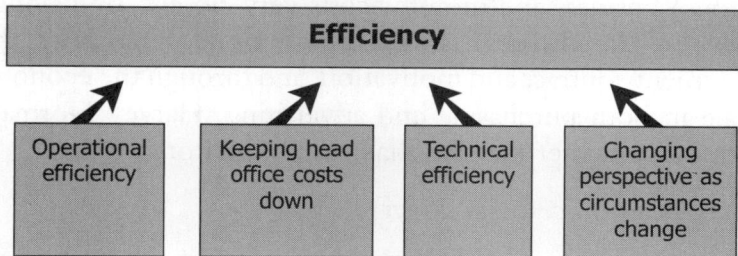

Efficiency			
Operational efficiency	Keeping head office costs down	Technical efficiency	Changing perspective as circumstances change

Operational efficiency

Operational efficiency is the use of operating systems that work to achieve their expected objectives, which could be related to cost, quality, speed or service. For the Salvation Army, where every dollar contributed and used on administration is a dollar that cannot be used on providing services to the needy, having efficient administration is important for relative success. The Salvation Army has a very low administrative cost ratio (around 17¢ of every dollar raised is spent on administration, less than its competitors). Of course, one way in which the Salvation Army achieves this is through the use of volunteers and low-paid employees, but its competitors also have access to similar volunteer or low-paid structures.

Harvey Norman achieves operating efficiency completely differently. Harvey Norman representatives are involved in discussions with suppliers in conjunction with franchisees to determine product ranges and buying deals, although the actual product purchasing is done by the franchisees at their total discretion. Harvey Norman franchisees own their own business, which is a separate legal entity for each franchisee, employ their own staff, order and own their own stock and maintain their own information systems. They obtain finance from a Harvey Norman subsidiary as part of their franchise arrangements and they benefit from generic Harvey Norman advertising. They also place and pay for their own local advertising. Harvey Norman franchisees achieve higher levels of earnings due to the fact that they run their own business and monitor costs very closely. By having its people be franchisees, thus fundamentally changing their employment contract and motivation, and through the economies of scale in both purchasing and advertising, Harvey Norman is able to make higher margins than its competitors.

Keeping head office costs down

One aspect of operational efficiency is keeping head office costs down, particularly for diversified corporations. During our research interviews, we were surprised by the relatively low-key head offices and the modest quality of the offices which most of these winning organisations had. For instance:

- Woolworths and Harvey Norman are renowned for their low-cost head offices. Woolworths is in a low-quality building above one of its modest city stores. Harvey Norman is in Homebush, an outer working class suburb of Sydney.
- John Menadue, CEO of Qantas in the mid-1980s, moved the Qantas head office from the centre of Sydney to the airport, to link it more closely with operations.
- Rio Tinto split its divisions off from the head office and forced them to move away so that they focused more on the business and less on head office politics.

Commenting on his attitude to head office costs, Gerry Harvey said:

> The rent here is very cheap. It's in my nature to be frugal with money... I don't have this great urge to have these things. In a perverse sort of way I would feel better in a housing commission home with no furniture. (Condon, 2002)

Technical efficiency

Efficiency is not just about low absolute operating costs. Using better quality technical systems can result in more efficient outcomes, in terms of delivering results.

For example, Qantas knows it cannot compete with the cost structures of Asian international competitors (or, now, its domestic low-cost competitors). So 'efficiency' for Qantas is primarily about technical efficiency – safety, yield management systems, reservation systems, operational logistics, plane turnaround times, lost luggage, etc. This can be matched against Qantas' value proposition of high-quality customer service, which requires different measurements than does a value proposition of low cost.

Rio Tinto aims to achieve operational efficiency using an almost completely opposite approach. Rio Tinto believes that hiring the very best people with good remuneration will be more than repaid through the resulting high levels of innovation and productivity which will enable Rio Tinto to deliver low-cost operating mines. In general, Rio Tinto will not start a mine unless it is in the bottom quartile of world operating costs... yet it does this while employing well rewarded people.

NAB focuses on getting its operating costs down and keeping its operating costs below those of key competitors, primarily through the use of better technology systems and processes. 'Simplify, standardise and automate' is one of its catchcries for focusing on this.

Changing perspectives on operating and technical efficiency

Of course, should the external environment change, the concepts of technical and operating efficiency may need to change too.

35

For instance, during the 1970s and 1980s CRA was very much focused on technical efficiency, without great concern for its commercial results. It believed that the resources slump, which was caused by the OPEC cartel-inspired oil price crisis that began in the early 1970s, would eventually end and that high global resources demand growth would return. This did not happen. Instead, the world became much more efficient at resource use. Eventually, in the early 1990s CRA came to realise that it needed to make a more reasonable ROE, and not just be a very technically efficient miner. A Rio Tinto executive said:

> Return on capital is much more important than we appreciated. Business is not just cost control and operating efficiency. Our previous 'Rolls Royce' approach to mine production systems was not necessary in all areas.

Beginning with one very troublesome project – the Marandoo iron ore mine in the Pilbara which was commissioned in 1992 – CRA found that it needed to substantially reduce costs to make the project viable. It found that it could cut 30 per cent off its capital costs by applying much more rigorous financial analysis – primarily its focus had been on technical analysis – without affecting the technical efficiency of the operation. Applying this type of logic to all other future capital – and operating – investments, Rio Tinto has subsequently greatly improved its financial performance, despite low growth and low prices in resources for long periods.

Telstra is another organisation which has been focused on technical efficiency for most of its life. As the setter of industry technical standards in its old role as the government-owned monopoly provider, Telstra provided high technical standards for the whole Australian telecommunications system. In recent years, however, due to the change in its ownership and the fall-off in industry growth rates, it has had to rebalance its focus to become much more commercially oriented.

Taking personal responsibility

Of course, many organisations have good processes and good technical and operating systems that can provide efficient operations. Yet somehow they rarely work to the degree they should. Why is that?

The third important factor for getting outcomes from a system is the way that people in the system behave. Results cannot be delivered simply by having a great system. People are needed to operate the system or to use the system's outputs. So the attitudes which people take to the system will significantly affect the outcomes from the systems... and the results which will be delivered.

To get effective execution, people need to take responsibility for the performance of the organisation, or at least their part of it. Is that the case in your organisation? Who is 'responsible'? What happens if results don't meet expectations? Usually the answer in most organisations is 'not much'. So is it any real surprise that plans do not actually come to fruition?

An important factor in people taking responsibility is open and direct feedback from management during planning and execution about what is working and what is not.

Most organisations don't take plans seriously. They are seen as mere guides to get the action started, and no-one necessarily feels personally committed or personally responsible for them.

By contrast, people in the winning organisations will do almost anything to make the outcome occur, once it has been approved. At Lend Lease, Brambles and Macquarie, there is a feeling that, once the project has been approved, the organisation trusts and empowers the people responsible to get the results which they have said will occur. They have created little business units within the large organisation (see the 'No cross-subsidisation' section for a detailed discussion) and provided opportunities for their people to take action. And the people have great incentives to deliver – personal financial gain, the opportunity for promotion and personal satisfaction from being responsible and achieving results. As a result, responsible managers (and people) work incredibly hard to overcome any unforeseen difficulties to ensure that the projected outcomes occur.

As one ex–Lend Lease executive said:

> It was an exciting opportunity to be there (straight out of university). You were able to be a decision-maker. It was not about the pay. It was about the opportunities, about career development.

A similar approach exists at Macquarie. A person whose project is approved through the Macquarie system knows that they are expected to achieve the approved outcomes. They know their personal performance will be evaluated against the achievement or otherwise on that project. Further, they know that their remuneration will significantly depend on that evaluation, so they have a very large personal incentive to ensure that the project meets its projected targets (see Chapter 8 for a discussion on incentive systems).

At organisations like Qantas, Telstra, the Salvation Army and Woolworths, this responsibility is generated more through the pride, commitment and the 'cause' which people feel about providing a valued community service. At Qantas, people (still) feel that it is an airline that 'belongs' to the Australian people, that they have a responsibility to Australians to operate Qantas successfully and serve Australians. At Telstra, people (still) feel a responsibility for the quality of the whole Australian telecommunications system and to make sure it works well. At the Salvation Army, people feel a great desire to help others, particularly those less fortunate than themselves. At Woolworths, people feel that they act as the agent for the customer in securing food and other products at good prices.

Good management control systems

To check whether they have clear processes which are efficiently undertaken by responsible people, winning organisations need good management control systems. Controls begin during the planning and approval process. Illustration 2.2 highlights the Lend Lease system of management controls in some detail.

Illustration 2.2 – Management control systems in project approval at Lend Lease

Lend Lease's business is heavily project based and Lend Lease is credited with developing most of the major elements of project management used in Australia. It is very difficult to get a project approved at Lend Lease, because:

- an enormous amount of due diligence is required to be undertaken in order to understand all the risks
- it must be clear that the project has drawn on existing expertise and experience within Lend Lease
- the project faces high financial hurdles for approval
- the project must have access to the management and organisational expertise necessary to carry it out
- there must be an exit strategy available, in case the project does not meet expectations.

Thus, before a project is approved, a great deal of work has taken place to minimise the chance of failure.

When a project is approved within Lend Lease, the operating schedules and financial outcomes which form part of that approval are expected to be achieved. They are not simply guidelines or hoped-for outcomes. And someone is responsible for those outcomes. Knowing how seriously these plans are regarded, that person will move heaven and earth to ensure that the project meets its planned outcome.

During the life of the project, Lend Lease conducts weekly project review meetings. Everyone with a responsibility for the project must be there but equally, no-one must be present at the meeting who does not have a role – there are no passengers! Everyone must contribute to the meeting and everyone must perform to the weekly plan.

Finally, Lend Lease systems are tremendously detailed and are being continually improved. They are backed up with strong links to key performance indicators (KPIs) and big incentives for achieving outcomes.

It is much easier to measure project performance directly in an organisation like this than it is in an organisation like a bank, where 'performance' – say for a loan or a customer – may not be clear for several years. On the other hand, each project is unique, so the chance of failure is much higher, as precedent is of limited value in projects.

Control systems are very different at Qantas, as its activity is based on a very large number of much smaller transactions that must be managed for success. Qantas regards its revenue/yield management system as one of the causes of its success (though this is only a relatively recent development, so that it can only be the cause of recent success, not of how Qantas managed to be a winning organisation prior to this period). Its yield management systems enable Qantas to continuously change the variety and quantity of fares available on every flight, based on actual bookings received. Particular fares can be closed off or opened up daily if demand changes warrant this. While this may be frustrating for passengers who are waiting and planning and suddenly find fares are not available, it simply reflects demand from other passengers... who *are* satisfied! Qantas' reservations systems and operational information systems are similarly highly regarded.

From a logistics perspective, it is interesting to reflect on how smoothly Qantas handled the tumultuous period between mid-2000 and early 2002. This included:

- the domestic airfare war begun in mid-2000
- Qantas' acquisition of Impulse Airlines as a result
- the September 11, 2001 terrorist crisis (when planes were not allowed to take off or land in the US for several days)
- the maintenance groundings of Ansett at Christmas 2000 and Easter 2001
- Ansett's cessation of flying in September 2001 and again finally in February 2002.

Qantas' ability to handle the rapid increases in customer enquiries and significant changes in passenger numbers and aircraft movements in these very short time periods was remarkable... for the lack of disruption that occurred within the industry. Of course, Qantas had some practice at this with its experience of the 1989 pilots' strike and the 1990–92 entries and collapses of Compass and Compass Mark 2.

Rigorously measuring performance

Rigorous application

In using systems and processes to get results, what makes winning organisations different from their competitors? It is not that they have unique systems or procedures. It is not that their IT systems or capabilities are superior. Indeed, our winning organisations in general were rather dismissive of the value of their IT efforts, even when outside organisations believed they had a competitive advantage in this area.

The difference is the rigour and discipline which they use to make the systems work. One Macquarie executive said:

> We make sure the conflict (i.e. differences between executives and areas) happens. Most mistakes in companies are a result of not voicing concerns early enough. You have to bring this conflict to the surface.

Rio Tinto conducts three separate evaluations of risk before approving a project – a technical, financial and business case analysis. Each analysis is done by independent groups and is completed before the project goes to Rio's investment committee. Interestingly, its close competitor BHP Billiton, stung by a string of poor major project outcomes during the 1990s, announced in April 2002 that it would be instituting a similar system.

Rio Tinto also undergoes a rigorous planning, rather than budgeting, process. It considers what is happening in the industry, how the product is positioned within the industry and what the goal is for positioning the particular Rio Tinto product within the industry. As we have shown in Illustration 2.1, Rio Tinto has a great history of bringing in major projects on time and on budget.

Woolworths has a system of 'Everyday Low Prices' in its Big W stores. This system is based on market-leading Wal-Mart's similar system in the US. It took 12 years to develop, because it is a complete logistics system involving the co-operation of suppliers, not a short-term discounting price initiative.

Key performance indicators?

Using a control system to measure performance requires that some target measures exist. Key performance indicators (KPIs) provide the final link in the chain of performance measurement. The development of KPIs, however, is a relatively recent managerial phenomenon. This project did not find that KPIs were regarded as critical to success, relative to some of the other issues discussed here. We suspect that best practice has not yet evolved in this area.

Woolworths is developing a system of no more than four KPIs for its top managers, gradually cascading these down to lower levels in the organisation. At least one of those KPIs has to be qualitative. NAB is another which limits the number of KPIs – in this case to not more than five areas and not more than three measures each – all quantifiable and all objective. These are reviewed on a three-monthly basis. Organisations such as Brambles and Macquarie have very few KPIs, primarily centred on growth, profits and return on investment. One interviewee commented on the Brambles approach:

> There's a heavy emphasis on financials forecasting. Brambles is tough on the numbers but it is OK to change the forecast beforehand if times are tough. But to not meet the target without having changed the forecast is considered bad management. If you don't ask for help, you better get it right.

(Note throughout that all references to Brambles relate to the 'old' Brambles, pre–August 2001 – things may be rather different in the 'new' company created by the merger with GKN.)

Handling mistakes positively

Winning organisations are not error-free in their execution. What do they do when they make an error? Four elements consistently arose in our discussions (see Figure 2.3).

They were:

- People who make a mistake need to admit it early.
- Something must be done to fix the mistake as best as possible.
- The organisation needs to learn from a mistake and do so quickly.
- Making the same mistake twice, or three mistakes in total, is grounds for dismissal.

Again, how different is this from most organisations, where often people don't admit errors, errors are hidden until the last possible moment, the organisation doesn't learn from errors and mistakes are often repeated.

Figure 2.3 – Handling mistakes

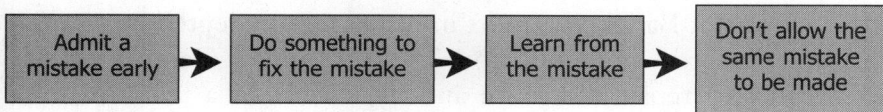

| Admit a mistake early | Do something to fix the mistake | Learn from the mistake | Don't allow the same mistake to be made |

Admit a mistake early on

This equates to the well-known 'no surprises' rule. Managers don't like to be surprised, at least not with bad news. People who are aware of errors made or problems looming in their own areas need to admit/own up to the mistake early so that action can be taken to correct it, minimise its effects, or prepare for the widespread recognition of that error, particularly publicly. Said one executive:

> One of the only ways to get fired from this organisation is to keep a problem hidden in the bottom drawer and not let anyone know about it. If we know about it, we can do something about it. The earlier we know, the more chance there is we can do something and the smaller the total cost is likely to be.

Brambles put it slightly more clearly:

> Above all, staff are advised to adhere to the doctrine of 'no surprises' – in traditional Brambles language, the 'primary

arse-covering rule'; own up immediately if something has gone
wrong and you will be helped, not crucified. Fail to draw attention
to the error or stupidity and there is a strong likelihood of
crucifixion. (Carew, 2000, p. 237–38)

The difficulty for the person – and the reason why people are so
reluctant to admit to mistakes – is that their career is likely to be
affected in the short term. Consequently, there is a significant
personal incentive in most organisations – and even in some of
the winning organisations – to hope the mistake is not discovered,
that it fixes itself, or that the individual has changed roles before it
is discovered and blame can be sheeted home. So the culture has
to support admitting a mistake without it being career-limiting.

Fix the mistake as best as possible

Winning organisations don't make mistakes very often, but when
they do, they fix them quickly. When Qantas had a plane slide off
the runway at Bangkok airport in heavy rain in September 1999,
its safety record – and reputation – was threatened. Qantas worked
feverishly to repair the plane and fly it out. As a result of this
event, Qantas significantly reviewed its maintenance and safety
procedures to minimise the chance of a recurrence.

Learn from the mistake

After minimising the costs of a mistake, a winning organisation
learns from it, in order not only that the mistake will not happen
again, but that any changes that might need to occur to systems
are made... Winning organisations enquire into their mistakes early
and quickly. They see mistakes as opportunities to improve.
Macquarie said that, once it had addressed a mistake, it undertook
an investigation, with a full written report being prepared within
four to six weeks.

At Brambles and Lend Lease, provided the person responsible for
the error could learn from it, it can actually be seen as a positive
experience in the longer term for a person to have survived a
mistake and prospered subsequently. To have demonstrated the
ability to fight back after adversity or to demonstrate success after

44

a mistake is not uncommon. One example of surviving adversity was Malcolm Gibb at Brambles (see Illustration 2.3).

Illustration 2.3 – From 'Death Row' to CEO (almost)

Malcolm Gibb was in charge of a major Brambles Industrial Services job in Sydney which went badly wrong. He was sent to what Brambles called 'Death Row' – level 14 administration in Brambles' head office. Eventually CEO Oliver Richter asked Gibb to 'do something with industrial waste in Melbourne', not exactly regarded as a plum job within the organisation. He took Gary Pemberton, who later became a CEO at Brambles and Chair of Qantas, with him. What is now Cleanaway Waste Management, one of Brambles' major divisions and greatest successes, was born under Gibb's leadership. When Richter retired, Gibb and Pemberton were both considered as his replacement.

In this respect, it is interesting and disappointing to see NAB's long and delayed time scale in 2002 for coming to terms with its debacle in the US over its failed Homeside acquisition. Here, while the enquiry was carried out by a relatively independent group, the causes of the debacle have not yet been made fully public, despite promises to do so. However, it is fair to say that, once NAB became aware of the problem, it moved rapidly to solve it.

Three strikes and you're out

This baseball phrase was popularised by US politicians in regard to the requirement that lawbreakers go to jail on their third conviction for an offence, regardless of the circumstances. Several of the winning organisations use variations of this 'rule'. The idea is that, while it is okay – even good – to make one mistake and learn from it, three mistakes of any significant type would be enough to get you removed from the company. Even making the same mistake twice would have the same result.

45

Winning organisations take positive action to get rid of people who do not meet their standards. Unlike regular organisations, they do not simply move the person sideways or to another division or position. They do not leave the person to carry on. They do not promote the person in order to move them on! This sends clear signals to the organisation: performance matters. Mistakes affect performance. Don't make too many of them. We care, we are monitoring performance and we will take action.

Interestingly, winning organisations — which might appear 'hard' and 'tough' from this discussion — do not in practice seem to fire many people. They do not have a 'hire and fire' culture. People who underperform (as opposed to making big mistakes) are often not dealt with perhaps as appropriately as they should be. The focus is on the big deals and getting them right, rather than worrying about the mid-range or lower-range performers. Some of the winning organisations considered themselves too 'soft' on their weaker people... but they did not see this issue as a particular constraint on their success.

No cross-subsidisation

A final factor emerged as being different for winning organisations in executing to deliver results. Not only is there a concern across the whole organisation about delivering results, this is also expected to occur at each unit. We term this the 'no cross-subsidisation' approach. Essentially, the poor performance of a business unit will not be allowed to drag down the overall performance of the organisation (or at least not for very long). Every business unit needs to meet the standards. No business wants to carry passengers.

In contrast, many large organisations have at least one unit which is not performing well. A typical managerial response if this issue is raised is that the organisation can 'carry' the unit while it finds its feet/improves/turns around/waits out an industry slump. This is the classic diversification argument. By averaging out performance across units, diversification reduces risk (volatility) for the whole portfolio. What is not explained by this 'risk reduction' argument is that the cost of this is a lower overall portfolio performance than would be obtained if the loss-maker was sold off or did not exist.

Such non-performing units within organisations are not well regarded within the organisation, even if some internal logic exists to explain the 'value' of the unit. Being manager of such a unit is not much fun. Peers tend to give little weight to that manager's arguments, feeling that such managers have to constantly justify their existence using all manner of arguments.

In the winning organisations, this game is played differently. At diversified corporations like Brambles and Lend Lease, it is well established that each unit has to pay its own way. At Brambles, the criteria are strictly financial. Meet your own profitability and ROE targets and everything is fine. At Lend Lease, the criteria are not simply financial, but they do include strict financials. Units are begun or closed, based on their ability to support themselves.

'No cross-subsidisation' also holds true at what are regarded as conventionally integrated organisations:

- At the Salvation Army, if a particular church unit cannot support itself, it will be closed. (Similarly, new units are opened if it is expected that there will be enough of a base to support it.)

- Harvey Norman, through its franchise system, treats every store as an independent entity. Franchisees who do not meet targets are replaced and turnover is very high, as it is difficult to find franchisees who can suddenly run their own small business to the level desired by Harvey Norman.

- Qantas expands and contracts routes regularly, based on route profitability. For instance, when the Asian financial crisis hit Korea, Qantas withdrew from Korea in 48 hours, based on assessments of expected future losses.

This concept of 'no cross-subsidisation' has received report from Jack Welch, former CEO of General Electric, the most highly rated diversified conglomerate and one of the companies in both

47

the *In Search of Excellence* and *Built to Last* high-performing company samples. In his memoirs, Welch (2001) says:

> My 'big' message... was intended to describe the winners of the future... The managements ... that hang on to losers for whatever reason – tradition, sentiment, their own management weaknesses – won't be around in 1990. (p. 106)

This led to his initial corporate strategy for GE of being number one or number two in the industry: 'fix, sell or close' each business in the corporation. He also says:

> Making tough-minded decisions about people and plants is a prerequisite to earning the right to talk about soft values, like 'excellence' or 'the learning organisation'. Soft stuff won't work if it doesn't follow demonstrated toughness. It works only in a performance-based culture. (p. 124–25)

In talking about how ideas are spread through the businesses, he notes that plants are rated against each other. As 'no-one wants to be last', everyone rushes off to find out what the best-performing plants are doing, so that their practices can be replicated in lower-performing plants. This is also done in the knowledge that, if performance does not reach acceptable standards, the business or unit will be closed or sold.

Acting as small businesses within a large organisation

This 'no cross-subsidisation' principle leads unit managers to care deeply about the results of their own unit – and to act as a small business within a larger organisation. This helps to explain why unit managers are so motivated to get the results which are in their forecasts. If they don't, and that outcome persists for any time, it is likely that the organisation will close the unit, leaving the manager without a clear position. By contrast, in most organisations losses or low performance are tolerated, and there is no motivation for the unit leader to fix the problems! The unit becomes an accepted drag on organisational performance.

Macquarie believes that one of the foundations of its success is this idea: the creation of a small business entrepreneurial environment. It currently views itself as an organisation of 45 businesses, in which the operating decisions are made by those closest to the clients, markets or business problems. This entrepreneurial environment – coupled with rigorous project evaluation by the centre – encourages rigorous execution of projects and acceptance of individual responsibility in delivering results.

Lend Lease had a similar philosophy until its recent conversion to a global organisation following the sale of MLC and the acquisition of Bovis. Brambles is another example, until its own recent international/global reorganisation following its merger with GKN. For instance, at one point in the Waste Management division, Brambles had 14 different companies in five states of Australia – all with different names.

Throughout its history, Brambles has attracted the type of people who are drawn to operating their own business. Speaking of the Brambles system of small businesses, one interviewee said:

> Managers see the businesses as their own businesses, as independent business units. It is up to you to grow them. Growth is expected – not so much incremental growth as growth through new deals.

This system was established in the early stages of the growth of Brambles. Warwick Holcroft, who became CEO in 1962 was:

> not content to entrust key positions to people who were merely good managers or good accountants – each had to possess an aptitude for the skills of the other... 'We try to make all our managers as close to being proprietors as possible, but one thing we can't do is substitute proprietor's capital'... That's one of the reasons we introduced stock options. (Carew, 2000, p. 26)

Qantas is another example of this approach. While appearing to be a single integrated business, under current CEO Geoff Dixon Qantas has been putting many operating units up for competitive tender, allowing both outside organisations and the current management and staff to compete to provide the service. The result for Qantas has been that some units have been outsourced while in others, although the current staff have won the tender, substantial changes in work practices and cost savings have occurred. This has both improved the efficiencies of the business units and also aligned the behaviour and interests of those in the units with that of Qantas as a business.

SUMMARY AND KEY MESSAGES FOR LEADERS

To summarise, the ability to execute effectively, to do what you say, to deliver results on time and on budget is a critical differentiator between winning organisations and others. In this chapter we focused on the set of internal processes that facilitate execution. Having clear processes starts the process off. Being efficient in operations and in the technical systems used will assist in getting outcomes. Having people who take responsibility for the outcomes of the work they do helps to ensure that the systems achieve what they are able to do. Having good control systems and measuring performance rigorously round out the processes needed, if all goes well. When mistakes are made, winning organisations see them as opportunities to learn, not to blame. Finally, structuring around small units to encourage and allow personal responsibility to flourish, and to prevent cross-subsidisation of business units, forces execution across the board.

The messages for leaders from this chapter are:

- Focus on execution to deliver results. Do what you say. Get the job done, on time and on budget.
- The keys to delivering results are to:
  - Have clear processes which are accepted
  - Be operationally and technically efficient
  - Ensure people take personal responsibility for their work
  - Have good management control systems
  - Rigorously measure performance
  - When mistakes are made:
    - > Encourage people to admit a mistake early on
    - > Fix the mistake as best as possible

> Learn from the mistake, after minimising its effects
> Be prepared to take tough action on those who make more than one significant mistake

- Don't cross-subsidise businesses or even units.
- Develop a small business atmosphere within the framework and advantages which the large organisation possesses.

3

PERFECT ALIGNMENT
Align everything
Consistency

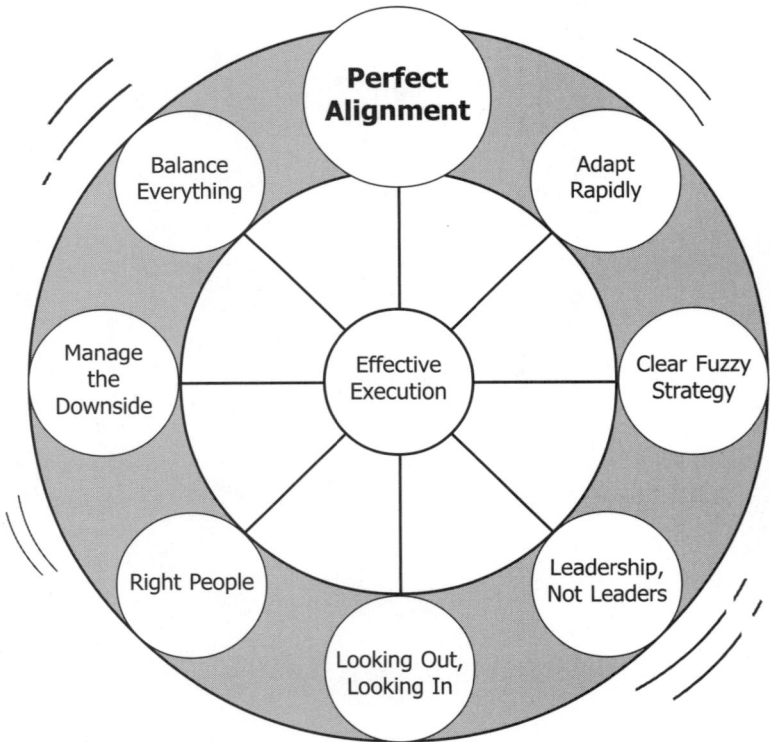

During the course of our research, we found our thinking drawn to the fact that each organisation we analysed was so consistent in what it did. Consistency comes out in many ways – consistency of leadership, consistency of strategy, consistency of process, consistency of balance, etc. Our interviews confirmed this, with consistency being mentioned by most interviewees in some shape or form. As a result, we came to the view that consistency had value by itself, regardless of the specifics of exactly what it was that was consistent.

As we refined our view over time, we realised that it was not static consistency that we were observing. After all, each of the organisations has changed radically over its lifetime. It was consistency *for the situation*. But the term 'consistency' has a static feel to it. People think that it means the same thing over and over.

The reason the organisations are consistent is that their parts and activities are closely aligned with each other. We also found that this alignment developed over time. As some element of the organisation changed (e.g. external conditions, its strategy, its leadership), the organisation was able to realign itself to the new situation, so that it could again achieve consistency.

So we came to the view that *alignment* was a better description of the element we were observing. And what we saw in these winning organisations was not just alignment, but alignment of everything – *perfect alignment*. Aligning everything to achieve consistency makes for the operational efficiency and commonality of purpose which is needed to execute and deliver results.

In this chapter we'll begin by understanding how our idea of alignment fits with previous studies. We'll then discuss what has to be aligned – what is 'everything'? Then we'll consider what we are aligning everything to – what starts this process? Finally we'll consider how realignment occurs over time.

THE HISTORY OF 'ALIGNMENT'

Alignment is not a new idea. Peters and Waterman (1982) developed the famous '7S' model. In this model, all the Ss – strategy, systems, style, staff, skills, structure and shared values – are connected by double-headed arrows to demonstrate that each one affects all of the others. Thus in order to deliver results, the concept behind the model is to line up – or align – all the Ss in the same direction, so they are consistent with each other, supporting each other.

It turns out in practice that 'lining up the Ss' – getting alignment across the organisation – is incredibly difficult. This is one of the reasons why implementing strategy is so difficult, and why delivering results distinguishes winning organisations from others. But it is surprising how little attention is given to this issue in the practice of managing organisations well.

Collins and Porras (1994) address the issue of alignment through the idea of 'cult-like cultures', which they describe as:

> ...a series of practices that create an almost cult-like environment around the core ideology in highly visionary companies. These practices tend to vigorously screen out those who do not fit with the ideology (either before hiring or early in their careers). They also instil an intense sense of loyalty and influence the behaviour of those remaining inside the company to be congruent with the core ideology, consistent over time, and carried out zealously. (p. 123)

While again not specifically referring to alignment, Collins and Porras refer to 'tightness of fit' as being a key characteristic of these 'cult-like cultures', enabling them to develop the 'congruence' which is observed.

In Australia, Hubbard (2000) developed and adapted the 7S model further (see Figure 3.1). The 7S model focuses on the internals of the organisation – but internal consistency is not enough. To create value for customers, the organisation must deliver what is wanted externally by customers. Hubbard's model effectively integrates three separate sets of ideas:

- The 'Environment – Strategy – Capability' (E-S-C) strategic analysis model, which seeks both external consistency and internal alignment.
- The 7S internal implementation model. This model better reflects what each 'S' was actually intended to convey:
  - 'Capabilities' replaces 'Skills'
  - 'People' replaces 'Staff'

- 'Culture' replaces 'Shared Values'
- 'Leadership' replaces 'Style'.
- Two new elements – perception and communication – are included. These are key elements that influence whether or not an organisation can actually deliver the results it wishes. Will people see the issues which the organisation faces (perception), so that they are able to address them? Will people understand what the organisation is trying to do (communication) in order that they can carry it out?

This work expands the number of elements that are identified as needing to be aligned.

Figure 3.1 – Hubbard's model of strategic implementation

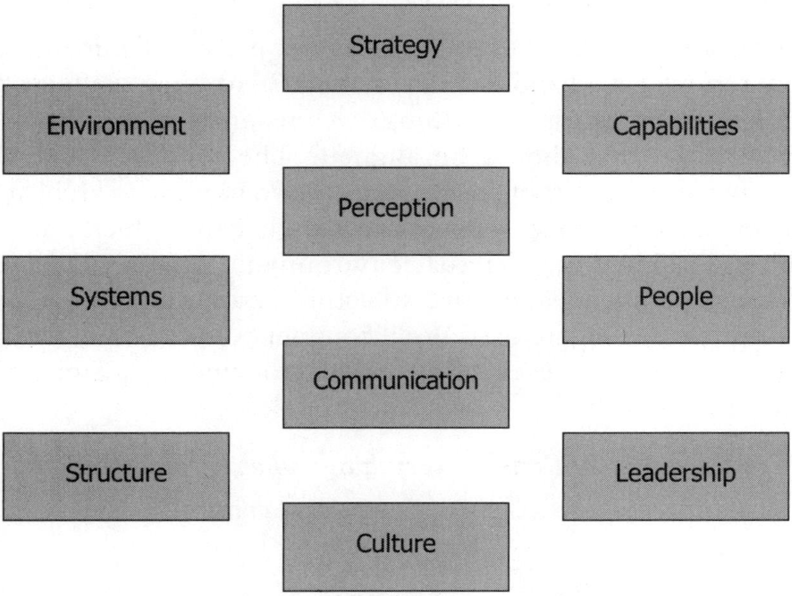

From these models, we can see that alignment and consistency are not new ideas. But they are ideas which are difficult to implement and ideas which are undervalued in the continual quest for the new and the different.

Many people find the concept of consistency boring. Yet consistency is critical, particularly for organisations like Telstra or Woolworths which depend on a very large number of sales of very small units. One of the biggest problems which these types of organisations face is how to deliver consistency of service to go with consistency of product. We all know how difficult it is to deliver service consistency in large organisations.

Similarly, alignment is also much less exciting as a management initiative than new product development or innovation or change. Yet our study finds that – in fact – alignment is more important than these ideas. The ability to line up all the activities within the organisation so that they are internally and externally consistent is a daunting task! No wonder so few organisations are able to do this and that those who do are winning organisations.

WHAT IS 'EVERYTHING'?

It is easy to say 'align everything' to get perfect alignment, but how can we get a handle on 'everything'? How can we focus on the key elements of 'everything', yet retain the idea that it is 'everything' that should be aligned? The models which we introduced at the start of the chapter – the 7S model and Hubbard's implementation model – cover the key elements which must be addressed. They are external environment, strategy, culture, systems, people, leadership, structure, communications and perception (see Figure 3.2). We'll comment on each one, though not all were seen to be equally important to winning organisations from the research.

Figure 3.2 – Aligning everything: what is 'everything'?

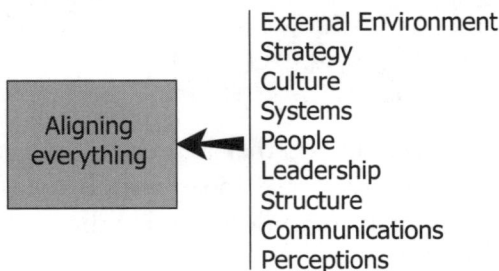

Aligning everything ← External Environment
Strategy
Culture
Systems
People
Leadership
Structure
Communications
Perceptions

External alignment

One point that was clear from our research is reflected in our winning framework: winning organisations are externally focused as well as trying to align everything internally. We cover the issue of external focus in detail in Chapter 7. From an alignment perspective, winning organisations are focused externally on customers and their needs. Qantas, Telstra, Woolworths and NAB all face mass consumer markets. For them, market research into the ever-changing needs of customers is very important and they spend a lot of time and money on it. Of these organisations, Woolworths relies most on customer feedback to its people, while the others have focused on more formal market research mechanisms. Since Woolworths regards itself as the buying agent for customers – rather than a retailer selling to customers – it is likely to be much more responsive to customer needs than other retailers. Another example of external alignment is given in Illustration 3.1, which shows how NAB aligned its home mortgage product to what customers wanted.

---

*Illustration 3.1 – Developing products
that customers actually want*

NAB achieved a significant advantage from its Tailored Home Loan package (which became known as 'Aussie mortgage loans' in the industry) for retail customers. Beginning in the late 1980s, NAB developed the first customer-based information file, followed shortly afterwards by its Customer and Management Service System (CAMS) in 1989. However, it was not until the early 1990s that the Tailored Home Loan was developed. This product relies on a choice-modelling technique which is built into the software to price different choices. It enables NAB customers to make their mortgage home loans much more flexible than those of competitor products, meeting the specific needs of particular individuals. It has only been quite recently that competitors have offered similar products. Building on this market research, more recently NAB has begun to actively segment its organisation to match the customer segments identified from its CRM systems, enabling it to serve its defined customer segments better than competitors.

In terms of external alignment, the Salvation Army is rather like Woolworths. It relies on its people being available to the community and being aware of the welfare needs of the society. The slogan 'Thank God for the Salvos' reflects the grateful attitude which the public has to the organisation and its services. It has often been the first or only organisation to tackle difficult problems in society, such as providing family welfare, crisis counselling, court services, detoxification services and safe housing for victims of violence and survivors of suicide. Over time, the range and size of services offered by the Salvation Army has expanded dramatically to reflect increasing and broadening community needs. Its ability to get the job done has meant that it is well supported by governments and by corporate sponsors, raising over $150 million per annum.

External alignment is more than just about customers though. For instance, both Qantas (for most of its life) and Telstra (which still does) have had government owners who have determined or influenced the strategy for the organisation, regardless of what customers might have wanted. Rio Tinto's strategy is very much constrained by what local communities want in locations where it wishes to mine.

This external orientation – and the ability of the internal organisation to deliver the products and services which are wanted, rather than those the organisation can produce – is a critical part of alignment that is not reflected in the original 7S model, but which is vital for winning organisations.

We turn now to the internal elements that need to be aligned – strategy, culture, systems, people, leadership, structure, communication and perception.

Aligning strategy

As with external focus, strategy is an important element of the winning framework for our winning organisations and we discuss its importance in detail in Chapter 5. Strategy setting must take account of the external environment, of the capabilities of the organisation, of its people resources and of the culture, systems and structures which exist. It is no good proposing a wonderful strategy if the organisation cannot deliver it!

For instance, the Salvation Army is very short of resources to meet its strategy to help alleviate suffering. But the government is outsourcing many of its welfare functions in the belief that other organisations can perform them more efficiently. The Salvation Army is a prime outsourcing candidate and now receives over half of its funds from various governments to undertake a variety of welfare initiatives. However, it still has to say 'no' to a number of initiatives which it would like to pursue but for which it does not have the funds.

Qantas has always had a strategy based on high-quality customer service. Yet there are significant signs that low-cost airlines have a winning formula which is gradually emerging in this industry. Qantas' response has been to re-establish the Australian Airlines brand to act as a low-cost – but not low service – airline to fly to international destinations which Qantas cannot afford to service with its own high-cost structure. Similarly, its acquisition and absorption of low-cost domestic competitor Impulse Airlines under the Qantas brand while offering its services on low demand routes, enables Qantas to 'bend' its strategy to meet its culture while also addressing emerging market needs.

Aligning culture

Culture is the most difficult aspect to change in an organisation. Hence, aligning it – or more likely realigning it – is the most difficult area to address. All the winning organisations in our research spoke of the importance of their culture. This is because it is aligned to what they want to achieve. But how do they align it in the first place? What would an organisation have to address if it wished to align the culture?

First, the organisation needs to have a clear view of where it wants to go and what it wants to achieve. For instance, the Salvation Army wishes to alleviate human suffering and distress by supporting needy and disadvantaged people, while preaching the gospel of Jesus Christ.

59

Second, this strategy needs to be communicated widely to people throughout the organisation by the leadership (not just the CEO). This communication needs to be continuous and through many channels and people. It needs to be consistent throughout. Most of the CEOs and senior managers we talked to said that a key part of their role is to communicate, communicate and communicate what the organisation is trying to do, why it is trying to do that and how people fit into that picture.

Third, there is the issue of understanding what the culture currently is. What do we want to keep? What do we want to change? For instance, for the Salvation Army, the uniform is a key part of their culture. It is readily identifiable. It immediately recalls the history and good image of the organisation. It is consistent with the 'Army' style of the organisation, as are the titles which its people use (Colonel, Lieutenant Colonel, Major, Captain, etc.). But in the 2000s, the idea of dress discipline and uniforms that don't change is seen as old-fashioned, a turn-off for young people in particular. Should the Salvation Army keep its uniform, which has been a key element of its culture, or should it change to reflect modern society?

Almost at the other end of the cultural spectrum, Macquarie has a very clear view of its culture and what it seeks from its people culturally. Like the Salvation Army, this has largely remained unchanged since Macquarie was set up. Macquarie sees its independence and flexibility as key cultural advantages compared to its international competitors. Macquarie believes its management philosophy of:

- loose/tight management structure,
- full service in Australia and focused service internationally,
- commitment to growth,
- focus on great people,
- formula-based profit-sharing remuneration system, and
- small business entrepreneurial environment,

represents the cultural keys to its success. However, originally it focused on a small number of niche markets in Australia... and provided no international service... so its culture is actually changing, slowly, over time.

In distinct contrast to Macquarie's culture is the culture of retail banking industry competitor NAB. The National Australia Bank's culture stems from its 150 years of Scottish Presbyterianism. Though it has acquired many banks in its history, including several overseas, its culture is very tight and is focused on:

- keeping costs low,
- strong discipline, and
- a very cautious approach to risk.

These values provided it with opportunities to buy some UK and US banks during the late 1980s and early 1990s, when other banks did not have the resources and were suffering significant loan losses due to poorer credit assessment than NAB.

What these examples show is that aligning culture is not a case of copying someone else's culture. It is not a case of finding the one 'right' culture. It is having a culture which is appropriate for the situation the organisation is in or wishes to be in.

One of the biggest challenges faced by Australian organisations is that, as they go overseas as part of their strategic cycle – particularly by acquiring other organisations – their need to incorporate or allow for the differing cultures and values of the employees they may acquire or hire is often overlooked at the managerial level. The managers tend to remain all Australian, yet the organisation seeks to be international/global. As we see organisations such as Brambles, Lend Lease, Rio Tinto, Westfield, NAB, Macquarie and others becoming increasingly international, their cultures will need to change to reflect this at the highest level. Illustration 3.2 shows how Lend Lease has introduced international directors to align its board with its international strategy.

Illustration 3.2 – Lend Lease aligns its board to its strategy

Lend Lease has appointed several international board members, increasing in number slowly over time, reflecting its international strategy. These include:

Yong Hau Chua – appointed 1994 from Singapore

Diane Grady – appointed 1994 from the US

Rudi Mueller – appointed 1996 from Switzerland

Albert Aiello – appointed in 1998 from the US

Jill Ker Conway – appointed 1992 from the US (though she is an Australian national).

Thus, of a board of 12, almost half are international. In addition, a number of others have worked for other organisations overseas.

Aligning systems

Systems are a key factor in aligning everything. Systems are pervasive. Consequently, unless they support the other elements, there is little chance of the ideas and wishes of the people and leaders in the organisation actually occurring.

There are many different ideas about what 'systems' means. Is it IT systems? Financial systems? Processes? We think of systems in terms of four different types (see Figure 3.3):

- operating systems
- management information systems
- decision-making systems
- reward systems.

While they are all important in operating an organisation, for winning organisations the emphasis is on some of these systems more than others. That is, although winning organisations have all of these systems, and understand their interconnections and their need to align, excellence in some systems distinguishes winning organisations from normal organisations.

Figure 3.3 – A framework of interacting internal systems that need to be aligned

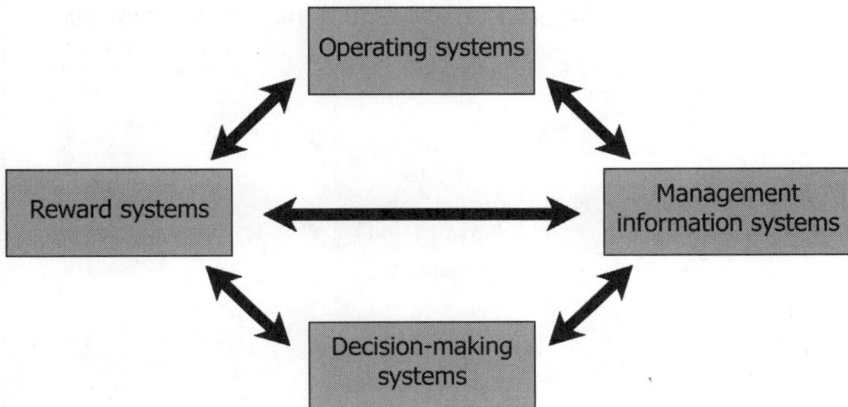

In Chapter 2 we discussed the importance of operational efficiency in delivering results. This efficiency comes from having good operating systems in place. All the organisations had good operating systems in place, but they took this for granted. They did not see operating systems by themselves as giving them particular advantage, except in rare cases, such as NAB with its Tailored Home Loan (see Illustration 3.1).

Management Information Systems (MIS) rest on the quality of operating systems. Again, no organisation claimed that its success was due to its superior MIS, at least in terms of any formal IT-based systems. Winning organisations were in general rather critical of the value of their IT-based systems. Qantas, with its yield management systems, was an exception. In general, however, technology per se does not seem to be a route to being a winning organisation.

'Decision-making systems' refers to the process of how decisions are made as well as the structure of decision-making in the organisation. Decision-making involves the use of the information from the formal MIS, but it also requires the subjective analysis of and judgement about qualitative factors external – and internal –

to the organisation, which do not appear in any formal MIS (see Figure 3.4).

Figure 3.4 – What makes good decision-making systems

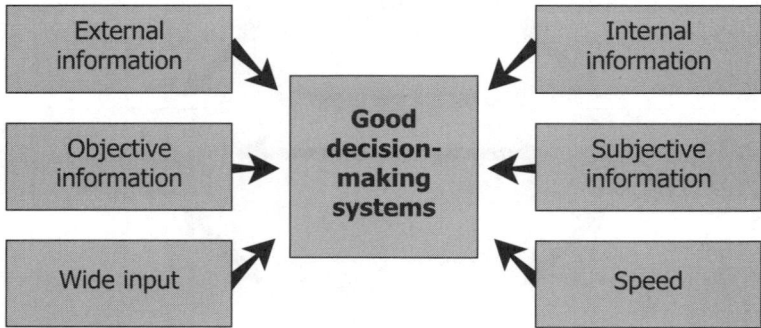

We have noted that the winning organisations are very externally oriented. This helps them include a lot of external information from the industry and elsewhere when forming decisions. For instance, unlike its major competitors, NAB has ownership of major banks in other countries. This gives NAB a better handle on events and issues in the international financial services industry, which it can then reflect back into decision-making in the Australian setting.

Good decision-making needs both the objective and the subjective view. Rio Tinto exemplifies the best of objective approaches in its mine development decisions. Using three separate analyses – a technical, a financial and a business case analysis – each of which is independent, maximises its chances of making the right decision. Macquarie similarly has its centralised Risk Management function assess any major investment proposal, in addition to considering the proposal from the sponsor division, thus providing at least two opinions on the proposal.

Nevertheless, despite attempts to get objective information, in the end decision-making is subjective. The value of having different perspectives, of being externally focused, of being concerned with rapid adaptation and of having clear strategy and the right people all help to make the final subjective decisions right much more often than wrong.

A third aspect of decision-making is speed. Quickest is not necessarily best in decision-making, but opportunities do pass by slow decision-makers. Having bureaucratic processes and layers of decision-making are two ways to slow decision-making. Brambles, Lend Lease, Westfield and Macquarie all minimise the layers and the bureaucracy, while maximising the personal responsibility of the proposal's proponents to improve speed and trying to ensure that only good proposals come forward. Illustration 3.3 shows how Westfield typically moves quickly in its decision-making.

> ### Illustration 3.3 – Westfield: A quick 'no' better than a slow 'yes'
>
> Westfield believes in commitment, not committees – entrepreneurial and active rather than institutional and passive. Frank Lowy once said he would rather have a quick 'no' than a slow 'yes'. The company's decision-making is highly centralised, but the centre is well aware that it needs to regularly go into the field and keep in touch with the business at the grassroots level. The keys to decisions are the thoughts and ideas of individuals, shared within the group and refined over time, using a 'toe in the water' approach to pilot new ideas.

In its quest to become more commercially oriented, Qantas has rapidly improved its ability to make quick decisions. After the terrorist attacks on September 11, 2001, American Airlines cancelled its order for new Boeing 737-800s to completely replace all its 737-400s. Qantas had been planning to replace a large part of its fleet in the next couple of years. It saw an opportunity to take advantage of Boeing's sudden shortage of customers. Within three weeks, the $1.5 billion decision to replace the fleet had been made and within three months the first planes began to arrive, in February 2002.

'Reward systems' is an area of systems which is both of great general interest and, more importantly, one of significant importance for winning organisations. Since the late 1980s, there has been a major shift in attitudes towards remuneration in Australia (and overseas). Some of the main causes of this have been:

- *The introduction of the Enterprise Bargaining Award system in 1987.* This encouraged and enabled individual organisations to bargain directly with their own people, rather than be limited to the existing framework of arbitrated industry-wide awards, where all organisations, whether efficient or not, flexible or not, skilled or not, well-managed or not, paid the same rate for the same work classification.

- *The Silicon Valley dotcom-inspired fashion for options.* While share options have been available for many years to a limited number of senior managers in listed companies, the IT/dotcom/IPO explosion during the 1990s made options a very rewarding way of being paid. They provided very high returns for those prepared to take high risk... and became available for a lot of people who would not previously have been able to receive them.

- *The privatisation fashion.* The privatisation of many Government and mutual organisations also led many people working in organisations to change their views (positively and negatively) about the commercial value of their work. The wide boost in share ownership which followed these privatisations (Commonwealth Bank, Qantas, Telstra, AMP, NRMA and Colonial in particular) also changed attitudes towards pay and expectations of organisational performance. Many employees became share owners and the differences between the interests of these two groups was significantly decreased.

- *The 1990s booming stock market.* Though the Australian stock market did not increase as much as its overseas counterparts, it rose rapidly. This encouraged the options concept and the share-owning concept to spill over into all types of organisations.

- *The willingness of employees to share risk and responsibility and the expectation that they will do so.* As a result of the previous points, people have become educated about the rewards for taking risk... and many have decided to accept more risk. Profit-sharing and bonuses have become widespread elements of rewards. Australia has become the country with the largest percentage of share owners per capita in the world. Compulsory superannuation, which was introduced in 1986 and rose to 9 per cent of salary in 2002, coupled with the view that retirees have a responsibility to look after themselves rather than rely on a government pension, has also been a key factor.

One outcome of these changes has been a huge increase in remuneration at the top end of most industries and a change in the structure of remuneration. Part of this is due to performance differentials, part is due to share price increases from share options, part is due to the recognition of increased risk in work and part to the fact that people who have a clear financial reward are often motivated to produce a lot more.

Another outcome is that there has been a big swing towards 'variable remuneration', i.e. where only part of the remuneration is conventional fixed salary while part is pay for personal performance and part is pay for sharemarket performance (see Figure 3.5).

However, a key finding from our research is that, while we found that all the winning organisations (except the Salvation Army) have embraced this concept, we were surprised to find that neither high pay nor high financial rewards were universally perceived to be critical to success.

Figure 3.5 – Reward systems: then and now

Then	Now

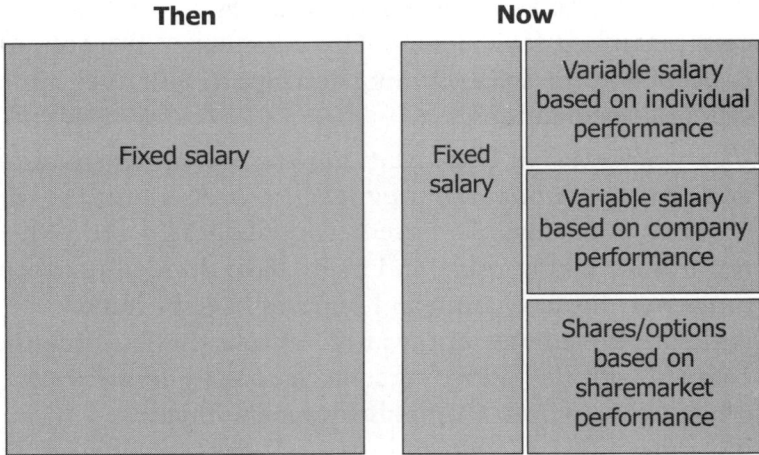

Interestingly, at all organisations, staff turnover was relatively low for the particular industry, regardless of their remuneration attitude.

Some organisations clearly pay and reward well. The Macquarie 'millionaires' club' is at one extreme, with Rio Tinto and Westfield also renowned as high payers. Brambles, Lend Lease and Harvey Norman provide high incentives, but base remuneration is not known to be high. At Woolworths, Qantas, Telstra and NAB, opportunities for promotion based on hard work and satisfaction from being involved in a cause in a good organisation are regarded as part of the remuneration. The Salvation Army, however, pays very poorly, due to the values of its religious background. It would seem un-Christian for Salvation Army people to be paid well when those they were helping were in dire need, especially when the money for those salaries comes directly out of donations. The Salvation Army clearly expects its people to get personal satisfaction from the 'cause' they serve and many non-officers accept lower-paid roles with the organisation as their way of contributing to society.

The concept of 'reward', then, seems to be much broader than simply either fixed salary or even total remuneration (see Figure 3.6). The remuneration formula varies. Personal satisfaction – which is not paid for by the organisation – is a part of the total 'reward'. There are personal costs too. For instance, large dollar rewards are usually associated with extremely long hours, large amounts of travel away from home, high stress levels and increased insecurity. Organisations which can show that they have a good cause, which are good organisations to work for and/or which are doing well, are always likely to attract and retain people. Clearly though, an organisation like Macquarie would not get the people it wanted by offering the Salvation Army pay levels. But neither would the reverse be true!

Figure 3.6 – Components of total reward

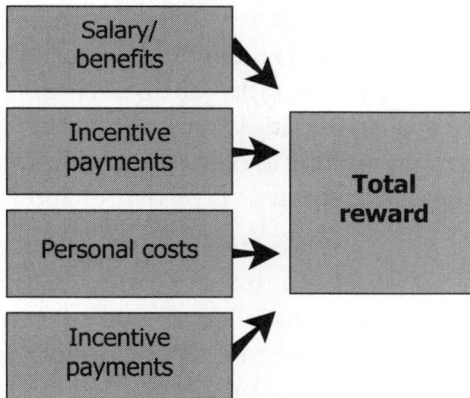

In summary, systems are important and aligning systems is essential. The key systems that make a difference for winning organisations are decision-making systems and reward systems. Decision-making systems are based on objective information where possible. They take into account a variety of perspectives – both internal and external – and decisions are made quickly. Reward systems define 'reward' widely to include non-financial elements, align employee interests with the organisation's interests and have a large variable component. The package, not the level of pay, is the critical element.

Aligning people

We use the term 'people' deliberately, rather than the more common 'workforce', 'workers', 'employees' or 'staff', in order to try to focus on the whole person rather than focusing on that part of the person who works, or highlighting any classification differences between types of people employed at a particular organisation. 'People' also includes 'managers', unless we wish to distinguish 'leadership' as a guiding group. This was the terminology used by executives in interviews and it reflects a subtle, but significant, difference in attitudes. In these organisations, people really are important. This is not just lip service. We were also impressed by the lack of 'them' and 'us' that exists in winning organisations. Managers see themselves as responsible for the wellbeing of their people.

Like external focus, strategy and leadership, 'people' was highlighted in the research as an element of critical importance in its own right. Chapter 8 talks about 'right' people, their commitment to the organisation and about the way people in winning organisations are proud of their organisation. The detailed discussion of the people element is in that chapter.

In terms of aligning people, the key issue is developing or maintaining that alignment in times of change. Telstra has shrunk from over 90,000 people to less than 40,000 over the last 10 years. Interestingly, in a highly unionised environment, there have been no major industrial relations problems during this very large downsizing. This 'non-news' item is a remarkable achievement.

Brambles and Lend Lease have also had remarkable relationships with unions by either involving them in the process (Lend Lease) or talking directly, openly and honestly to them. One Brambles publication stated:

> Brambles was instrumental with Bill Kelty [then Federal Secretary of the ACTU] in totally restructuring the award system for the transport industry... Pemberton [then Brambles CEO] was pushing co-operation. He believed in keeping relations with the unions open and strong... Pat Geraghty [then Secretary of the Transport Workers Union] was blown away by Pemberton's sharing of information and Brambles is probably alone in having such solid relations with the maritime unions. Pemberton's approach of being so open and determined meant that he overcame all the obstacles. (Carew, 2000, p. 154)

On the other hand, to overcome disastrous industrial relations and continued disruption at its mine sites in Australia over many years, CRA took the complete reverse tack. Through the use of the principles of 'time span of discretion' of Elliott Jaques (1989), it has defined the role of a manager at various levels. It has also tried to define clear roles and responsibilities consistently for each level of a consistent structure. From this Rio Tinto has introduced a system of individual contracts into a number of its operations to replace the industry awards. This has had the effect of directly linking managers and their people at each unit – leading to improved working relationships and increased productivity. Where collective agreements have been maintained, as in the coal operations, they have been revised to promote maximum operational flexibility.

What these examples show is that there is no one right 'formula'. The commonality here is the willingness to talk with and negotiate with people directly – which is generally regarded as the best way – or with unions, seeking win/win situations, even when overall job losses are a clearly necessary outcome. Unions or people were only blamed for problems once in all our interviews – by a long-retired executive.

Other issues in aligning people – hiring, training, promoting, rewarding and supporting them – are covered in detail in Chapter 8.

Aligning leadership

As with people, leadership is highlighted in the research as another element of critical importance in its own right. Leadership is much more than the CEO or even the top management team. Leadership is discussed in detail in Chapter 6.

While leadership is, and must be, involved in doing the 'aligning', it is important that the leadership team itself is aligned. John Saunders and Frank Lowy provide a perfect example at Westfield. As joint CEOs, they had separate offices with a meeting room in between. They were closely involved with all phases of the work, so they were not remote to people or the technicalities of the decisions. Decisions were always made jointly. It was only when

Lowy's three sons entered the business and Frank Lowy had expanded his capabilities and horizons beyond those of Saunders, who remained an instinctive manager, that the partnership ceased to work satisfactorily.

This ability to discuss ideas is critical in organisations. At Westfield, when decisions have to be made, all those involved in the decision are invited to a formal meeting. A wide-ranging discussion is held, where every view is expected to be offered and every view is listened to. A decision is then made by the leadership if consensus has not been reached. Using this approach, the outcomes are then 'owned' by the team.

At Telstra, Frank Blount spent a great deal of time aligning his own leadership team, recognising that without a cohesive, focused leadership team, his chances of pushing major change through the organisation were significantly reduced.

At Lend Lease, before a proposal is put up for approval, it is expected that the proposer will have consulted with everyone in the organisation who has experience in any aspect of the project's activities, so that all previous available knowledge is brought to bear on the proposal. Not to consult widely is considered an organisational sin. A similar view is taken at Brambles.

We noted during our interviews that there were significant differences in the views held by the current leadership at some of our winning organisations. This is not really surprising. Not every CEO and top management team at every winning organisation throughout its history has been happy or agreed! Indeed, the histories which we read of Woolworths and Brambles indicate violent and significant disagreements at board and top management team levels. For instance, in summarising the role of Woolworths' co-founder Percy Christmas as CEO, Murray commented:

> Woolworths was never a one-man band, rather a team operation comprising tough-minded individuals whose board meetings were still remembered more than 50 years later... as being of table-pounding, door-slamming intensity. Yet the tensions were ultimately creative. (Murray, 1999, p. 14)

No organisation progresses evenly throughout time. There are spurts and setbacks for all organisations. What sets the winning organisations apart is their ability to overcome such differences and move forward. For instance:

- Woolworths was almost out of business on several occasions in its history and was proposed for takeover by Coles by co-founder and CEO Percy Christmas to the board in 1936. This proposal was thwarted by the board.

- Rio Tinto survived extremely lean years throughout the 1980s, believing that the resources cycle would turn upwards again shortly, before eventually coming to focus directly on the commercial aspects of its operations during the 1990s.

- Westfield lost millions from 1986–89 when it diversified by buying a controlling shareholding in the Channel Ten television network and starting a listed cashbox investment company.

- Qantas and Australian Airlines were competitors when they were merged by their common parent (Qantas was allied with Ansett at the time, so Australian Airlines was very much the opposition). The merger was extremely acrimonious, described by one of our interviewees as the 'red and blue wars' (reflecting the different colour schemes of the two organisations).

But it is also true that it is much more enjoyable to be on a winning team, to have a unified leadership and a leadership which is aligned to the rest of the organisation than the reverse!

Aligning structure

The dominant finding about structure from the research is that structure is not an important element for winning organisations. Structures are constantly being changed and realigned in most of the winning organisations (the Salvation Army is the notable exception and Rio Tinto has a structured view of the roles of particular job levels – see Chapter 4).

73

These organisations see structure as supporting the activities – aligning to them – rather than having the idea that there is any one 'ideal' structure. For instance, Macquarie develops a new division or a new group as new ideas come to the surface. As groups or divisions feel that a new structure would work better, it is introduced. Consequently, Macquarie is constantly changing its structures to fit the perceived needs of the people. One Macquarie executive said:

> Structure is determined by what each group wants. The restructure that formed my division occurred because two divisions had merged under joint heads and it didn't work. So they asked Big Al to fix it and he said, "What do you want me to do?" So one group said they'd be happy to come in with us and I agreed, so that's what we did.

Another said:

> We are not very tolerant of timewasting, of committees, or of bureaucracy around here.

Lend Lease and Brambles have had similar views, at least prior to the recent internationalisation/globalisation of their businesses. One ex–Lend Lease executive said:

> They're always changing, restructuring. It's a part of life. They are very quick to adapt.

Westfield, Woolworths, NAB, the Salvation Army and Harvey Norman tend to evolve new business units with similar operations to their existing ones, so that new structure only emerges to manage the increasing number of (similar) units. These organisations are operating domestic or multi-domestic businesses, rather than international/global businesses, and so find different structures more appropriate.

Qantas and Telstra have been changing their structures rapidly, reflecting the changing orientations of their organisations since privatisation and the rapid changes in each of their markets. These organisations are very young in their current formats and are still searching for the best structures.

Having been global for over five years now, Rio Tinto is developing a fixed structure around global product lines.

In summary, the above variety of approaches shows that structures are not key to success. Nor, in most cases, are they a particular drag on efficiency in winning organisations. As we reported in Chapter 1, structure is essentially a non-factor in terms of differentiating the practice of winning organisations. Structures evolve to align to changing needs, such as changing strategy. Most organisations spend far too much time worrying about structure. Focusing on people would be much more valuable.

Using communication to align the organisation

Most CEOs (and senior managers) say one of their main tasks is to communicate, communicate, communicate. Executives at all the winning organisations mentioned the importance of communication with each other and with their people in terms of aligning organisational activity and behaviour. Most felt more needed to be done. But they also felt that the amount of communication was never sufficient. Getting the senior leadership out amongst the people is seen as critical to facilitate the opportunities for communication.

Several have formal methods of doing this. For instance, Macquarie has its CEO present at every management development program and runs lunches and discussion groups throughout the year to promote two-way communication. When trying to develop the new culture at the newly merged Australian and Qantas, James Strong indicated in a letter to all the people how important he saw communication:

> There is one essential ingredient of management in every instance, and that is the best possible communications within the group... the same success stories have the common ingredient of investing a lot of time and resources in people, communicating both ways, training, involving and encouraging individuals to meet their maximum potential... I will spend a month each year on the road, talking to them at every major location via 50 to 100 presentations... (*The Australian Way*, December 1993)

Rio Tinto uses its own managers to 'teach' management development programs, rather than bringing in outside experts. It also has regular video or telephone conferences to overcome the tyranny of distance between the London head office and its global operations. And the CEO normally visits several sites when he is in Australia (and similarly elsewhere in the world).

In summary, winning organisations see communication as important. They undertake a lot of activity to support that belief. But there are no specific or unique practices here which are widely practised.

Aligning perceptions

During our interviews, we noticed that all the interviewees presented virtually the same picture of the causes of success for the organisation and its history, despite their different backgrounds and work histories. In one or two cases, there was less than complete agreement. As pointed out earlier, this is as we would expect. Organisations do not do equally well all the time and views about them vary. Drawing on our experience of other organisations – where differences in perception are the norm rather than the exception – we felt confident when we heard similar perceptions from our interviewees (and held similar ones ourselves!).

Sharing a common understanding of the situation is essential if correct analysis and decision-making is to follow. Having an external focus, bringing in external views, sharing these views and communicating frequently help to develop common perceptions. So do hiring practices, providing training and management development experiences and the consistency of the actions which the organisation undertakes.

ALIGNMENT TO WHAT?

Having found that in winning organisations everything is aligned, what is it that they are all aligned to? What is it that drives alignment? Three possible contenders emerge (see Figure 3.8):

- alignment to strategy

- alignment to culture
- alignment to leadership.

Figure 3.8 – Alignment to what?

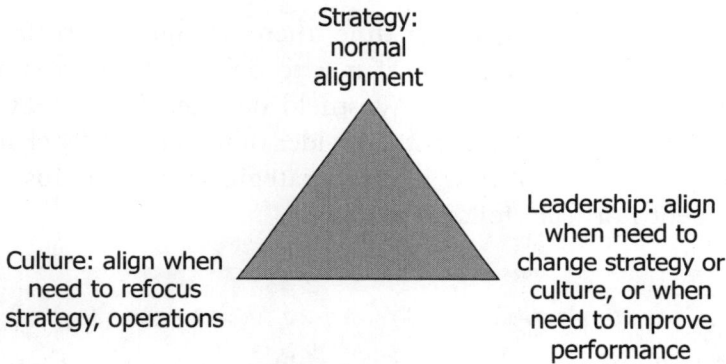

Strategy:
normal
alignment

Culture: align when
need to refocus
strategy, operations

Leadership: align
when need to
change strategy or
culture, or when
need to improve
performance

Each winning organisation is in a different position in its strategic cycle and its industry. Consequently, what drives alignment will vary for each organisation and circumstance. Emphasis on one aspect will, at least for the time, reduce the emphasis on the other two. However, since we seek to align everything, the issue of what we are aligning to is about timing differences, not conceptual differences.

Aligning to strategy?

Standard research suggests that alignment should normally be to the strategy of the organisation. We note from the original 7S model that the development of strategy is itself affected by the other Ss, so that the internal alignment of the Ss may determine or, at minimum, constrain strategy options and development.

What we find in the winning organisations is a consistency of strategy over time and, where there is change, an incremental change (see Chapter 4). The strategy will change over time, for a variety of reasons:

- changes in external pressures and opportunities
- changes in leadership
- changes in the capabilities which the organisation develops

77

- changes in the values and culture which the organisation possesses
- changes in the people, systems, processes and structures of the organisation.

As the strategy changes over time, there is a need to realign the activities of the organisation if it is to deliver the new strategy. Illustration 3.4 shows how Westfield changed its strategy over time, requiring a realignment. This idea of incrementally changing strategy is also captured in the strategic cycle. In this sense, alignment normally follows strategy.

Illustration 3.4 – Westfield goes to the US

By the 1970s Westfield was concerned about the limited future growth potential of Australia. Westfield had been interested in entering the US shopping centre market for some time. John Saunders and Frank Lowy had been attending the International Shopping Centre Convention in the US since the late 1950s. They were interested in entering the US market, using a 'toe in the water' strategy.

In 1972, the Australian government began to reduce currency regulations and restrictions, facilitating the development of international business from Australia. In 1976 Westfield bought Trumbull Shopping Park in Connecticut for $US21 million, beginning its development in the US. To support this development it established Westfield America Trust as a separate company to hold all the US assets and to gain funding in the US specifically for US assets. By 2000 it had increased from 1 to 39 shopping centres and was one of the biggest players in the US industry.

Aligning to culture?

Another possibility is that everything should be aligned to the culture of the organisation. This is essentially Collins and Porras' argument – preserve the core ideology and stimulate progress in every other area of the organisation's activities. A former Lend Lease executive said:

> [Lend Lease] has a unique entrepreneurial culture that embraces challenge and innovation, that empowers people. The culture is the core of the company. It is the competitive advantage of the company.

The difficulty with this is that, periodically, the values of the organisation and the associated culture need to change. The obvious examples in the winning organisations are the originally government-owned organisations of Telstra and Qantas (see Illustration 3.5 for some detail about Telstra's cultural change).

Illustration 3.5 – Cultural change at Telstra

Telstra's original strategy was very consistent for over 70 years – provide a phone for every home in Australia. But by around 1990, this strategy had been achieved. Coupled with this was the emerging deregulation of the industry and the proposed privatisation of the organisation.

What should Telstra have done? The high-quality engineering and technical standards that had been built up around providing phone connections were no longer of such high value.

The values and culture had to change from that of a government-owned monopoly, where people worked for life, to that of a commercially oriented, publicly listed organisation in one of the fastest-growing, newly deregulated, industries in the world. This explosive growth was also based on a dramatic change in product mix – from local fixed-line phone calls to global mobile communications.

How well would your organisation have fared/be faring faced with this tremendous change in the fundamentals of the organisation and the environment it faced?

So aligning everything to existing values and culture is problematic in changing environments. As values and culture are the hardest elements of an organisation to actually change, they will limit the change that is possible and certainly limit the speed of change. And inability to change speedily could consign an organisation to its deathbed if its industry faced some fundamental upheaval.

Aligning to leadership?

A third possibility, coming from the 'one great leader' theory of organisations, is that as CEOs change, strategy changes, so alignment should be to the CEO – the one great leader. Clearly, in practice, a new CEO can affect or change the organisation incrementally or dramatically, requiring significant changes to achieve realignment. But organisations survive CEOs, and often the direction of the organisation is actually little changed by different CEOs, even when they appear to be proposing major change. And of course CEOs are themselves reacting to external changes as well as following their own perceptions, preferences, values and styles.

We have already noted that one thing winning organisations are not about is the one great charismatic leader. Consequently, while many of the CEOs – and their leadership teams – over the long histories of these organisations have influenced their direction, very few have made such radical changes that the organisation is little recognised from what it was before. For instance, Qantas has had four CEOs over the last 15 years. Their main contributions have been:

- *John Menadue* – aligning the head office with operations; increasing the focus on Asian routes
- *John Ward* – presiding over the integration of Qantas and Australian Airlines
- *James Strong* – making the integration work; developing common high service standards and a sense of commercial reality as Qantas became a listed company
- *Geoff Dixon* – focusing on commercial performance while preserving high service standards; surviving a domestic airfare war; managing the consequences of September 11, 2001 and the collapse of Ansett.

None of them actually changed the fundamental direction of the organisation substantially. Yet all faced significant challenges during their periods in office. Therefore, we do not think that it is really about aligning everything to the leadership. We see leadership as a catalyst and an influencer in the alignment process, but not the focus of the alignment.

To sum up, the underlying process is normally to align 'everything' to the strategy, recognising that the strategy will itself change over time. Being dynamic, however, alignment is constantly changing. Attempting to align everything to achieve perfect alignment is a formidable task. That so few organisations come close to achieving it suggests the size of this task is very great. Alignment – and the consistency that follows from it – needs more attention in management practice.

ALIGNMENT OVER TIME

So far we have been considering alignment of activities to the current or desired (short-term or medium-term) future position of the organisation. That is, we know what we are trying to do. What do we have to align to make it happen in the near future?

As we have seen, the winning organisations have grown and developed a long way from their original business. For people working in these organisations, the changes have indeed been significant. Growth and expansion have brought opportunities, but most of the organisations have also sold and/or closed businesses (and hence people have been transferred into other organisations, or lost their jobs). Some organisations have been involved in continual job reductions, in the pursuit of increased operational efficiency.

How is alignment managed over time and over a changing range of businesses and business situations? Our study shows that:

- Rapid adaptation is one of the keys for winning organisations. The ability of these organisations to adapt rapidly to planned and unplanned changes is a key of their success.

81

- These organisations are oriented to the external world. Consequently, they are more aware of the opportunities – and the threats – which exist. This enables them to prepare more carefully for contingencies. A focus on managing risk also helps.

- The ability to change over time is influenced by the choice of the CEO and the leadership team. Most of the organisations felt that their line of CEOs had been 'right for the time', even though the thrust of each CEO was actually different. This is consistent with the strategic cycle of development. Different stages in the cycle require different capabilities and different visions for the future, and new CEOs develop new strategies to meet those different visions.

- As winning organisations proceed overseas as part of their strategic cycle, the type of people they require in terms of capabilities, attitudes and often nationality is different.

  As winning organisations diversify their businesses, or focus them, the type of people and leaders needed also changes.

  Winning organisations are always developing their people, communicating with them about where the organisation is going and what will be needed, and providing them with opportunities for personal growth.

- Communication is vital. Managers often underestimate the intelligence and understanding of their people. People generally have a very good idea of the state of the business and what changes are being considered.

  Managers apply the 'no surprises' rule to their people too. They try to keep their people as informed as possible, to give them the opportunity to change work practices if this is important, to adapt to a new environment if this is important. And if they must close down or sell businesses, they try to ensure that their ex-employees are well treated.

Winning organisations do not have magic formulas for realigning over time. There are many elements to be addressed. They execute, rapidly adjust to external information, choose their leadership well, choose and manage their people well and communicate widely and frequently.

SUMMARY AND KEY MESSAGES FOR LEADERS

Alignment is a difficult concept to get your hands on, especially when 'everything' needs to be aligned. But alignment is necessary to 'execute to deliver results' efficiently and effectively. The key elements to align are strategy, culture, systems, people, leadership, structure, communications and perception. Alignment must be external as well as internal. Alignment should normally be to strategy, but the roles of culture and leadership are important at different times in driving alignment.

The key messages from this chapter are:

- Everything must be aligned.
- Alignment must be to external forces as well as internal factors.
- Strategy should normally be the driver of alignment, but culture, values and leadership at times may be valid drivers.
- Culture is the most difficult area to align, if change is required. Understanding the real culture is the starting point.
- Systems are crucial foundations. Decision-making systems and reward systems are critically important. A wide view of 'reward' should be taken.
- Aligning people is essential for delivering results.
- Leadership must be a major player in the alignment process.
- No particular structural solution is best. Structure should be flexible enough to meet specific short-term needs. Much time is wasted on restructuring.
- Communication of messages throughout the organisation by leaders is an essential element of success.

- The role of aligning perceptions is often overlooked in alignment – not everyone sees things the same way and this must be addressed in aligning everything.
- In times of change, everything must be realigned to the new situation.

4

ADAPT RAPIDLY
Adapt! Adapt! Adapt!

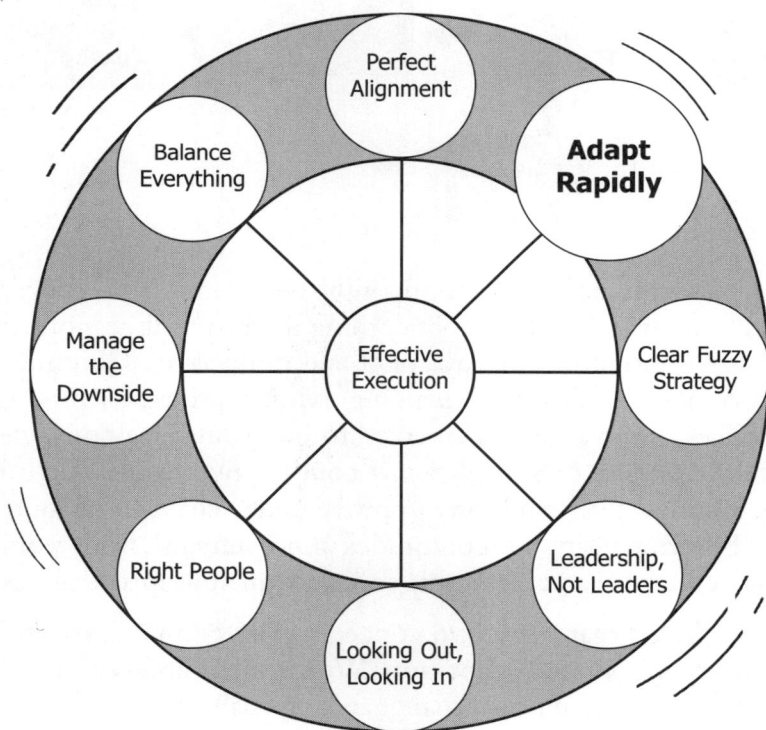

Closely related to 'perfect alignment' is our finding that winning organisations adapt rapidly. As mentioned in Chapter 3, not only do they need to be aligned to be consistent, but they also have to be able to adapt over time... and then realign to become consistent again! But even more important than having this ability to adapt is being able to adapt rapidly. Many organisations struggle with the ability to adapt, but that is exactly what these organisations are able to do – change quickly to meet new situations (see Figure 4.1).

Figure 4.1 – The process of rapid adaptation

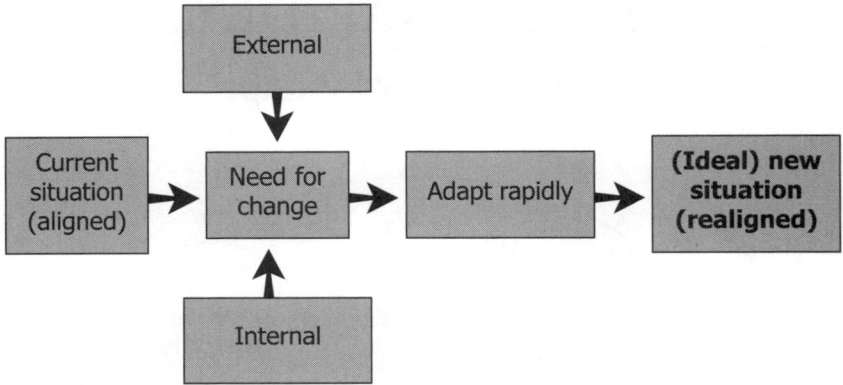

What causes this rapid adaptation, or the need for it? Two concepts related to rapid adaptation kept coming up in our discussions and analysis – continuous improvement and innovation. Continuous improvement is related to changing existing processes, products or services. Innovation is perceived to be about developing *new* products, services or processes. Of course, any change might be termed 'innovative' while any improvement, whatever its source, might be termed part of a 'continuous improvement'. Both require people, creativity and leadership to create an appropriate culture.

We concluded that these two concepts were components of the larger concept of rapid adaptation. We view the ability to rapidly adapt to external or internal change, big or small, as a key capability for these winning organisations and one of the reasons why they are able to stay ahead of competitors.

In this chapter, we'll first focus on the idea of 'rapid' – what it is that enables winning organisations to be quick in changing. Then we'll look at what constitutes 'adaptation' – the ways in which adaptation takes place and what it is that enables/encourages winning organisations to rapidly adapt, and adapt, and adapt (see Figure 4.2).

Figure 4.2 – The factors behind adapting rapidly

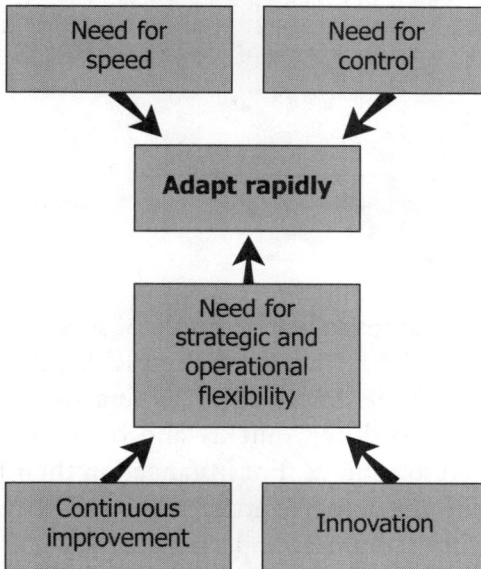

WHAT IS 'RAPID'?

What does 'rapid' mean? We have said that a key aspect of the ability of winning organisations to adapt is the speed at which they can do it. Winning organisations have a sense of urgency in everything they do. Part of this is attitudinal – they simply expect that things can be done more quickly than in other organisations. Coupled with this is that they have a clear idea of what it is that the organisation wants to do, both strategically and operationally. Part of it is organisational – they set themselves up to be able to do things quickly by having good systems, good people and good structures. Another part of it is having the resources to be able to carry out what they want to do (see Figure 4.3).

Figure 4.3 – Factors enabling speed in adaptation

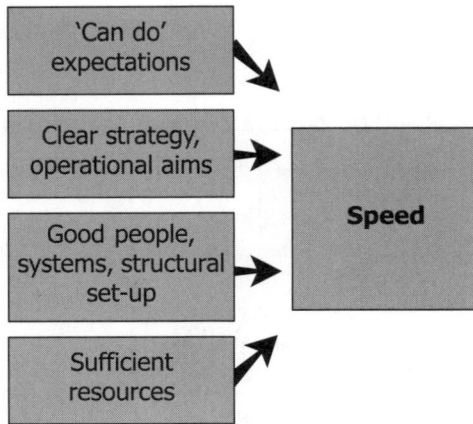

Westfield provides an excellent example of speed. Its emphasis on speed comes from the founders of Westfield, John Saunders and Frank Lowy, who were described as 'hyperactive and in a hurry'. They expected to do things quickly and they had clear views of what they wanted to achieve. For instance, on their first trip to the US to investigate shopping centres, they would typically record the layout with both a camera and a notebook... and they even did the same thing with the motels they stayed in! (One of Westfield's first projects was the Shore Inn motel.) They sought both to understand what existed and why, and also how the layout could be improved. In the evenings, Frank and John would discuss their findings and work out how they would improve the layout if they were in charge. Frank Lowy described his own attitude to speed:

> I have this force within that constantly drives me to improve, not necessarily for financial gain but for being able to do more... I can't sit around and do nothing. My mind just doesn't rest, whether it's five o'clock in the morning or midnight, I still give all I have to everything I do. (Margo, 2000, p. 185–186)
>
> I drive myself and spare no effort. It is sheer slog that allows for no laziness of mind or body. I allow myself no latitude and give up all comforts, day and night, until I achieve the goal. (Margo, 2000, p. 254)

This approach pervades Westfield management. Commenting on the roles of his three sons, who became joint managing directors during the 1990s, he said:

> We eat, sleep and talk business. This is not an eight-hour-a-day commitment. We are at it 24 hours, on the weekend too. The business hovers over us constantly. (Margo, 2000, p. 264)

This constant involvement means that many more decisions can be made in the same chronological time period than in a normal organisation which only works eight to ten hours a day five days a week. Some of the non-executive directors commented on their experience of the results of this speed at Westfield:

> Each time we have a meeting there is a new deal on the table... These deals... are concrete, formidably researched and entirely reality-based. It's impressive. *Carla Zampatti*
> (Anon, *The Detailed Westfield Story*, p. 131)

> When I think of Westfield, I think of great activity. *Rob Ferguson*
> (Anon, *The Detailed Westfield Story*, p. 130)

> During my board membership there has never been a dull moment ... Most of the centres have been upgraded or are in the process of doing so, and at the same time all options of further expansion are on the table. I sometimes have the feeling that we are playing soccer with more than one ball. Directors asked management many times if they could cope with this ... management proved to be completely in control. *Herman Huizinga*
> (Anon, *The Detailed Westfield Story*, p. 139)

This intensity of activity leads to speed of decision-making. The fact that Westfield does everything possible in-house also assists the speed of the total process. Illustration 4.1 gives an example of how this works for a major project.

Speed and control

Many organisations can do things quickly. They rush about in a state of chaos, and somehow the job gets done, but it is exhausting, costly, inefficient and often out of control. In winning organisations, speed comes with control too. For instance, Westfield used the critical path method to plan the development of its first shopping centre in 1966, and has been using this technique ever since to minimise development and redevelopment time. When Westfield is redeveloping its centres, it tries to minimise disruption to the trading time. Therefore, the construction shift starts at the end of the trading day. It continues throughout the night, clearing up before the start of the next trading day.

Illustration 4.1 – How Westfield speeds up the development process

When Westfield buys a shopping centre, it does not begin to think about how improvements can be made. It has already worked out how it will improve the centre in great detail and embarks upon that improvement process as soon as possible after the centre is acquired. For instance, when it purchased the Garden State Plaza centre in New Jersey in 1986, it immediately embarked on a plan to increase mall space and attract upscale retailers to improve the quality of the centre. This was all done by its in-house development, design and construction team, enabling much quicker implementation than if outside contractors had to be involved.

A typical innovation was the conversion of a former truck tunnel under the property into a basement shopping level, resulting in 140,000 square feet of new space with 50 new specialist retailers.

Upscale clothing retailer Nordstrom was targeted as an anchor tenant. Nordstrom had no locations in the north-east of the US at the time. Through intense personal lobbying and selling of the benefits to Nordstrom's owners, Nordstrom was encouraged to make a quick decision to take up the opportunity. The addition of Nordstrom provided the attraction for other upscale stores, including clothing company Neiman Marcus, and many other subsequent changes and expansions.

By the end of the process (the plans were completed in 1989 but the improvement process continued until 1997) Garden State Plaza had become the dominant shopping centre in its area.

This focus on speed without losing control of operational detail is seen in other winning organisations. When Woolworths planned to open its first shopping complex in Newcastle in 1964, senior management feared a disaster due to lack of an anchor magnet store (Murray 1999). These fears surfaced at a planning meeting only four months before opening. Following discussions after the meeting about what to do, a proposal to rectify the problem was on CEO Theo Kelly's desk by the following morning. By midday, Kelly indicated preliminary approval. A meeting was held the next day and the proposal – to develop Woolworth's own 'magnet' store – was approved. What should it be called? 'Big W' was suggested, based on a US idea called Big E. Kelly approved the name over the weekend and the centre opened on schedule – Big W was born.

Emergency relief services in Australia cater to unexpected and significant events that cannot be planned for. Speed and control are essential to meet each emergency. The Salvation Army is one of the best placed organisations in the community to respond. It has a clear command structure that readily translates into an efficient field operation during an emergency and it is readily identified as an organisation that helps in times of need. The Salvation Army sees this capability as one of its services and plans for emergencies of all types.

Telstra and Qantas also have excellent reputations for assisting in emergencies. When community emergencies occur, Telstra is expected to be able to restore communications in minimum time. The fact that it is able to do this is due to the attitudes of its people – they feel a responsibility to the country to do whatever it takes to solve the emergency. One Telstra executive said:

> Telstra people rise to the needs of the community. There is a real empathy between Telstra workers and the community. There is an expectation that the 'mail will get through'. Telstra workers work really hard to overcome crises, but those stories never appear in the newspaper.

Qantas people have a similar view. Qantas has detailed contingency plans at all times to cope with unexpected maintenance needs, weather problems and missed connections, as well as with industry

91

disasters. Margaret Jackson, chair of Qantas, commented on the events of September 2001:

> On Sunday September 9, Qantas was invited to buy Ansett for $1... On Tuesday, September 11 the terrorist attack on the US took place. The next day, Wednesday September 12, an administrator was appointed to Ansett. On Friday September 14, Ansett was grounded...
>
> Qantas embarked on a huge logistical exercise...We transferred 2,600 anxious passengers to and from the US. We transferred 115,000 Ansett domestic passengers free or at a steep discount. We operated an additional 196 regional flights. We arranged for services to 22 regional destinations previously served only by Ansett...
>
> ...We managed well because we were managing well before. We had programs in place...
>
> But when the crisis hit we no longer had the luxury of long lead times for making decisions. Decisions that we might once have agonised over were made in two days. If they proved wrong, we made new ones.
>
> It was vital to keep staff and the community informed... Even with such intense communication... we had to let go and rely on each other... We had to trust our senior executives. (Jackson, 2002, p. 5)

FLEXIBILITY: THE ABILITY TO ADAPT

In order to adapt, an organisation must be prepared to change. How is it able to change? The winning organisations are committed to their strategy but show considerable flexibility within their aims. That is, they do not see flexibility as a virtue by itself, but as a capability to be used to achieve a particular end goal or position that is carefully thought out, or to take advantage of an opportunity that fits with the values of the organisation.

Flexibility within winning organisations is a consequence of both customer demands and internal expectations that the organisation will be able to meet those demands. Therefore, they force themselves to be flexible to achieve this. But what is 'flexibility'? How are winning organisations flexible? We see two types of flexibility – strategic and operational flexibility (see Figure 4.4).

Figure 4.4 – Types of flexibility

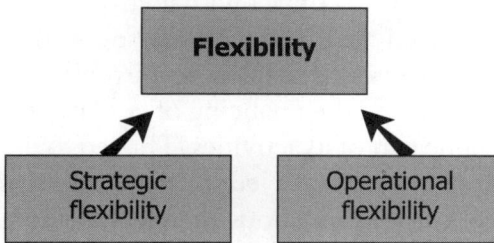

Strategic flexibility

Of the two types – strategic and operational flexibility – strategic flexibility is the more challenging issue. How can you be 'strategically flexible' when you have a clear strategy? The answer is 'over time'. Woolworths provides a good example (see Illustration 4.2).

For Macquarie, flexibility is a key element in the development of its strategy. The choice of products and services which Macquarie offers depends not on top-down planning of the senior management team, but on bottom-up, entrepreneurial efforts of Macquarie people. Before establishing Macquarie, co-founders Mark Johnson and David Clarke had worked for other merchant banks and had learned what they didn't like in the processes of merchant banking organisations. Their concept for overcoming these deficiencies – to hire bright people, empower them to use their ideas, reward them using a profit-sharing formula agreed to by shareholders, yet to be cheaper than international competitors, and maintain a very high ethical reputation and control risk centrally – did not specify any particular products or services. Hill Samuel (the original name of what is now Macquarie) searched for niches in Australian banking to begin its growth. Over time, it has covered many niches, so much so that it now regards itself as a full-line investment bank in Australia... but a niche player overseas.

One example of how this process of generating ideas works is shown in Figure 4.5, a diagram of how Macquarie moved from gold futures to agricultural commodities. One product Macquarie already offered was gold futures. Arbitraging of this product by Macquarie staff led

93

to actual physical trading of gold becoming another business. This brought the company into contact with gold-producing companies. Macquarie discovered that these businesses wanted to sell gold forward over longer periods than were currently available, and so gold mine assessment and the financing of gold mines (against future production) became part of its activities. This led to the development of the derivatives business. This led to Macquarie thinking it could apply this model to other precious metals, such as silver. This led to Macquarie applying it to base metals as well, which resulted in the company doing international business in these metals. This then led to a similar business in agricultural commodities. None of this was planned by the centre or the CEO, though each stage was approved centrally to control risk.

Illustration 4.2 – Never say never

During the early part of Woolworths' life, CEO Percy Christmas stated vehemently that the company would never enter food retailing as it knew nothing about food. Despite this statement, Woolworths did in fact sell very minor amounts of food in its variety stores.

Then in 1957, an 'egg war' broke out in Sydney as Woolworths imported cheaper eggs from Victoria into NSW. Despite bans being put in place by the Transport Workers Union and the NSW Egg Board, Woolworths reached a compromise agreement that allowed it to sell cheap eggs... so long as it was with some other product!

A Woolworths executive had recently visited the US and had recommended entry into supermarkets. The success in lowering egg prices substantially and the resulting publicity, coupled with this report, encouraged Woolworths to set up its first food supermarket in Sydney that year. The acquisition shortly after of 32 Brisbane Cash and Carry food stores from under the nose of arch-rival Coles signalled Woolworths' substantial entry into food. Woolworths came to dominate food retailing in Queensland and is now the dominant food retailer in Australia... and 85 per cent of its total sales now come from food!

Figure 4.5 – Strategic flexibility at Macquarie Bank

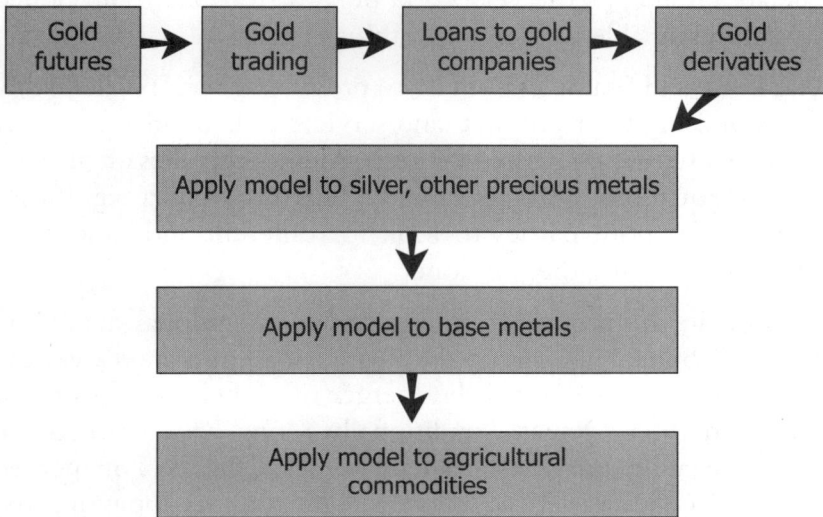

```
┌──────────┐    ┌──────────┐    ┌──────────────┐    ┌──────────────┐
│   Gold   │ →  │   Gold   │ →  │ Loans to gold│ →  │     Gold     │
│ futures  │    │ trading  │    │  companies   │    │  derivatives │
└──────────┘    └──────────┘    └──────────────┘    └──────────────┘
                                                            ↓
┌────────────────────────────────────────────────────────┐
│   Apply model to silver, other precious metals           │
└────────────────────────────────────────────────────────┘
                          ↓
┌────────────────────────────────────────────────────────┐
│              Apply model to base metals                  │
└────────────────────────────────────────────────────────┘
                          ↓
┌────────────────────────────────────────────────────────┐
│           Apply model to agricultural                    │
│               commodities                                │
└────────────────────────────────────────────────────────┘
```

There are many other examples. Harvey Norman was long opposed to entry into computer retailing. Yet it changed its mind and now it has over 50 per cent of the personal computer retail market. Lend Lease decided funds management would be the key plank of its portfolio of businesses, using MLC as its vehicle. Yet, in 2000, Lend Lease changed its strategy to become a global real estate player. It sold MLC, which was focused on Australian general investment and accounted for around 50 per cent of its total profits, to NAB, because it no longer fitted its new global strategy.

Operational flexibility

Operational flexibility is a more traditional concept of flexibility and easier to appreciate. Yet it too flies in the face of conventional wisdom. Traditional operations-dominated approaches seek economies of scale and scope, and focus on a small product range to achieve efficiencies. Flexibility, however, does not allow maximum economies of scale to be pursued.

But flexibility has a different value, especially in such a small market as Australia. Here, the opportunities for specialising and using long runs or large volumes to take advantage of economies of scale are limited, so the very good organisations often developed through being able to do a lot of things well.

Lend Lease and Brambles both try to provide operational flexibility by customising their products and services to particular customer needs. Lend Lease also shares any savings which it makes on planned construction costs with its clients. This provides a significant incentive for both parties to look for different and innovative solutions to getting the job done.

Qantas is in the process of improving its operational flexibility, which has helped it come to dominate the local market over the last five to ten years. With the merger of Qantas and Australian Airlines in 1993, Qantas – traditionally a long-haul international airline – began to operate short-haul domestic flights. The merged entity had a wide variety of different flight patterns, types of plane and types of people (both in terms of skills and desires). While this flies in the face of the concepts of focus and specialisation, it gave Qantas a very interesting – and highly valuable – degree of operating flexibility. When demand is very high on domestic routes, some capacity may be diverted from international routes and/or different plane types may be used so that, for the same landing slot, more passengers can be handled. For start-up international routes with low demand, some smaller planes from the short-haul operation can be used to test out commercial viability. The wider range of routes – and wider range of staff – also improves opportunities to progress for those who perform well. One of the reasons Qantas was able to handle the almost simultaneous domestic collapse of rival Ansett, and the collapse of international travel following the World Trade Center attacks in 2001, was its ability to rapidly divert capacity from international routes to meet the unexpected domestic demand.

The constant restructuring of organisations is another indicator of flexibility that we observed in the winning organisations. Restructuring is not seen by winning organisations as a strategic solution but as a short-term tactical response, taken in stride, to improve efficiency by being flexible.

ADAPTATION BY CONTINUOUS IMPROVEMENT

Adaptation can be achieved by either continuous improvement or by innovation (see Figure 4.6).

Figure 4.6 – Continuous improvement and innovation give rapid adaptation

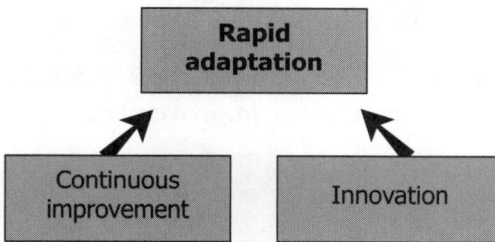

We see 'continuous improvement' as consisting of the vast array of small and continuous changes that an organisation makes to improve its performance. We see 'innovation' as significant new ideas introduced to the organisation. Let's look first at the role of continuous improvement in adaptation, as this is the less well understood approach to creating value and delivering results.

The history of continuous improvement

At one level, continuous improvement is simply a mantra. Of course, every organisation wants to 'improve' and do so constantly. Who can disagree with this statement of desire?

The origins of the term are mainly associated with the quality movement and its plan–do–check–act cycle (see Figure 4.7). This technique of continuous improvement encourages organisations to consider that better results can be achieved by:

- Planning before 'doing' the event. What do we want to achieve? How are we going to do it?

97

- After 'doing', 'checking' back against the plan. Was the outcome satisfactory? What do we need to do now to improve our performance?
- 'Act' again, after making any corrections considered necessary.

In this way, if action is unsatisfactory (i.e. it does not meet targets or benchmarks), it can be reviewed before being repeated, with the aim of improving the outcome each time. When the target or benchmark is reached, it can then be raised to a higher level to continue the improvement process.

Figure 4.7 – The plan-do-check-act cycle of continuous improvement

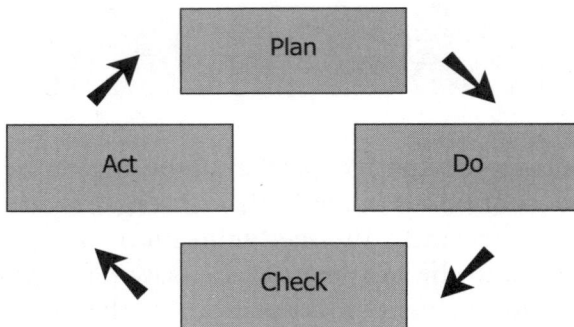

But in practice this cycle rarely happens in most organisations. While there is lots of 'doing' and some 'planning', our experience is that there is not a lot of 'checking' done – there is little post-implementation review and summarising of lessons learnt before doing it next time – and even more rarely are changes made before the next 'act' occurs.

Collins and Porras supported the importance of this concept when they identified 'good enough never is' as one of their elements for success. They said:

Our research findings clearly support the concept of continuous improvement... it is an institutionalized habit – a disciplined way of life – ingrained into the fabric of the organization and reinforced by tangible mechanisms that create discontent with the status quo... visionary companies apply the concept of self-improvement in a much broader sense than just process improvement... it means doing *everything* possible to make the company stronger tomorrow than it is today. (p. 186)

Continuous improvement in winning organisations

Practice in winning organisations is different. All the phases of the plan–do–check–act cycle are important and they are executed. But there are some surprises. For instance, our research showed that winning organisations spend little time benchmarking against competitors. They are too busy running their own races. When we raised the issue of competitors in our interviews, we were surprised that interviewees had little to say and seemed relatively unaware of the details of their close competitors. What they were passionate about was their own performance and position against their own targets, goals and strategies.

Despite this lack of direct external comparison, they were quite critical of themselves. Winning organisations don't praise themselves greatly. They set quite demanding targets. That's one of the reasons why they keep improving! They may be doing well but they feel that they can do better and must do better if they are to maintain their position or improve it. This is consistent with the findings of Collins and Porras who said:

Visionary companies, we learned, attain their extraordinary position not so much because of superior insight or special 'secrets' of success, *but largely because of the simple fact that they are so terribly demanding of themselves.* (p. 186)

In many ways, winning organisations are concerned with creating their own future, not benchmarking against laggards. Their focus is on their future and the future of their industry and how they can maintain or improve their position in it. But they are ahead of the game. They are defining the rules of the game. By being leaders, and maintaining focus on real continuous improvement, these organisations are hard to catch.

How do winning organisations continuously improve?

So how do these organisations continuously improve to meet and exceed the changing expectations of customers? Figure 4.8 outlines the key internal factors which our study found. They are:

- having a culture of change
- being dissatisfied with their own performance
- having growth as a driver
- having good people
- having good systems
- having a cost focus, and
- planning for continual upgrading.

Figure 4.8 – Internal drivers of continuous improvement

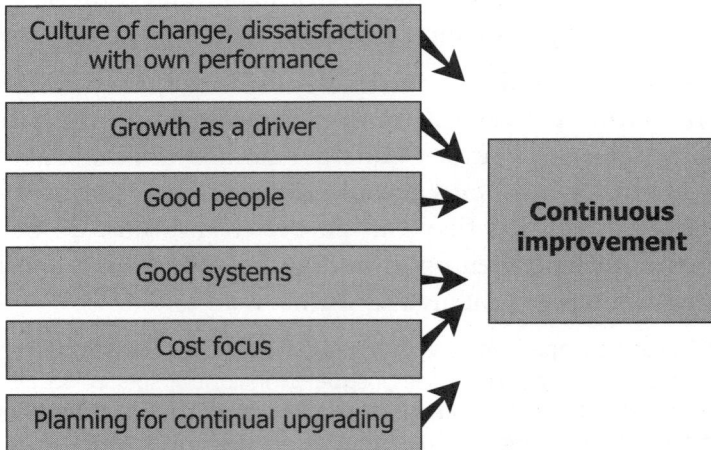

At its best, continuous improvement is a significant element of the organisation's culture. In such a culture – a culture of change and dissatisfaction with the current situation, however good it may seem to outsiders – people continue to seek new ways of operating. New opportunities are continually spotted in such a culture. No sooner is one idea implemented than another is underway (in practice there are many ideas in various stages of implementation simultaneously).

Westfield created a new area in the centre court of its shopping centre at Tuggerah, ACT, when it introduced a 'lifestyle' section instead of a 'fashion' area. It was so successful that Westfield took it to the Marion centre in Adelaide and extended it so that it became the best in the country. The concept was next taken to Southland in Melbourne where, with more improvements, it was called 'The Street'. After further refinements it was taken to Carousel in Perth, then Burwood, Sydney. Said one executive:

> We watch, we monitor and we anticipate where change is coming from. From this and from constantly talking to retailers, we keep our competitive edge.

Having growth as a driver also creates the need for continuous improvement. For instance, in 1984 Brambles held a planning workshop in Manly. After two days of discussion, little had been achieved. After dinner that night, one executive said that if they were any good as a management team and an organisation, they should be able to add $100 million profit in five years. At that time, profit was $30 million. The challenge was taken up by those at the table and the 'Manly Manifesto', as it became known, was drawn up on paper napkins, identifying intentions, capabilities, financial objectives and possible acquisitions. Next day the plan was hammered into shape with clear details. CEO Gary Pemberton said:

> It doesn't sound like a big deal but it has a very dramatic effect on people to go to the end and work back. It changes the perception of what is possible, it forces people to think about big things, not about the little things. (Carew, 2000, p. 146)

The plan was achieved by 1989, as per the challenge.

Good people and good systems are other key components of winning organisations that we have commented on in earlier chapters. Macquarie, which has growth as a driver, hires good people and heavily incentivises them to seek that growth. Interestingly, in both Macquarie and Brambles, the growth target is largely a consolidation of bottom–up business level plans rather

101

than a centrally determined target. This suggests again how powerful the combination of good people and good systems can be.

Another way to continuously improve is to focus on cost control. This is quite a different emphasis but it can be equally effective. Being tight with costs can force organisations to look for new ways to decrease their costs or improve their productivity. Woolworths, for example, is a technology leader in its industry and seeks to achieve cost efficiencies by using the latest technology in the key areas of its business. In the 1920s, it was the first store in the world to acquire receipt-printing machines. In the 1950s, it had the largest punched-card stock control operation in the world. In the 1960s, it was one of the first in Australia to adopt computers and one of the first to adapt them to its broader needs rather than simply mechanising the accounting system. In the 1980s, it was a leader in the use of scanning technology.

NAB is very cost focused and became the national cost leader in its industry through the use of technology (with the slogan 'simplify, standardise, automate'), large amounts of training and rigorous measurement. Operational improvements made in one area of its business are moved to another business.

Qantas has spent much of the last 10 years focusing on cost control, to improve its commercial returns. In the early 1990s, Qantas set up 20 continuous improvement teams to establish world best practice in engineering and maintenance. Yield improvements, working with Boeing to achieve 'industry leader' status in engineering and maintenance, and improving scheduling techniques are some of the means it has used.

Planning for continual upgrading is another valuable way to continuously improve. Westfield never rests in regard to improving its shopping centres, with around 30 per cent under redevelopment at any one time. It believes that each centre has a life of only 7 to 10 years before needing renovation.

ADAPTATION VIA INNOVATION

Adaptation is not just continually improving what already exists. The second approach to achieving successful adaptation is innovation. Winning organisations are innovative. However this innovation is not big bang/big idea innovation. This finding is consistent with earlier research findings about innovation in Australian business by Carnegie et al (1993), who undertook a major study of leading innovators in Australia. Illustration 4.3 summarises their findings on innovation and compares them with ours.

We categorise innovation into the following types (see Figure 4.9):

- borrowing ideas from overseas
- process innovations
- incremental product and service innovations.

Figure 4.9 – Sources of innovation for winning organisations

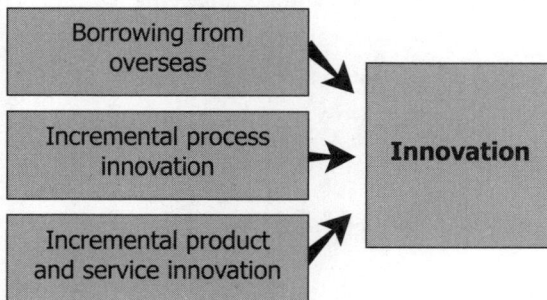

Borrowing ideas from overseas

A classic approach to 'innovation' in Australia is to find an idea overseas, to copy it and to offer it in Australia. Several of the winning organisations used this approach to get started. The original ideas that started Woolworths (cheap variety stores) and Westfield (mall shopping centres) as corporations came from overseas. The Salvation Army (church and welfare), Rio Tinto (mining) and Macquarie (investment banking) all began as subsidiaries of overseas organisations. Dick Dusseldorp came to

103

Australia as a representative of a Dutch construction firm looking
for opportunities. He found construction opportunities, stayed...
and Lend Lease began.

Illustration 4.3 – Innovation in Australia

Carnegie et al defined innovation very broadly as "something
that is new or improved done by an enterprise to create
significantly added value either directly for the enterprise or
indirectly for its customers" (p. 3). In our study, this would cover
both continuous improvement and innovation.

The work was based on a largely qualitative study of 120
businesses of leading innovators. They classified innovation into
the following types:

- creating better processes
- providing new and improved products and services
- combined process and product innovation
- technological breakthroughs
- market-driven continuous product and service improvement
- across the board improvement.

The key findings were:

- 90 per cent of innovation is the result of incremental
  improvement
- five major themes are important for innovation:
    - focusing on customers
    - building a competitive supply system
    - sustaining innovative leadership
    - building a systematic approach to innovation
    - committing scarce resources to competition.

Good leadership, good management and good employee relations
need to be in place to have an innovative culture.

Our research did not find much in the way of 'technological
breakthroughs' and we treat the last two categories as 'continuous
improvement' rather than 'innovation'.

The first Woolworths shop in Sydney was based on Cash and Carry, a business run by three of the founders (Ernest Williams, Percy Hall and Charles Humble) in Adelaide. But Hall had worked for F.W. Woolworth in the US and the UK. Woolworth was a 'five and ten cents' store – a discount variety store – which had 1,000 stores in the US by 1919. In searching for a name, they found that Woolworths was not registered in New South Wales so, since that best represented the type of business they sought to offer, they registered it and began business.

Most organisations continue to look at developments overseas, particularly, it seems, in the US. For instance the 'wheelie bins' now in common use for rubbish collection in Australia were discovered by Gary Pemberton in the US in the early 1970s (Carew 2000). Pemberton was impressed by the one-person trucks which operated the system so he bought three and shipped them to Australia. The bins were first introduced into industrial waste collections, as Brambles foresaw industrial relations problems if they were used in domestic waste first.

Another example is Woolworths, which modelled Big W on Wal-Mart (its rivals have competing Kmart and Target stores, which are also modelled on their US originators!), spending some 12 years to perfect the 'every day low price' logistical and merchandising system in Australia.

Why is borrowing from overseas so important as a source of innovation? While our study did not address this issue, we speculate that the small market size of Australia, the fragmented nature of the state-based market, the consequent lack of local research and development activity and the derivative and import-based nature of the society and business (Australia has been heavily dependent on its links with first the UK, then the US and now Japan and China) are key drivers of this approach to 'innovation'.

Process innovations

Several important innovations for winning organisations came through process, rather than the more conventionally understood and expected area of products and services. Process innovation was addressed by Carnegie et al as one of the major sources of Australian innovation, so our findings are consistent with those.

The co-founders of Harvey Norman – Gerry Harvey and Ian Norman – had previously owned and run Norman Ross – a precursor discount retail chain – from 1961 to 1982. This had been enormously successful in New South Wales and Queensland until it was acquired by Waltons Bond, a subsidiary of the diversified conglomerate Bond Corporation, and both Harvey and Norman were sacked. As no non-compete clause had been inserted in the takeover documentation, they established Harvey Norman in the same year... to compete in the same line of business.

However, they made one crucial change to the formula. They believed that the future of 'big ticket' retailing lay in smaller owner-operated stores, where the owner's expertise and dedication to personal service would be backed up by the financial muscle, buying power and management services ability of a larger organisation. The system they established has several unique features:

- franchisees are personally chosen
- each franchisee is limited to owning only one franchise
- people are charged only a small franchise fee for the privilege/opportunity of being a franchisee
- as part of the franchise agreement, franchisees provide certain information to the franchisor, enabling Harvey Norman to monitor franchise performance including sales, cash and stock levels, thus ensuring that franchisees do not get into financial difficulties
- Harvey Norman retains the right to withdraw franchises should they not comply with the franchise agreement requirements
- franchisees totally control their own purchasing decisions.

Harvey Norman has come to dominate its field... and its innovative system has not yet been replicated! In 1982, it opened the first complex in Sydney with seven franchises – hardware, furniture, bedding, electrical appliances, kitchen and bathroom renovations, and carpets. By 1988, when it listed, Harvey Norman had 12 complexes and, in 2002, had over 150 stores. Further, it had diversified by acquisition into other similar areas of retailing, where it was applying similar principles.

Lend Lease, Macquarie and Brambles similarly apply these principles of financial incentives to get people to see themselves as running little businesses within a large company framework, but they do not use the franchising concept. Brambles is very focused on units meeting financial criteria for the business and providing a value-for-money proposition in the services it offers. On the other hand, Lend Lease provides very high levels of welfare support for its high-quality people and has high-quality and customised large-scale construction projects. It sees itself as developing a 'community of interest' of stakeholders, rather than following the 'make a quid' strictly financial approach of Brambles (see Illustration 4.4).

Rio Tinto works in a commodity business. As such, it has very limited opportunities to develop new products or services. So its focus on innovation is also process-oriented. Rio Tinto's approach to management systems is unique (see Illustration 4.5), though it has recently begun to be applied at Telstra and some other major Australian organisations.

Rio Tinto has many other process innovations to its credit. Indeed, process innovation at its first mine at Broken Hill in 1905 enabled the company to commercially produce zinc when existing processes did not work. Currently it is working on two major innovations. They are the Mine of 2020, which is intended to be an environmentally sustainable mine, and the HIsmelt iron ore smelting process, which has been in development for almost 20 years and which is now proceeding to commercial plant status. These projects indicate the commitment necessary for research and development in this industry, which operates on extremely long time scales from discovery to mine development to full production. How many other Australian organisations would even be prepared to invest in this type of research with such long time scales?

> ## Illustration 4.4 – Process innovation: Lend Lease's 'community of interest'
>
> From its beginnings, Lend Lease has had a philosophy of a 'community of interests' – balancing the interests of its people, clients, suppliers, shareholders and the community. This is quite a different perspective to that of a financially oriented organisation.
>
> In terms of looking after its people, some of the examples of Lend Lease's innovative practices were that it:
>
> * hired the best people
> * offered shares to employees so that by 1981 employees were the largest shareholding group with 17 per cent of total shares
> * initiated a Building Trades productivity agreement in 1958, updated it in 1973 and established the ACTU/Lend Lease Foundation to develop training skills in 1983
> * introduced profit-sharing in 1973, raising this to 5 per cent of pre-tax profit in 1981
> * introduced a company-paid employee health plan for all Australian employees and their families in 1980
> * introduced disability insurance cover for subcontractors in 1982.

Incremental product and service innovation

The third area of innovation – products and services – is the most traditional perception of what innovation is. But the examples of winning organisations are of incremental innovation rather than fundamental innovation, consistent with the findings of Carnegie et al. Brambles has been the most successful of the winning organisations in using product and service innovations (see Illustration 4.6).

Lend Lease was the first company to turn the financing of its real estate assets into a property trust financial product. The innovation here was that the risk in construction and the risk in managing an existing asset are quite different. Capital can be raised more cheaply for the lower risk management of existing assets.

Illustration 4.5 – Process innovation: formalising the roles and responsibilities of management

Frustrated with high levels of industrial disputation, in the early 1980s, CRA/Rio Tinto's Tom Barlow recommended the work of Canadian academic Elliott Jaques to CEO Rod Carnegie, who was concerned about improving the financial performance of the organisation.

Jaques believed that the work of managers is to get their people to deliver the goals of the organisation. To do this, Jaques believes that getting the roles, accountabilities and structures right is critical. An effective structure makes clear who the manager is, what the manager is accountable for and who judges performance.

According to Jaques there are seven levels of work, each with a different time span of discretion (i.e. the time before a decision can be determined to be correct or not). The longer the time span of discretion, the more important the job. Job levels should be determined by time span of discretion. A person at one job level should manage people at lower levels. Each manager should judge the performance of their subordinates and, in turn, be judged by their manager.

CRA introduced this radical process of rigidly defining and practising the roles and responsibilities of management at the Woodlawn mine in 1984. When this pilot experiment was successful, the process was moved to other mines on a unit by unit basis, managed by the head office Organisation Development Unit, and accompanied by heavy amounts of staff training and development. At one location, the levels of management were reduced from 14 to 5.

As a result of the rigorous application of the Jaques organisation development process throughout the group, substantial improvements in efficiency, quality of work and people relationships were made. While the principles sound relatively simple, applying the principles to work roles is difficult and tends to upset existing embedded organisation processes which have simply grown up over the years.

Illustration 4.6 – Product and service innovation at Brambles

Brambles' international developments and extensions of the CHEP pallet system, Cleanaway waste management and Recall records management all represent products which, though they existed, have been taken to extraordinary levels by Brambles.

The humble CHEP pallet – a wooden pallet used to enable goods to be lifted and transported more easily – was introduced to Australia by US ships in 1943 when forklift trucks and pallets started to be used to unload ships instead of manual labour. The Australian government developed a pool of pallets and forklift trucks during the war to speed up ship movements. In 1946 the committee was renamed the Commonwealth Handling Equipment Pool (CHEP) and became a trading organisation. In 1958 the government decided to sell CHEP and Brambles was part of the successful consortium, buying out its partners' interests shortly after. Brambles' development of a national pool of pallets, its control and guarantee of supply of the pallets, its development of a variety of pallets for different product types and its market expansion of this pallet system throughout Europe, North America and now parts of Asia all represent product and service innovation to particular markets.

Brambles saw waste management as an extension of materials handling and transportation. In 1970 Brambles bought Purle Waste Disposals for $120,000. Purle was part of the UK Purle group which was the recognised world leader in waste management. The Brambles self-styled 'garbos' group, which became Cleanaway, had begun. Brambles' development of a wide variety of binning systems and collection systems, and its application of these ideas to different markets, are further examples of product and service innovation. Future CEOs Gary Pemberton and John Fletcher both came to prominence through this group.

Finally, when Brambles acquired Grace Bros Removals in 1983, it included box storage facilities. In 1991 Brambles bought the Vault Company in the US and several subsequent US acquisitions led to the development of Brambles' third major business – Recall records management – where a similar approach is being followed for both hard copy and electronic storage of records.

By separating the assets – creating General Property Trust (GPT) as a vehicle for managing property and selling the assets into GPT when they were constructed – Lend Lease was able to develop two related businesses with different costs of capital. Interestingly, Westfield followed this example a little later with the formation of Westfield Property Trust and then Westfield America Trust for its US assets.

Westfield provides another interesting example of incremental product and service innovation. While the original idea of modern shopping malls came from the US, Westfield has been constantly experimenting with the 'product' in Australia and has exported the concept of 'branding' the centre back to the US! In Australia, going to 'Westfield' has become synonymous with going shopping for retail customers. Using common signage, crossmarketing in newspaper, television and radio ads, clustering of centres in areas, making centres more social than competitor centres and using the continual improvement process to transfer learning from one centre to another rapidly have enabled Westfield to build its brand in the US, where it now has more centres than it does in Australia.

The Salvation Army is a good example of an organisation which sees the problem which the customer faces and comes up with innovative solutions. For instance, its 'Employment 2000' initiative was piloted in Perth in 1983! Research showed that employers of unqualified and low-skilled labour were primarily looking for people with positive work attitudes, while the long-term unemployed felt worthless, powerless and lacking in self-confidence. Employment 2000 trained disadvantaged people and aimed to place them in full-time employment. It had very high placement and success ratios.

Woolworths has primarily innovated by expanding its product and service range incrementally, with innovation of new products and services being more evident since the late 1990s. The most dramatic event that occurred was when Woolworths was doing quite poorly in the mid-1980s. It decided to focus on fresh food as a point of differentiation from arch-rival Coles. Since adopting the slogan, 'The Fresh Food People' in 1987, Woolworths has grown rapidly in a mature industry. Innovations have included:

- expansions into petrol retailing
- a banking alliance with the Commonwealth Bank
- an entry into wholesaling to independent competitor supermarkets and convenience store chains
- expansion into national liquor retailing
- expansion of Dick Smith electronics into superstore formats
- development of the Crazy Prices discount chain
- development of Metro small shop format shopping centres.

Each of these organisation examples represents incremental product or service innovation, but the application of that product or service to areas/services/industries well beyond its initial scope has made these innovations of great significance. Importantly, little of this is the result of fundamental research, or highly detailed market research or R&D programs. It is primarily based on an interesting formula:

- motivated, capable people, with the right attitude for the organisation's values and with credible expectations about future rewards
- seeing a problem from the customer's perspective
- applying some creative thinking
- large amounts of determination and effort
- a supportive, but not munificent, organisation (rewards are based on outcomes)
- leveraging a concept into other geographies and other industries.

Of these requirements, the only one in short supply in the community is likely to be the supportive organisation. All the others are widely available... but rarely combined to get the results which winning organisations achieve.

112

SUMMARY AND KEY MESSAGES FOR LEADERS

Winning organisations adapt rapidly and continuously over time. Rapid adaptation over time is based on speed of response and the flexibility to respond, aligning and realigning to deliver results. Speed with control is required. Both strategic and operational flexibility are demonstrated, through continuous improvement and innovation.

The key messages for leaders from this chapter are:

- Expect to have to change and adapt to new circumstances.
- Expect to have to adapt rapidly and continuously.
- Provide the supporting mechanisms of clear aims, good people, systems and resources to enable adaptation to happen quickly.
- Speedy actions and responses must come with control.
- Some flexibility of strategy is required over time.
- Develop a culture of continuous improvement.
- Seek innovation in process as well as in products and services.
- Seek innovations from overseas sources, as well as local research and development.

5

CLEAR FUZZY STRATEGY

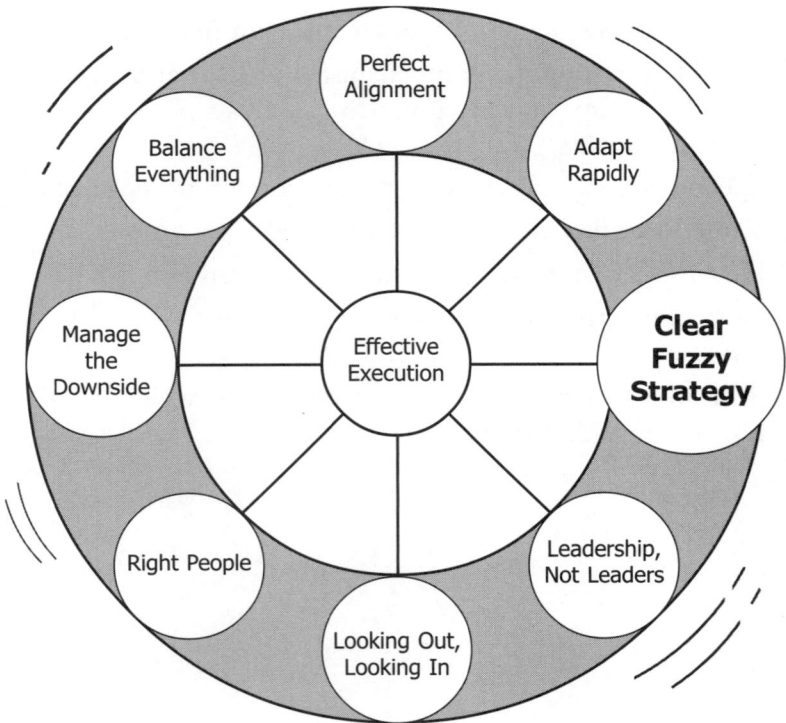

Everyone knows that strategy is important... what's different for winning organisations? Unfortunately, while many people think that 'strategy' is important – and it is – the concept of 'strategy' is not well understood. So the first issue we need to understand is just what 'strategy' is. Then we will look at how strategy for winning organisations is both clear and fuzzy. Strategy is a driver of direction and action for the organisation. We measure execution and results against the strategy. But, as the winning framework demonstrates, strategy is not the only driver and it's also influenced by the other elements in the framework. Finally in this chapter, we'll see that strategic issues vary throughout the strategic cycle and that even winning organisations make mistakes in strategy from time to time.

WHAT IS 'STRATEGY'?

The word 'strategy' is widely used – and abused – in organisations. One aspect that everyone agrees on is that 'strategy' is about the long term. But 'long term' itself is not an agreed-on concept, varying from two years in an internet/rapidly changing technology-based industry, to three to five years for 'normal' organisations, to 10-plus years for mining and other industries where decisions taken have very long-term effects.

Levels of strategy

One of the reasons for the confusion is that use of the word 'strategy' does not make clear what *level* of strategy is being discussed. There are four levels of strategy (see Figure 5.1):

- *Corporate or multibusiness strategy*. The key issues here are:
    - Do we want to grow?
    - What businesses should we have in our portfolio? What is our 'vision' of what the portfolio should be?
    - How is value created by having these several businesses collected together?
    - How do we want to position the corporation? (e.g. GE's famous 'number one or two in every industry we are in', News Corporation's 'a leading global media company')?
- *Business strategy*. The key issues here are:
    - Do we want to grow?
    - What products and services do we want to offer?

115

- What customers and markets do we want to serve?
- What generic strategy do we want to use to achieve this?
- What position do we want to hold in our industry?

- *Business unit or functional strategy.* The key issue here is: How do we best carry out our unit/function activities to deliver the business strategy of the organisation?
- *Personal strategy.* This is not part of 'strategy' for an organisation, but of course it is very important for the people who work in the organisation. Their behaviour and aims can significantly impact on whether or not the organisation is able to achieve its own strategy.

Figure 5.1 – Four levels of strategy

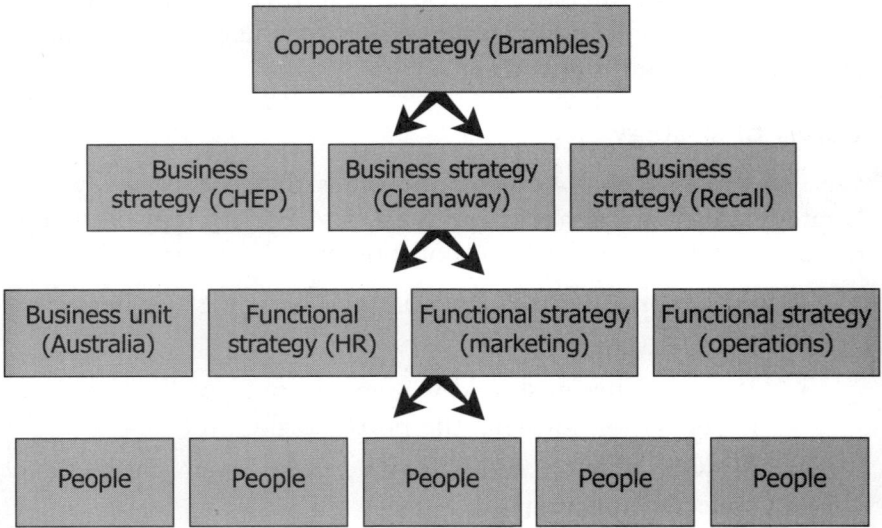

The main focus of strategic thinking is on the competitive positioning of the business in its industry, i.e. business–level strategy. However, most of the winning organisations are collections of several different businesses... so for them, corporate strategy is also an area we need to focus on. How do these organisations think about their corporate and business strategies? For the rest of the chapter, we will use the term 'strategy' to cover both business and corporate levels of strategy. We should not do this and would not if we were referring to a single organisation! However, as the winning organisations cover both businesses and corporations, we will combine them here to avoid confusion.

Confusion over 'strategy'

These different levels of strategy are one reason why the term 'strategy' might be confusing. Discussion about 'strategy' can be associated with quite different levels of organisational thinking and action.

While we have outlined a clear view of the different levels of strategy, unfortunately this is not clearly understood – or accepted – in general organisational practice. There are also many terms which are used to convey strategic concepts. For instance, apart from the terms used above for the different levels of strategy, the following terms are also used widely in practice to convey strategic ideas:

• goals
• objectives
• aims
• vision
• mission
• purpose
• strategic intent.

While one organisation may use one or more of these terms consistently over time, unfortunately there is simply no consistent agreement in practice – or in theory – about which are the 'right' terms to use for describing the essential features of what the organisation is trying to achieve, in the long term.

Even the studies we are linking to do not agree! While Peters and Waterman have 'strategy' as one of their 7Ss, Collins and Porras do not use the word!

117

Instead, they include:

* 'Purpose', which is defined as:

   The organization's fundamental reasons for existence beyond just making money – a perpetual guiding star on the horizon; not to be confused with specific goals or business strategies. (p. 73)

   In our view, this is clearly a major part of what 'strategy' is about.

* 'Big Hairy Audacious Goals' (BHAGs), which are described as:

   All companies have goals. But there is a difference between merely having a goal and becoming committed to a huge, daunting challenge – like a big mountain to climb. Think of the moon mission in the 1960s... a true BHAG is clear and compelling and serves as a unifying focal point of effort – often creating immense team spirit. It has a clear finish line... people like to shoot for finish lines. (p. 94)

   This could also be the essence of strategy, but to Collins and Porras it represents only a part of the totality of what an organisation might be pursuing in the long run.

So even the experts are confused! Is it any wonder 'strategy' is so poorly understood?

STRATEGY IS CLEAR

Our research found that, even though organisations often didn't have a specific statement of their strategy, such as a vision or mission statement, they were quite clear about the direction in which they were headed. Table 5.1 indicates the essence of the strategy followed by the organisations over the 20-year period we analysed in detail, and also how that strategy was conveyed to people outside the organisation. It shows two things. Firstly, that we are able to get at the essence of the strategy for a long period with a very few words! In this sense strategy is both clear... and quite stable. Secondly, it shows the variety of mechanisms used to communicate the essence of that strategy.

Table 5.1 – How 'strategy' was publicly conveyed during the period analysed

Organisation	Essence of Strategy 1980–2000	How Strategy is Conveyed
Brambles	Specialised industrial services	CEO reports
Harvey Norman	Specialist discount retailing	CEO reports
Lend Lease	Property construction, development and funds management	Chair and CEO reports
Macquarie	Niche-based financial services	CEO reports
National Australia Bank	Retail financial services	Some use of vision statement
Qantas	Australia's international airline	Earlier use of mission statement
Rio Tinto	Finding, mining and processing resources	Untitled statement at front of annual report
The Salvation Army	Preaching the gospel and alleviating hardship	Some use of mission statements
Telstra	Full range telecommunications	Variety of mechanisms used
Westfield	Shopping centre development and management	CEO reports
Woolworths	Food and general retailing	Variety – objectives, CEO reports, Chair reports

For instance, Westfield's strategy has always been about the development of regional shopping centres. It has always been highly vertically integrated in designing, constructing and managing them, with ownership separately held by associated property trusts (Westfield Property Trust for the Australian centres and Westfield America Trust and Westfield America Inc. for the American ones).

119

Woolworths has always been a retailer. Since the 1950s it has specialised in food retailing. In 1993, when it was relisted, Woolworths said:

> Woolworths is Australia's largest food retailer and, with its general merchandise and specialty retail groups, is the second largest retailer [in Australia]. (1993 annual report)

This statement was backed up by a set of objectives, a statement of culture and an operating philosophy. This is typical of the idiosyncratic nature of strategy statements. They are all individual in construction.

In 2001, Woolworths said:

> We're all here to deliver our customers a better shopping experience each and every time:
>
> - To continue to increase shareholder returns
> - To grow our enterprise
> - To improve operating efficiencies
> - To achieve world class retail operations.
>
> (2001 annual report)

While the words have changed – and they changed in most years – the intent and direction is clear and consistent – growth in retailing. Close analysis will note the dropping of 'food', 'general merchandise' and of 'Australia' from the 1993 statement. Woolworths has expanded its product and service range during the period to include petrol, liquor, banking services and shopping centre developments. During the period, CEO Reg Clairs saw Woolworths as a 'significant global supplier of food' by 2020. So we can see the consistency, but we also note the subtle changes that typically occur through development over time.

The Salvation Army has had several experiments with mission statements over the period we analysed, all with slight variations. However, the key elements have always been the same. In 1983 it said:

> ...primary aim [is] to preach the gospel of Jesus Christ to men and women untouched by ordinary religious efforts... From this

120

service to God flows service to man... The Army has always sought to make practical and spiritual responses appropriate to individual and community needs.

In 1995, the mission statement said:

The Salvation Army, an international movement, is an evangelical branch of the universal Christian Church. Its message is based on the Bible, its ministry motivated by the love of God. This mission is both spiritual and practical, encompassing the preaching of the gospel of Jesus Christ and alleviating human suffering and distress without discrimination.

This shows that it sees itself primarily as a church, but a church having a practical side, serving people who are suffering.

Macquarie Bank, which is quite a young organisation, has never had a mission or vision statement. However, it has developed its own statement – called 'What We Stand For', which states:

Macquarie Bank aspires to be a pre-eminent provider of financial services over the long haul. We recognise that, however our achievements to date are judged, the quest for improvement is never ending. The Macquarie culture is represented by the way in which we act and work together. The values to which we aspire can be summarised in six principles... integrity... client commitment... strive for profitability... fulfilment for our people... teamwork... highest standards... Our commitment to the six principles is vital for our continued growth and prosperity.

Here the first sentence clearly describes the strategy, while the rest of the statement describes how that strategy will be achieved from a process perspective. It is interesting to see the specific mention of continuous improvement, of culture and also of growth, all of which are common recurring themes in winning organisations, wherever they may be expressed or discussed.

How do vision and mission statements fit into 'strategy'?

Vision and mission statements are often proposed as providing the essence of the strategic direction for an organisation. Many organisations have spent a great deal of effort and expense developing vision and/or mission statements to try to articulate the direction in which their organisation is heading... how do they fit into this picture?

Surprisingly, our research found that vision and mission statements are rarely used to illuminate strategy in winning organisations. *None of the winning organisations consistently used either or both a mission or vision statement over the 20-year period we studied.* It was not that they simply changed the words in the statement. While some used one or both during part of the period, vision and mission statements are not seen to be of great importance.

Having a vision or mission statement is *not* a key to being a winning organisation. Time and money spent developing vision/mission statements may well be wasted. However, the reverse does not follow!

These organisations did have a clear view of their strategy... and strategy is important, as interviewees in the winning organisations confirmed. The examples above are clear statements of strategy, but they rarely involve vision or mission statements, as you could see from Table 5.1. Despite this, mission and vision statements can be useful methods of defining and communicating clear strategic views. There are no mechanical or consistent ways which winning organisations use to communicate strategy.

There is also a degree of fuzziness about the strategy of each. Indeed absolute clarity was not sought, primarily because of the perceived need to be open to relevant opportunities and not be completely locked in. This is consistent with the ideas of rapid adaptation, continuous improvement and innovation (see Chapter 4) and being externally focused (see Chapter 7).

Growth as a driver of strategy

One of the key findings about the winning organisations is that growth is a key driver of the organisation. This growth – of profits, not just sales – comes from the strategy (and the leadership). This is a key difference for winning organisations. Where other organisations are happy to accept lower rates of growth, or focus on sales growth, winning organisations are driving hard for high profit growth rates, which they manage to achieve without overstraining the organisation. For instance, Lend Lease, Brambles and Macquarie have had very long periods of profit increases before a reduction occurs.

Linking strategy and values

Our research found that the strategy and the values of the organisation were closely linked and aligned. We concluded that when strategy underwent significant change, such as a move from government to private ownership, when organisations developed overseas or when they realigned from multidomestic to global operations, values changed to adapt to the new perspective. We did not conclude that strategy should be aligned to values – rather the other way around (see Figure 5.2). However, strategy development is constrained by the current set of values and, for strategy to be implemented, values must be consistent with the strategy.

Figure 5.2 – The relationship between strategy and values

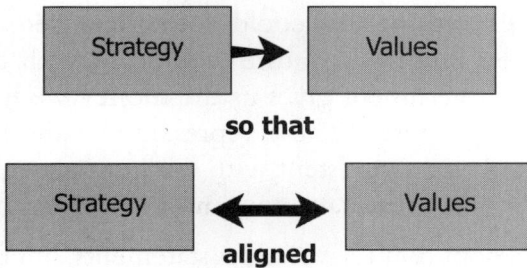

The studies of Collins and Porras and Peters and Waterman both emphasise the importance of values and of them being aligned with the strategy or core purpose. 'Shared values' is one of the Peters and Waterman 7Ss. Collins and Porras see 'core values' as part of the 'core ideology' of the organisation, along with 'purpose'.

All of the winning organisations have strong and clear values, whether explicit or implicit. The Macquarie statement given earlier includes its values. The Salvation Army has a separate list of values printed on cards for widespread distribution. The values are:

- human dignity
- justice
- hope
- compassion
- community.

When Telstra began its change process in the 1980s from being a government-owned public sector utility to a commercial – and eventually a publicly listed – organisation, it developed a Vision 2000 program with three explicit – and quite new – values:

- customers come first
- we make it possible
- business success builds our future.

For an engineering-oriented organisation at that time, the idea of 'customers come first' was a radical change. The idea that 'we make it possible' overturned the existing idea that the bureaucracy had rules for everything that could not be changed. The idea of 'business success builds our future' conflicted with the previous idea that 'the Government gives us the money we need to build the system we propose'. These represented radical changes in values, but they were consistent with the new strategic direction. Variations on these ideas have continued since that time.

Many organisations don't have values statements, but their implied values are heavily supportive of their strategy. Rio Tinto implies its values from the strategy statement – called 'The Way We Work' (see Illustration 5.1).

This is a rather long statement – certainly much longer than could be remembered by anyone! This long statement is supported by several pages more, covering transparency, corporate governance, accounting standards and internal financial control, a variety of policies and board committee terms of reference.

Illustration 5.1 – Rio Tinto's implied values: 'The Way We Work'

Rio Tinto publishes 'The Way We Work' on its internet site. It contains a clear view of the values, albeit implied, that Rio has:

Rio Tinto is a world leader in finding, mining and processing the earth's mineral resources.

In order to deliver superior returns to our shareholders over many years, we take a long-term and responsible approach to exploring for first class orebodies and to developing large, efficient operations capable of sustaining competitive advantage. In this way we help to meet the global need for minerals and metals which contribute to essential improvements in well-being, as well as making a direct contribution to economic development and employment in those countries where we invest.

Wherever we operate, we work as closely as possible with our hosts, respecting laws and customs and minimising adverse impacts, and ensuring transfer of benefits and enhancement of opportunities. We believe that our competitiveness and future success depend not only on our employees and the quality and diversity of our assets but also on our record as good neighbours and partners around the world.

Accordingly, we set ourselves high environmental and community standards. Our commitment to health, safety and the enhancement of the skills and capabilities of our employees is second to none in mining. We seek to make lasting contributions to local communities and to be sensitive to their culture and way of life.

But a careful analysis shows clearly both what the organisation plans to do, how it wants to position itself and what its values are. The values implied are:

- having a responsible approach to development
- having large, efficient operations

- helping to improve humanity's well-being
- making lasting contributions to the economies where it mines
- having respect and sensitivity for the laws, customs and way of life of host countries
- minimising adverse environmental and community impacts
- being a good neighbour
- being a good partner
- having the highest-quality health and safety for employees.

Another example is Lend Lease, which has always had a 'community of interest' approach to its businesses. In 1997, Lend Lease published a statement called 'Our Beliefs' which brought together some of the main values which have been running through the organisation since its inception (see Illustration 5.2).

Lend Lease said about these beliefs:

> If our beliefs are genuinely held and practised throughout the group, we will attract the best people to work for us, the quality of work will attract the attention of customers, demand for our services will grow and our global family will prosper – all of which contributes to delivering superior value for shareholders.

In summary, winning organisations have clear strategies but they are expressed in a wide variety of ways, and vision and mission statements, one of the standard recommended tools of strategy development and communication, are rarely used. Strategies vary over time, on an incremental basis. Growth – of profits – features in strategies. Strategies are linked closely to values. Sometimes values need to be realigned to strategies as they change.

STRATEGY IS FUZZY

While we have used the examples above to demonstrate 'clear' strategy, many people will feel that even these are open to interpretation. So it will almost certainly be obvious to you that the examples we have *not* included here are likely to be 'fuzzy'!

Illustration 5.2 – Lend Lease's beliefs

Belief	Observations
Sound corporate governance policy	We believe there is a strong link between good governance and performance.
Community of interest between shareholders and employees	We wish all employees to be shareholders, and they collectively own over 13 per cent of the issued capital. We aim for all to share annually in the profits.
Being a leading employer	A reputation that we have enjoyed domestically needs to be created globally.
A pillow stock, or no nasty surprises	We aim to increase earnings and earnings per share every year, irrespective of the economic climate.
Enhance the environment	We are conscious of the impact Lend Lease can have on the environment. We aim for it always to be positive.
Relationships	We cannot do it all ourselves. We need a number of special relationships that enhance our capabilities.
Collaboration	No individual has a monopoly on good ideas.
Let the community be the judge	We will only prosper with the support of the communities with which we interact.
Ethics and standards	We should not do anything that would diminish the pride our parents have in us.
Dare to be different	The theme of this report and the enemy of mediocrity.

The lack of a clear statement, such as a vision, mission or some other named statement, means that the issue of what the strategy of the organisation is remains open to interpretation. If there are inconsistent sets of words in the many statements issued by the organisation, it is likely that the organisation is not fixed, or clear, about its strategy.

We found that, while the winning organisations had clear strategy, there was a degree of fuzziness at the margins. There are at least three reasons why this might be so (see Figure 5.3):

- a desire to take advantage of opportunities that come up
- a desire to be flexible and adaptable at the highest level (see Chapter 4)
- the possibility that the organisation's strategy is not clear... or not known.

Figure 5.3 – Reasons for 'fuzzy' strategy

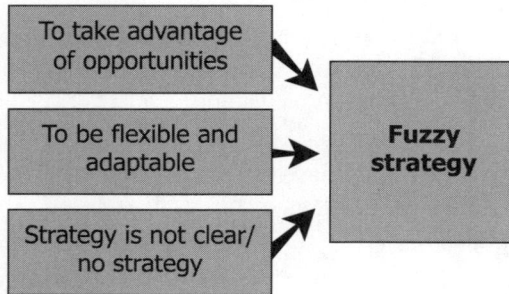

In most organisations, our experience is that it is the last reason which is the most common. But in the case of winning organisations, this is only true for short periods at most when they are adapting from one strategy to another, as they move from one stage of the strategic cycle to the next.

The desire to take advantage of opportunities

The first reason why organisations might want to have a fuzzy strategy is to be able to take advantage of future opportunities. These opportunities may not be predictable and being too fixed – not flexible enough – may lead organisations to pass opportunities by.

Brambles is a good example of a winning organisation that has not wanted to be too clear about its strategy so that it could take advantage of opportunities. CEO Gary Pemberton banned the word 'strategic' in the organisation. Successor CEO John Fletcher boasted of never having conducted a press conference, which reduced his risk of having to publicly define and narrow down his stated strategy.

The fundamental driver at Brambles has been growth of profits, though its set of products and services was described in its earlier days as 'dig, lift, load and haul' industrial services. Noticeably, what is now one of its major global businesses, Recall records management, does not fit into this... but Recall came into Brambles via a 'haul' operation (Grace Brothers Removals) and the managers in charge saw an opportunity to turn it into a separate business.

The same is true for each of the major businesses which Brambles has or had – they were all perceived as opportunities that were in some way linked to existing operations but which were new. CHEP was seen as a diversification of materials-handling techniques. Cleanaway was a diversification of industrial services. Groupe CAIB was seen as a geographic stepping stone into Europe (though Brambles had no railcars in its operations at the time).

Macquarie makes it clear that it depends on the entrepreneurial talents of its people to take advantage of opportunities, rather than having a fixed view of products and services. In its 1986 annual report, it said:

Macquarie Bank is a market maker... in the sense of developing new products and introducing innovations to existing markets. Macquarie Bank is regarded as one of the most creative financial institutions in Australia.

And in 1989 it said:

The Bank's aim is to maintain and diversify business activities while continuing to develop as a strong, reliable financial institution. The people at Macquarie are among the best in their respective fields. They share an ability to bring imagination and flair to their work, yet their entrepreneurial talents are guided by prudence and integrity.

These statements show the emphasis on innovation, imagination and flair as drivers of future business growth – not a top-down strategy but rather a focus on the development and creation of opportunities.

The desire for flexibility and adaptability

In some cases, fuzzy strategy is not due to the desire for opportunism but to the desire to be flexible. In Chapter 4 we noted the value of strategic flexibility in allowing winning organisations to rapidly adapt.

Harvey Norman and Woolworths define themselves simply as retailers, even though they are each focused on particular aspects and formats of retailing – in fact, they hardly touch each other in terms of products and services. This general description of 'retailing' allows them to be flexible and adaptable if new products or formats arise. Woolworths has used this flexibility to enter petrol retailing. The original idea was to use its own carparks to set up petrol retailing, and thus get a return from what is a non-producing asset! For Harvey Norman, the Loughran Group and the Joyce Mayne Group, acquired in 1998, have become the Domayne chain – a downmarket chain with similar types of goods as Harvey Norman. In 2001 it also bought Rebel Sport, a sports products retailer, and a new product range for Harvey Norman. These acquisitions have been incremental strategic developments – flexibility at the margin – rather than opportunism.

The Salvation Army makes it clear that it will care for people, but the specific services which it offers vary from period to period. It enters areas perceived to be of increasing need and sometimes withdraws when others, particularly governments, come along to take over or to do a better job. For instance, it has entered the drug rehabilitation and homeless youth service, reflecting increased demand for those services. It has also entered the unemployment service, as the government seeks to withdraw from that area. On the other hand, it has withdrawn from general hospital work, as that industry is consolidating and others can serve the need better.

Lack of strategy?

A third interpretation of the lack of clarity of strategy is that perhaps winning organisations don't actually have a strategy. This raises a crucial issue: can an organisation be successful without a strategy?

Are we just seeking strategy – and forcing ourselves to find something – even where there is actually none?

From both our own analysis and the interviews we conducted, we formed two conclusions. First, we concluded that all winning organisations do have a strategy and that strategy is important in guiding them for the long term. Second, we found that, because the organisations were in different positions in the strategic life cycle, because they faced different individual contexts, and because the concept of strategy is neither mechanical (like accounting) nor agreed on by theorists, the clarity of strategy varies over time.

However, apart from some diversification errors that we see as part of the strategic life cycle, strategy for winning organisations develops incrementally over time and is communicated with a high degree of clarity, but in different ways.

CLEAR *AND* FUZZY STRATEGY

So what does a clear *and* fuzzy strategy look like? Our research found that strategy needs to be clear enough to provide guidance to constrain the range of activities to those which already exist or can be easily and incrementally linked to current activities. (There are no cases of unrelated diversification in our winning organisations, suggesting this is not a likely strategy for success.)

It also needs to be fuzzy at the edges so that:

- opportunities that are related and/or incremental can be taken up
- innovation is encouraged
- the organisation is flexible enough to adapt to external changes (but not so flexible that anything goes as 'strategy')
- the organisation can change its strategy over time as it develops and grows.

How important is strategy?

Given the lack of clarity over what constitutes strategy, a major issue is how important strategy really is for organisational success.

While winning organisations have clear (and fuzzy) strategies, other organisations also have good strategies, but they are not represented here. Is 'good strategy' really a differentiator for winning organisations?

We concluded that, contrary to our prior beliefs and expectations, the ability to execute effectively is more important than the strategy. That's why it is in the centre of our winning framework and why we started the book with the chapter on effective execution. This is a critically important conclusion and flies in the face of conventional theory. Good strategy is a driver of success, but good strategy alone is not enough to guarantee success. Organisations need the other elements to get effective execution. Good strategy does, however, help alignment (see Chapter 3), encourage consistency and focus execution.

Who sets the strategy?

The theory is that the direction for the organisation – the strategy – is set at the top of the organisation, ideally via a vision or mission statement or at least a clear communication from the CEO or top management team. The lower levels of the organisation then 'fit' into this espoused strategy.

What we found was that the direction of the company was set in a variety of ways (see Table 5.2). In several cases – Brambles, Lend Lease and Macquarie – it was set by the actions of divisional managers and their divisions. The role of the top management was to encourage and reward people for entrepreneurial behaviour, set some general boundaries and manage risk.

In other cases – Harvey Norman, Qantas, Telstra, Woolworths, NAB and Westfield – strategy was tightly controlled at the top, as suggested by conventional theory. In yet other cases – the Salvation Army and Rio Tinto – strategy had mixed controllers. In these cases, the central head office tightly controlled major decisions and policies, but individual units had considerable flexibility to meet local needs and conditions.

Table 5.2 – Alternative approaches to setting strategy

	Conventional Strategy	Opportunistic Strategy	Mixed Strategy
Locus of control	Top management team	Divisions	Top and division
Role of top management team	Set direction Take control	Set general boundaries Encourage divisions Manage risk	Set general strategy Facilitate idea transfers Monitor for control
Role of divisions	Follow and implement direction	Determine what opportunities to pursue	Follow general strategy Customise to local opportunity Specialise in an area of competence

However, regardless of the strategy setting approach, in all cases execution and alignment were excellent! So we came to the conclusion that these factors were of primary importance. Having a good strategy is very helpful, because it provides guidance for alignment, consistency and execution. But many organisations have 'good strategy' and 'good strategy' by itself does not make for success. If faced with a conflict, go for effective execution over strategic clarity.

Passion: the missing ingredient?

One CEO we spoke to was quite clear about a particular element of the success of his organisation – passion. He said:

> You have to be passionate about the business you are in. You have to live and walk the talk. You can't just sit in the office analysing the numbers, mouthing the words. You have to really love the business if you want to inspire people to work with you.

An organisation which has a 'good strategy' but which is not passionate about it is unlikely to be successful. Good strategy must have a 'cause'. It must grab people. They must want to deliver it.

We found passion in all the winning organisations. And we see that the strategy must inspire the people in the organisation to want to make it work. Otherwise it will be a dry and sterile environment... and the strategy won't be delivered. We address passion in the chapters on people (Chapter 8) and, particularly, leadership (Chapter 6).

But again, passion itself is not enough. Passion without strategy is like a headless chicken – a lot of running and energy but not much result. There are plenty of organisations with passion... but without a strategy which would enable them to harness that passion and make the organisation more effective.

STRATEGY OVER TIME: THE STRATEGIC CYCLE

Organisations develop and grow. Strategy varies over time. We developed the strategic cycle to explain how strategies vary, the essence of which was given in Chapter 1 (see Figure 5.4). 'Winning' looks different at different stages of the cycle. In this section we'll follow the strategic evolution of some of the most highly developed of the winning organisations to explain in detail how the strategic cycle works for a particular organisation over a long period of time.

The strategic cycle for Brambles

In 1875, Walter Bramble began as a butcher in Newcastle. In 1916 W.E. Bramble & Sons was established when Walter's three sons entered the business, and it soon included a variety of small businesses, including transport and industrial services for large local companies such as BHP at Port Kembla and Wollongong.

Still based in Newcastle, in 1954 Brambles became a public company and the current organisation was born. Brambles was always seeking new outlets to diversify into.

Figure 5.4 – The strategic cycle of growing organisations

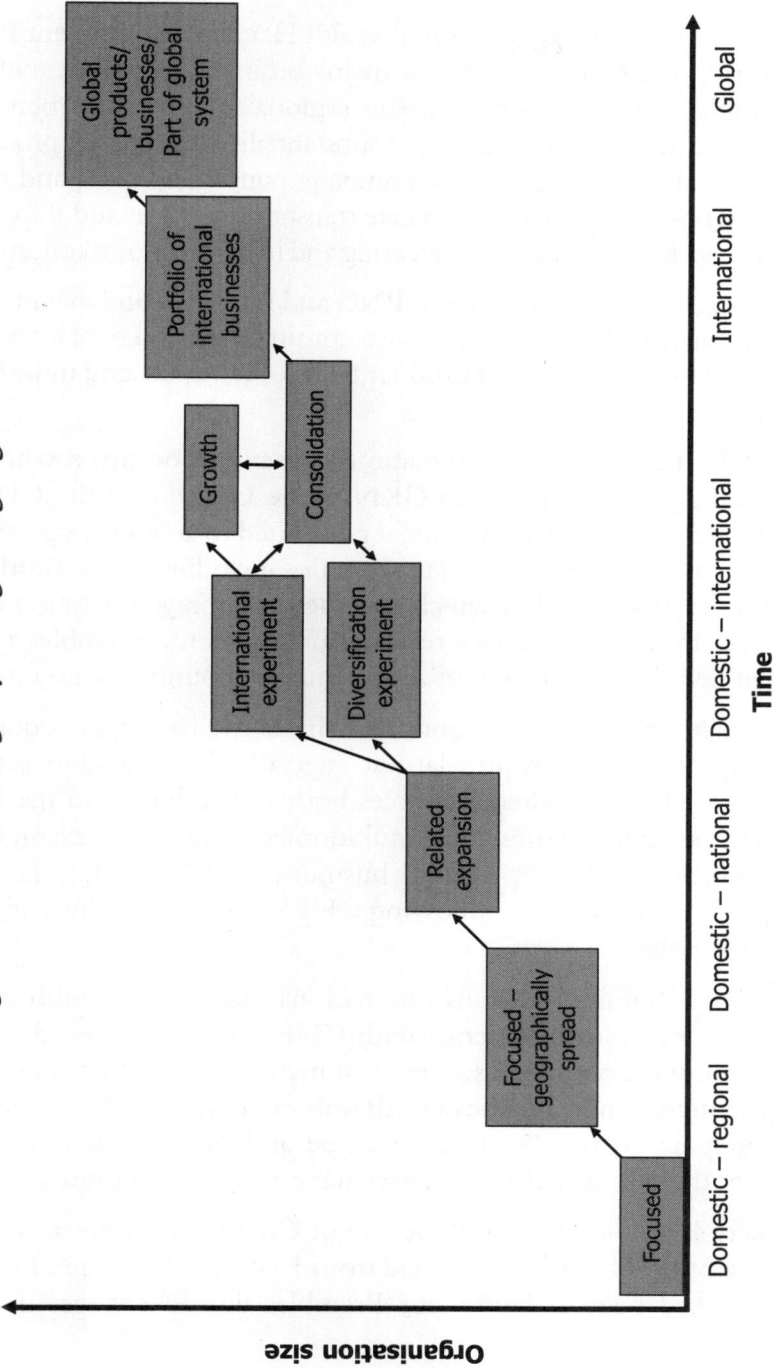

In 1958, it bought the Commonwealth Handling Equipment Pool (CHEP) and established it as a major business unit. This moved Brambles from being a domestic-regional company to being a domestic-national company and substantially changed its product mix. From 1961 to 1970, the company continued to expand into related businesses, such as interstate transport, customs and shipping agencies, steel fabrication engineering and industrial waste collection.

In 1971, it made acquisitions in PNG and New Zealand, beginning its international experiment. It also continued to make many other acquisitions in the related product fields of transport and industrial services.

In 1974, the first major international expansion occurred when it formed a joint venture with GKN in the UK to start the CHEP pallet system there. Meanwhile, it continued to acquire a variety of industrial services companies in Australia, including Grace Brothers transport group, within which was the box storage operation that eventually became Recall records management. Brambles then expanded the CHEP system across Europe, country by country.

International expansion continued. In 1984, Brambles acquired Groupe CAIB, Europe's largest specialised rail wagon rental service. This diversified Brambles both in products and markets and turned it into a substantial multidomestic company, expanding the portfolio of international businesses. In 1986, Cleanaway expanded into the UK, following CHEP, and further diversifying the international portfolio.

In 1989, Brambles took its international business portfolio from Europe into North America with CHEP (Canada, then the US the following year), Ensco environmental waste and some US equipment rental businesses. Brambles reorganised into three geographic areas – Australia, Europe and North America – to reflect the fact that the businesses were now all multidomestic.

Finally Brambles ran into a problem! Consolidation occurred in the early 1990s. Results declined from 1990 to 1997, when Ensco, which had been a disaster for Brambles due to changes in the environmental waste industry regulations, caused $A500 million to be written off. Several businesses were sold but records management, which trailed the other businesses in development, expanded rapidly into several different countries. Brambles also began to explore Asia and looked into airport privatisation in Australia as a potential new diversified business.

In 1999, the final phase began, with records management being established as a global product business headquartered in the US. CHEP also went global, followed by industrial services and equipment rental. Groupe CAIB was sold, as it was not seen as having the potential to go global.

In 2001, Brambles merged with its global CHEP partner, GKN, to bring the joint interests together into one company. Brambles held 57 per cent of the joint company. This move aimed to facilitate the joint venture moving 'as one' into further international markets. Figure 5.5 gives a visual representation of the strategic cycle developments for Brambles.

Growth comes from incremental related diversification

From the example we have just followed in detail it is clear that, in general, as the organisation grows it diversifies, but it does this incrementally or in a related manner. This idea was best expressed to us by a Macquarie executive who said:

> In terms of expanding the businesses we are in, we think in terms of 'adjacency' and whether we have the relevant competency or could get the relevant competencies. 'Adjacency' to us means expanding one step at a time, which reduces the risk.

With Brambles (and Lend Lease, Rio and others), each diversification was perceived to be related to the businesses they were already in. Brambles' initial informal definition of its areas of business as 'dig, lift, load and haul' industrial services; the encouragement of managers seeing themselves running their own businesses; the focus on profit growth, not just growth; and the focus on services to customers and building customer relationships all provided powerful levers not just for expansion, but for related expansion.

137

Figure 5.5 – Brambles' strategic cycle of development

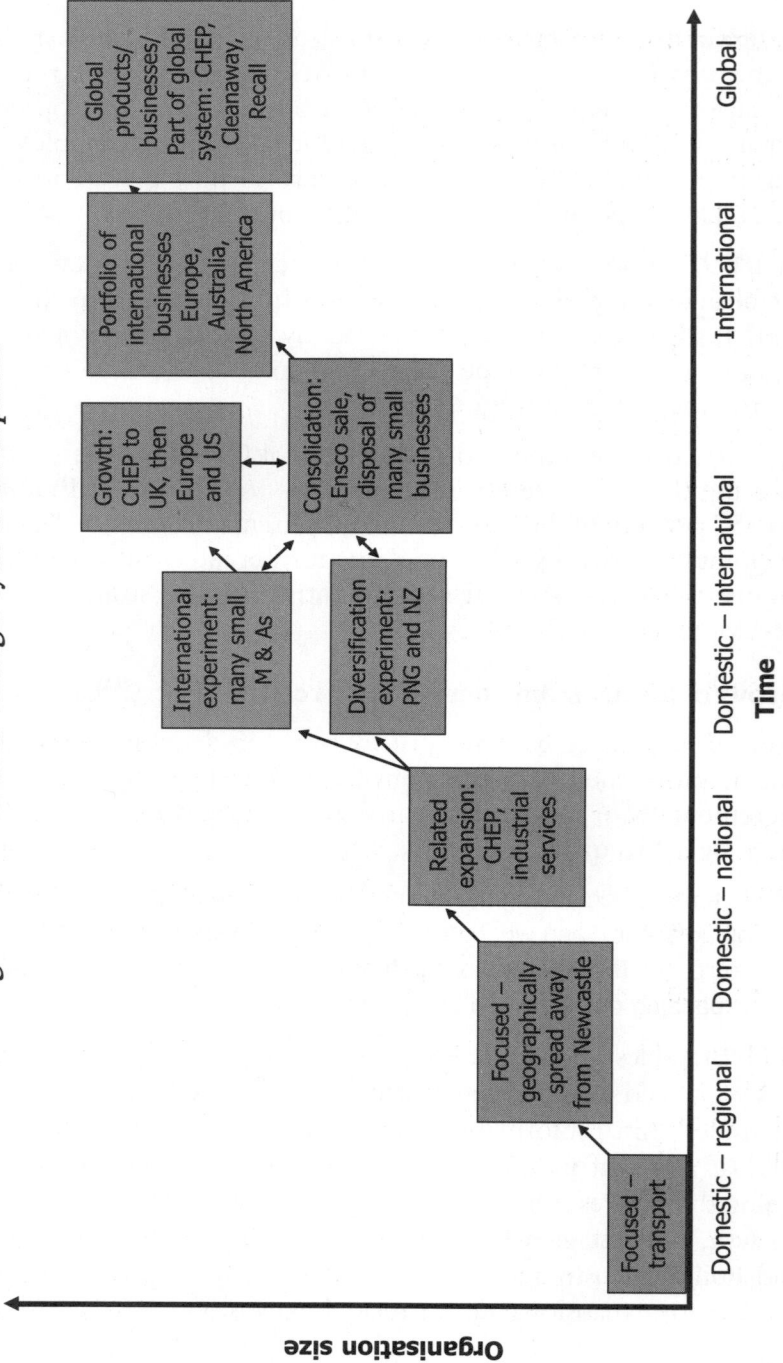

Australian organisations becoming global?

Rio is the most developed of all the winning organisations in terms of the strategic cycle, having gone global in 1995 when it was reacquired by its parent. Lend Lease is the next closest to global development, but it only developed a global strategy in 2000.

The fact that:

- Rio was reacquired by its international parent RTZ,
- Lend Lease has acquired major construction company Bovis, and
- Brambles has merged with its joint venture partner, GKN

suggest that, for Australian organisations, the global stage may well need to be reached by merger or acquisition with other major industry players. The BHP Billiton and News Corporation cases lend credence to this scenario, but it is untested at this time and by our research.

MISTAKES IN THE STRATEGIC CYCLE

The strategic cycle shows a period of consolidation which organisations all seem to go through. None of these winning organisations has simply proceeded in a forward direction without having to retreat from some business areas. They are not infallible. There are two types of 'mistakes' that appear – unrelated diversifications and overseas related diversifications.

Unrelated diversification

The more difficult mistake to understand is where the organisation diversifies into unrelated areas, despite its history of success in related businesses and despite the known history of the failure of unrelated diversification.

A good example of this is Westfield (see Figure 5.6). After 20 years of success in building shopping centres, in 1981 Westfield took a minority interest in an oil prospect and also entered another consortium in the heavy construction and civil engineering

139

industry, specialising in resource and energy development. In 1983, it took another minority interest in an oil and gas pipeline. In 1986, it launched a 'cashbox' company – an investment company in which investors backed the management team, not knowing exactly what that management team might do with the money invested. They were an extremely popular idea at the time. Westfield Capital Corporation, as it was known, bought into media, retail and manufacturing companies and ended up owning Channel Ten in 1987 just before the sharemarket crash.

Figure 5.6 – Westfield's unusual diversification period

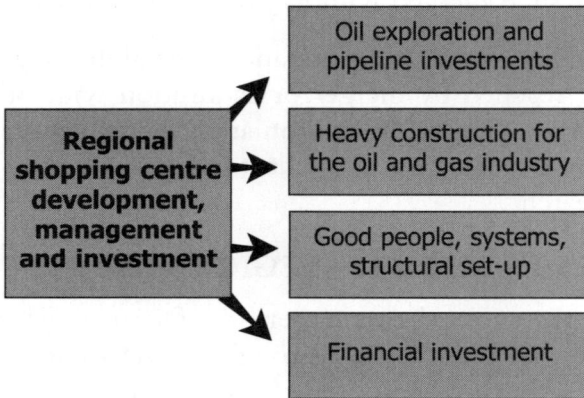

Why did it do this? It is easy to forget that at the start of the 1980s Australia was expected to experience a 'resources boom' and that in the mid-1980s, the sharemarket and general economic boom led people – even experienced managers – to believe in an unbelievably golden future. (The cash box/sharemarket boom was of course repeated again with the dotcom boom of the late 1990s). At these times, managers begin to believe they can manage anything. Investing in good managers in an unknown industry is viewed as a way to 'free ride' on their success.

Westfield appears to have been caught up in both of these fashionable trends – resources and cash boxes. By 1989 it had sold out of all these investments, making a huge loss ($500 million) on the media investment (which ironically has done very well since, under media industry management), though the resource industry investments did adequately well.

Since then, Westfield has remained focused on its shopping centres with only one other minor non-core activity – a minority joint venture investment in Intencity, a high technology leisure entertainment chain of retail shops.

It is worth noting the time period involved. While the 'consolidation' took only two years, the whole episode of unrelated expansion took almost 10 years... Strategic decisions, good or bad, have long-term effects of some magnitude. That's one good reason which alone indicates why strategy is important!

Related diversifications overseas

The second type of mistake occurs when organisations pursue their own businesses, but into unfamiliar overseas markets. Most Australian businesses focused on Australia until the 1980s. At this time trade barriers began to be reduced, discouraging inefficient industries in Australia, and the finance industry was opened up through such fundamental reforms as floating the dollar, allowing the entry of foreign banks and freeing up interest rate and investment restrictions (see Chapter 11 for more on this). This allowed and encouraged Australian organisations to begin to explore taking their businesses overseas.

The fact that this exposure to international opportunities has occurred in only the last 20 years means that the experience of international Australian businesses is quite immature, even now. It is not surprising that many Australian businesses have found it difficult to succeed overseas, given this lack of history and experience.

Even winning organisations have found it difficult to be successful overseas, even in businesses which they understand locally. Brambles' failure with US waste management company Ensco is one of the biggest by the winning organisations, costing Brambles around $500 million. Ensco was the first hostile takeover Brambles had ever made. It took three years from the time the idea was broached for Brambles to conclude the acquisition. During that time, cheaper rival technologies had been allowed to enter the market, so that Ensco's market position was no longer favourable. In addition, other competitors had entered the industry which, by the time of acquisition, was heavily over capacity.

Most recently, NAB's failure with Homeside in 2002, a mortgage consolidator in the US, is another even more costly example. NAB wrote off around $4 billion due to technical miscalculations in Homeside's pricing model and lack of control of the subsidiary from head office. Coupled with NAB's (profitable) sale of Michigan National Bank, which means a total retreat from the US, it suggests that NAB is currently in the 'consolidation' phase of the strategic cycle. That NAB first invested overseas in 1987 and in the US in 1995 indicates the difficulty of being successful overseas, even for winning organisations. It is a long, slow process.

Telstra's investment in Pacific Century Cyber Works (PCCW) in 2000 and in Clear and Reach in New Zealand in 2001, coupled with its more minor investments in Vietnam and other countries in the 1990s, have yet to demonstrate any significant return, even though these are businesses in which Telstra is intimately involved in Australia. Telstra is also in the 'consolidation' stage.

Qantas has periodically flirted with the strategy of being an 'around the world' airline on its own, but when times have been tough in the industry, it has withdrawn from many routes. Recognising its limited resources (and the constraints of its ability to undertake market development in the industry), it went through a period of focusing on Asia on its own in the late 1980s, then as part of the British Airways–Qantas alliance in the mid-1990s, and then for the Oneworld alliance in the late 1990s. But Qantas again withdrew from Asian routes during the 1997 and 2001 Asian crises. In Qantas' case it is relatively easy to withdraw, as it has little capital tied up. However, its signal of lack of commitment and the evident lack of profitability in overseas markets again suggest the difficulty of operating overseas, even in one's own industry.

So why do these failures occur when these organisations have very successful track records at home and they are expanding in their own industries? The key reasons seem to be:

- lack of understanding of the social and business culture of the country in question
- lack of understanding of the specifics of the industry in that country
- having a poor understanding of the business partner in the joint venture (if applicable)
- paying too much/being too optimistic about the likelihood of being able to turnaround or change the company that has been acquired.

All this suggests caution is important in overseas expansion... and we'll address that in Chapter 9, on risk management.

Realignment during a major strategy change versus mistakes

As organisations move through the strategic cycle, the change in perception required for each new stage at the point where they make the transition from one stage to another has significant implications for some of the businesses in their current portfolios.

Perhaps the clearest example of this is Lend Lease. In 1998, Lend Lease said it was 'creating a global niche strategy as a property investment manager'. In 1999 it said it had 'two core areas of activity – financial services and real estate'. In 2000, Lend Lease's strategy was to be a 'global real estate company' with three activities:

- real estate investment and funds management
- project management and construction
- property development.

Here we see the gradual emergence of a truly global strategy... and the consequent sale of its Australian-based financial services company, MLC, in 2000. In this case, Lend Lease sold the company which was responsible for almost half of its total profits to focus on strategy at a new level – global products – instead of remaining a multidomestic organisation.

Brambles similarly decided to focus on four global product businesses. This required the sale of its European rail wagon rental business – Groupe CAIB – which had also been responsible for a significant part of its profits. However, Brambles did not see this business 'fitting' into a global structure, so it had to sell, for strategic consistency.

Another case is Rio Tinto. As Rio Tinto continues to go global following the merger of CRA with its UK parent RTZ in 1995, it focuses on large-scale long-life mines. Its policy is to encourage the development of large mines where economies of scale allow it to be globally competitive. So quite a number of its smaller assets have been sold since 1995 as this realignment to a global product strategy takes place.

These are not 'mistakes'. They represent the internal effects of important strategy changes. They confirm the central role that strategy plays in organisational development – but they do result in substantial change in the business portfolio.

SUMMARY AND KEY MESSAGES FOR LEADERS

Strategy is an important element of the framework... but, contrary to the belief of strategists, it is not the most important. Strategy is a driver of effective execution, but the other elements are needed if effective execution is to occur. An organisation's strategy must be aligned with its values, and growth – of profits, not sales – must be a key element in it.

Strategy in winning organisations is clear, but it is also fuzzy at the margin to allow for opportunities, innovation and the need for future flexibility. Vision, mission and other statements are not used greatly, but clear and consistent strategies do exist across long time periods.

Strategy varies over time depending on the stage of the strategic cycle. Even winning organisations make mistakes, which cause them to consolidate their position for a period of time.

The key messages for leaders from this chapter are:

- Have a clear strategy, but allow for some flexibility at the margin to adapt to opportunities and allow for development through the strategic cycle.
- Ensure that this strategy is clearly understood throughout the organisation.
- Ensure that the strategy and values are aligned.
- Emphasise profitable growth, not growth by itself.
- Be passionate about the organisation's direction.
- Be careful when going overseas – be prepared to develop slowly, incur losses and consolidate for some years.
- Be clear about what not to do – don't diversify into areas you don't know, especially in times of high business fashion.

6

LEADERSHIP, NOT LEADERS
Captain-coach leadership

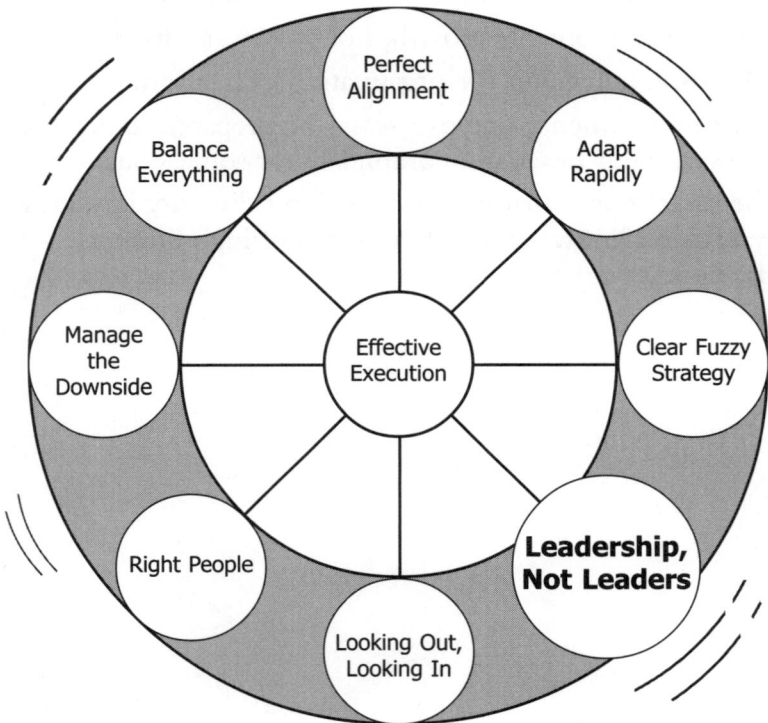

In organisation after organisation as we analysed our findings, we came up with the elements in our framework above... except for leadership. So we asked ourselves, "How is it possible for these results to come about? Where did the strategy come from?

Who hired those right people? How was the organisation externally focused?"

We realised that clearly leadership must be an important factor, since it is often the driver of the other factors. The question was, "Is it the 'leaders' themselves who are the cause of the success of the organisations, or is it leadership as a whole?" We found that there were many good CEOs – which is the conventional view of 'leader' – in all the organisations. We wondered whether the success of the organisation might be due to the catalytic or visionary influence of perhaps a single one of these CEOs in each organisation.

What we found was an emphasis on team leadership, not individual leaders, and not just a single visionary leader. So we call this element 'leadership, not leaders' to focus on the characteristics of leadership, not on a single leader. Indeed, each leader and leadership team in the winning organisations faced quite different circumstances from their predecessors – and successors. We concluded that leadership needs to be 'right for the time'. There is no single magic leadership formula. We found no one size that fitted all. Perhaps this explains why the search for common leader characteristics across past individual CEOs was singularly unsuccessful.

We also found that the leadership styles needed in Australia are different. 'Captain–coach leadership' – where the leaders are part of the team, on the field of play, yet leading and coaching at the same time – is the style of leadership that people seek and that winning organisations provide.

In this chapter we'll first look at exactly what we mean by 'leadership' and discuss the four levels of leadership that exist. We'll then consider the findings on leadership by previous studies of successful organisations. Then we look at the leadership capabilities that distinguished winning organisations in our study. As we are concerned with the long term, we also consider how leadership style and characteristics change over time. We examine the internal leadership programs of several of the winning

147

organisations, and consider these as possible role models for developing future leadership from within. We'll conclude by considering whether – despite all the above – there really is or has been one dominant leader for each organisation. We reject this conclusion, but think the debate is worth having, as we know many people think this is what good organisations are about!

WHO/WHAT IS 'LEADERSHIP'?

The term 'leadership' is used frequently and often its use is confused, much as use of the term 'strategy' is confused. We see 'leadership' as 'behaviour of the key group of people in the organisation that positions the organisation for its future'. We distinguish this from 'management' which we see as 'behaviour that enables the organisation to carry out its current activities most efficiently'. Leadership is about the future. Management is about the present. While both are necessary, the future of the organisation depends on its ability to move forward, not just to undertake its current tasks efficiently.

This does not define any particular organisational position as 'the' or 'a' leader. You do not have to be CEO to be a leader, but you do have to be acting in such a way that it helps the organisation position itself for the future. Indeed, our definition specifically suggests that it is a group of people, not just a single position, that constitutes the leadership of the organisation.

Levels of leadership

We see four levels of 'leadership' (see Figure 6.1):

- *The CEO.* This is the conventional, and media-based, view of leadership. The CEO-as-leader view personalises the organisation, and whatever the organisation does is seen to be the responsibility of, and caused by, the CEO. At one level (that of ultimate organisational responsibility), this is true. At another level it is ludicrous, but it makes good media copy. Rupert Murdoch is News Corporation.

Bill Gates is Microsoft. While we agree that the role of CEO is the most influential and is one of the keys to how an organisation will behave, we reject this view that leadership is just the CEO.

- *The top management team.* A more realistic view of leadership is that the top management team around the CEO (and including the CEO) is responsible for the organisation's performance. The 'team' generally consists of those who report to the CEO, but sometimes it can include others and sometimes not all of those.

- *All business unit leaders.* What good organisations seek now is for all business unit leaders to pursue leader behaviour. Those who are able to do so are likely to rise up the management ranks into the top management team. In winning organisations, many of the business unit managers do exhibit leader behaviour – that's one of the key reasons why they are able to execute and deliver results! But it's too hard for the media, or others outside the organisation, to focus on such a large group or identify the high-flyers with potential, so most of these names are unknown in the public discussion of leadership.

- *The board of directors.* Another group which has received limited attention until recently has been the board. The board is often viewed as just a rubber stamp unless the executives are doing poorly. A more modern view is that the quality of the board and its relationship with the top management team is an important part of business success. There is very little attention focused on boards in terms of their actual contribution to good organisational performance. However, as board decisions are collective, good and bad directors can be painted with the same brush.

So 'leadership' is much more than just the CEO leader. Within each organisation, the 'leadership' will be a different group of individuals, at different levels, coming from the four levels identified here. Who is the 'leadership' group in your organisation?

Figure 6.1 – Four levels of leadership

Leadership is a team-based capability

Why do we focus on a group of leaders? The executives in all the winning organisations talked about their leadership teams rather than individuals, both in external reporting and in interviews. In reflecting on his years as CEO of Macquarie, and on the role of CEO, Allan Moss said:

> Our success has been very much a team effort... (Moss, 2001)

Reflecting on what a fortune-teller would have told him in 1977 when he joined the organisation about his role as CEO in 2001, he said that his role as CEO did not seem as important as might be expected:

> She would have replied: "From what I see, you don't do a lot. You read a fair bit, you spend some time staring at what appears to be a small television screen. A lot of your day involves meeting with people but you usually do much more listening than talking. You have a lot of lunches with people but they cannot be important because you don't get to drink much alcohol. However, there is one productive activity – you do quite a lot of typing."

At Westfield, while Frank Lowy is acknowledged as the driver of the business since the original partnership with John Saunders ended in the mid-1980s, the style of decision-making shows that it is not simply Lowy's ideas which are accepted. Large meetings are called to discuss key issues. Everyone is expected to contribute and Lowy is widely acknowledged as a good listener, keen to learn. The resulting decisions are likely to benefit from the wide input and few bad decisions have been made.

The role of boards in leadership teams

How do boards fit into the leadership of winning organisations? Though only some of the winning organisations talked about the value of their boards, we found that several board members were represented on more than one of the winning organisation boards over time (see Table 6.1). We think this is no coincidence. Winning organisations are likely to value good people from other winning organisations! For instance, Gary Pemberton went from being CEO of Brambles to being Chair of Qantas. James Strong went from being CEO of Qantas to being Chair of Woolworths. Don Argus went from being CEO of NAB to being Chair of Brambles. Those who are on the boards of winning organisations would also be sought after by other organisations seeking to learn from their experiences of those winning organisations.

Table 6.1 – Some common board members in winning organisations

Person	Boards
Margaret Jackson	Telstra, Qantas
James Strong	Qantas, Woolworths
Gary Pemberton	Brambles, Qantas
John Ralph	CRA, Telstra
John Morshel	Lend Lease, Rio Tinto
Diane Grady	Lend Lease, Woolworths

PREVIOUS FINDINGS ON LEADERSHIP

Both Peters and Waterman and Collins and Porras included leadership as a key element in their models of their successful organisations. Leadership is one of the elements of the 7Ss under the term 'style' and Peters and Waterman see leadership as the driver of the eight elements they identify in their 'excellent' organisations.

Collins and Porras include 'clock building, not time telling' in their model. They say:

> Having a great idea or being a charismatic visionary leader is 'time telling'; building a company that can prosper far beyond the presence of any single leader... is 'clock building'.
>
> ...instead of concentrating on acquiring the individual personality traits of visionary leadership, they take an architectural approach and concentrate on building the organizational traits of visionary companies.
>
> ...we found that creating and building a visionary company absolutely does not require *either* a great idea or a great and charismatic leader. (p. 23)

In commenting on 'home grown management' – another factor in their model – they say:

> In short, it is not the quality of leadership that most separates the visionary companies from the comparison companies. It is the *continuity* of quality leadership that matters... (p. 173)

So leadership has been identified as an important factor in the prior studies and the focus is also on building the organisation, rather than on the charisma of the individual. In his most recent work, Collins (2001) again found this, developing a concept he called 'Level 5 leadership': 'a paradoxical combination of personal humility and professional will'. However, Collins was referring here to an individual, rather than a leadership team.

AUSTRALIAN LEADERSHIP TEAM CAPABILITIES

The previous studies are all from the US. What are the capabilities that leadership teams of winning organisations in Australia emphasise? From our research we found the following factors were the important capabilities (see Figure 6.2). Leadership teams in winning organisations:

- have captain–coach leaders
- build the business, not their own careers
- are grown from within and have long internal experience
- walk the talk

152

- are passionate for the cause
- are decisive
- have a long-term view
- communicate
- are consistent
- have few trappings.

Of course there are many other characteristics that 'leaders' have. For instance, this list doesn't mention competence, responsibility, or ability to influence! But these are the ones that our research found make the difference from leaders and leadership teams in normal organisations. We'll explore each of these ideas below.

Figure 6.2 – Key capabilities of leadership teams of winning organisations

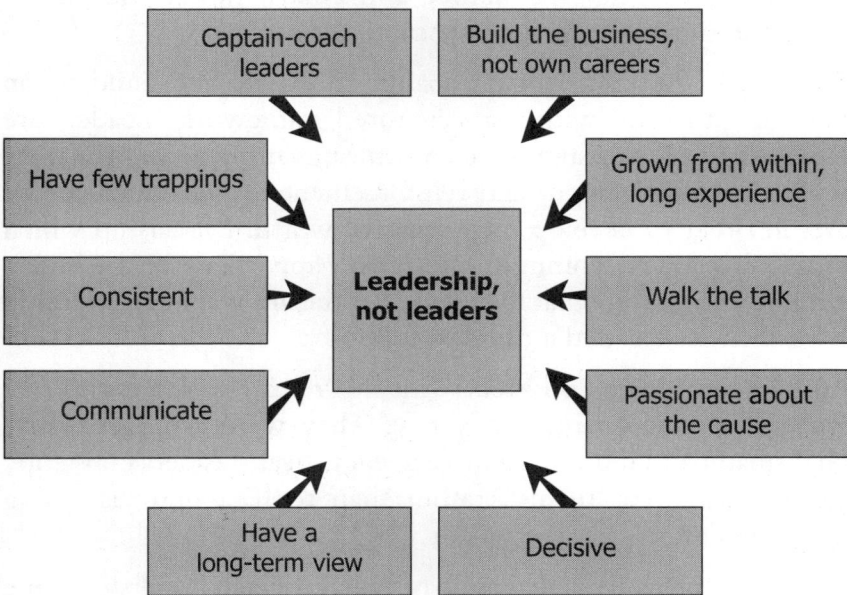

Captain-coach leadership

A key difference in the leadership capabilities emerges between US studies and our study relating to the style of leadership. The Telstra archetype study was conducted in the early 1990s to see what the differences were between Australian expectations of leadership and those of other countries (see Illustration 6.1).

The study showed that Australians want their organisational leaders to be coaches – people who exhort them and encourage them to improve performance – rather than generals providing a vision and telling them what to do. They also want their leaders to be players on the ground during the game, showing captaincy skills in the field, supporting them during the play and sharing the work involved, not generals who are removed from the battle. It is a very egalitarian view of leadership, consistent with the historical value of mateship in the Australian culture. This view applied to leadership in general, not just to the CEO or to the top management team.

The study also found that, unlike Americans, Australians view change negatively, not positively. Australians view change as a cause of insecurity, instability and chaos, rather than as an opportunity or a challenge, as Americans do.

As a result, Australians want change to evolve and build on an existing situation, within a structured framework. Leaders are expected to provide support and nurturing during times of change, with acknowledgement and reinforcement of who their people are, in order to develop their sense of worth. Leadership which creates instability, communicates crisis, apportions blame and is authoritarian is not what they seek. Australians want a relationship with their leaders and a cause to follow.

Our findings were consistent with this research. We found that leaders were surprisingly low key. They were not particularly charismatic and did not seem very egotistical. Leaders constantly referred to their 'teams', rather than to 'I' when discussing achievements.

Macquarie provides an example of captain–coach leadership. One Macquarie executive said:

> The role of leadership here is to create an environment that is supportive of entrepreneurs. This is a collegiate environment, not an individual one and it is definitely not an environment of command and control.

154

Illustration 6.1 – The Telstra archetype study: desired leadership style in Australia

Telstra contracted for some research to be performed during the early 1990s to explore the 'mental highways' which were shared by its people, compared with those in other countries, and to gain a greater understanding of how Australia's unique cultural characteristics should shape its approach to business effectiveness. The study was based on a similar study done for AT&T during the 1980s.

What Telstra staff wanted from their leadership was:

- a 'cause' which had social and/or moral implications for why the organisation was moving in a particular direction
- acknowledgement of who they were
- clear guidelines about their direction
- constructive feedback on what they were engaged in.

Telstra termed this 'captain-coach' leadership – a leader who creates stability by:

- explaining reality
- defusing crises
- creating a goal or cause to strive for
- providing clear instructions
- providing a sharp focus on how to achieve results
- providing support and nurturing through difficult times
- acknowledging and reinforcing who its people are
- adding, growing and helping to develop their sense of self-worth.

What they did not want was a leader who:

- communicated crisis
- created instability
- focused on results
- provided unclear instructions
- apportioned blame
- provided no or negative feedback
- was authoritarian.

Another said:

> [The leadership team] doesn't really like to tell you what to do. The idea is to let each business operate like a small business. Each business can control its own costs.

One of the founders of the firm confirmed this:

> There is a collegial decision-making process. It is consensual, not decided by the CEO... There are very little top-down imposed decisions ... If you're in the 'brains for rent' business, a dictator style of leadership does not work.

Finally, the view of the CEO at the time of writing was:

> We started out as a professional partnership doing M&A and we have retained that philosophy.

CRA (now Rio Tinto) provides us with another example. In 1986, it had already formed the public view that the role of 'manager' was to be a leader and also a coach. In 1993, CRA said in its annual report:

> An important part of our management process philosophy is to encourage a commonality of interest among all the people who work in our businesses. We are promoting managerial behaviour that breaks down the distinctions between different classes of employees: we want coaches, not bosses.

A Rio Tinto executive confirmed this view:

> Leaders are expected to lead. They have a lot of discretion. But other things are more important than [individual] leaders. For instance, the ability to listen, teamwork, operations, being well-rounded people... our ability to critique the work and to improve it... This is due to self-empowered managers trained in the principles of management, which is mostly to do with working with people, i.e. teams and relationships with others downwards, sideways and upwards.

Building a sustainable business, not their own careers

The first factor given for success in *Built to Last* is 'clock building, not time telling', i.e. leaders are focusing on building the organisation (the clock), not simply reporting on where the organisation is up to (time telling). We also found this. The leadership team focuses on building a sustainable business, rather than egotistically promoting their own careers.

James Strong provides a good example. When he was trying to integrate Australian Airlines and Qantas in 1994, he published his views in *The Australian Way*, then the in-flight magazine for both airlines. Strong was speaking to employees as much as to customers, though. In the August 1994 edition, he said:

> It is always a delight to observe a group of people displaying true teamwork... In sport we see it as normal behaviour... Yet strangely we often do not apply the same rules to working together in organisations... One of the greatest shortcomings of any large organisational structure is the extent to which it will tolerate people who do not really care about their jobs or have regard for the impact of their uncaring behaviour on other people... If it was a small group, people would recognise that such behaviour is very dangerous to each of the other group members and the group as a whole. Yet because of the anonymity of a large organisation it may be tolerated by colleagues... It is up to leadership to be aware of and counteract the negatives, and build the positive benefit by a committed program of activities over a period of time, creating the right atmosphere.

In September 1994, he commented on the changes that he had introduced in his first year as CEO:

> The initial steps late in 1993 and early this year involved significant changes in structure and management appointments. These were designed to bring about a different style of managing, with a flatter organisational structure and more specialised management functions to concentrate attention on detailed areas of the business. As part of this focus on the detail of our passenger products and services... [we are] developing a series of improvements... It represents the most comprehensive overhaul since the early 1970s.

Brambles executives were known as never being afraid to 'get dirty' to build the business. The 'dig, lift, load and haul' philosophy of the early days, the 'garbo' mentality and the lean head office demonstrated the focus on building the business rather than enjoying the spoils of being CEO or of being in the top management team.

Home grown and stable

We found that the vast majority of leaders came from within the organisation, had been with the organisation for long periods and remained as CEO for long periods. Looking at CEOs as indicative of the leadership team, of the 40 CEOs over the 20 years in all 11 organisations, 37 – 93 per cent – came from inside the organisation.

This focus on promotion from within means that the organisation's strategic direction is likely to change incrementally, rather than dramatically. Of course, since the organisation is doing well and is externally focused, it only *needs* to change incrementally. Promotion from within also means that the organisation 'understands' the new CEO and vice versa – there are not likely to be many management changes at the top in this kind of incremental promotion, so the role of the specific individual CEO matters less.

When managers are brought in from outside, it is usually because the organisation is not performing well or it wants or needs to change significantly. Both Telstra and Qantas have been in that position over the last 10 years, resulting in some introduction of external people into the top of the organisation – Frank Blount at Telstra and James Strong at Qantas for example (though Strong had been on the board at Qantas and been CEO of Australian Airlines, which became part of Qantas). However, these are two of only three complete outsiders who have been recruited by winning organisations. Ziggy Switkowski, who followed Blount, was brought in from outside to a position reporting to Blount and had been with Telstra for two years before he was appointed CEO. Blount, Strong and Switkowski all brought in a number of outsiders into the top management team once they were appointed.

These findings are consistent with Collins and Porras' work. They said:

> Visionary companies develop, promote, and carefully select managerial talent grown from inside the company to a greater degree than the comparison companies... Of 113 chief executives... only 3.5 per cent came directly from outside the

company, versus 22.1 per cent of 140 CEOs at the comparison companies. (p. 173)

It is interesting to compare with competitors where those winning organisations have close competitors. Table 6.2 shows that competitor organisations were much more likely to bring in CEOs from outside. Again, this is consistent with the findings from *Built to Last.*

Table 6.2 – Winning organisations and competitors: where do their CEOs come from?

Winning org.	CEO in 2000	Inside/ outside	Competitors	Recent CEOs	Inside/ outside
Woolworths	Corbett	Inside	Coles Myer	Fletcher/ Eck/ Bartels	Outside/ Outside/ Outside
NAB	Cicutto	Inside	ANZ Westpac C'wealth	McFarlane Morgan Murray	Outside Outside Inside
Rio Tinto	Clifford	Inside	BHP Billiton	Anderson/ Gilbertson	Outside/ Inside
Qantas	Dixon	Inside	Air NZ/ Ansett	Eddington Toomey Norris	Outside Outside Outside

Most leaders have been with the organisation for a long period. Turnover in the winning organisations is lower than industry average. Much of what turnover there is occurs very early, as people who don't like the culture or who can't make it in the culture leave quickly.

CEOs at winning organisations lasted longer. Table 6.3 shows the range of numbers of CEOs over the last 20 years is two to five (excluding the Salvation Army, which has a policy of rotating CEOs) and the average CEO tenure is 9.8 years. This compares with the general average of around four years (at the time of writing). The advantage of leadership 'staying longer' is the ability

159

to use the information better to do more things during the period, as the learning period is reduced.

Table 6.3 – CEO tenure at winning organisations

Organisation	Number of CEOs Appointed 1980–2000	Average Tenure (years)
Brambles	3	10.7
Harvey Norman	3	19.0
Lend Lease	2	8.5
Macquarie	2	11.0
National Australia Bank	3	6.7
Qantas	4	5.0
Rio Tinto	3	8.7
Salvation Army	7	3.0
Telstra	4	6.0
Westfield	3	22.7
Woolworths	5	6.2

Walk the talk

Another noticeable feature of these leadership teams is their links to the people in their organisation, not just to the management team, and their ability to 'get dirty', as Brambles would say. The best example of 'walking the talk' is clearly the Salvation Army. Not only do the Salvation Army people receive low pay, which gives them a common viewpoint with their clients about the materialistic economy in which we live, but Army people are also expected to live their lives according to the values the organisation is promoting. The role of the family is paramount – with couples being required to both accept the role before one member can be promoted. Alcohol is banned. The uniform makes leader behaviour very conspicuous and easy to monitor in a doubting world.

When Woolworths was undergoing a turnaround in the mid-1980s, newly appointed Executive Chairman Paul Simon discovered that Woolworths had lost its price competitiveness and its closeness to the customer. He felt that Woolworths was no longer being run by merchants and traders but by people who analysed computer printouts. Managing Director Harry Watts, future CEO Reg Clairs and other senior executives went back to working in the stores. Clairs recalled:

> We got in at five in the morning. We unloaded trucks. We stacked the delicatessen. We stacked the fruit and vegetables. We made mince in the butcher's shop. We served customers on the check-out. We did all the basics. (Murray, 1999, p. 215)

Simon cut out the 'silver service, three-course lunch culture' that had evolved at head office. He cut out first-class travel, five-star hotels, insisted all company cars be Holdens and reduced the size of head office as he got the head office culture to align with the values of the stores.

In 2001, CEO Roger Corbett carried on this theme:

> I'm just a shopkeeper, not a great strategist... Every Saturday, I drive my car out the driveway and visit stores to see them as customers see them and to meet and speak with the staff. If I know how the store runs, then everyone will need to know about it.

Gerry Harvey part-owns one store in the Harvey Norman network. This enables him to keep a direct handle on what is happening in stores, gives him direct access to customers and forces him to think and act like a franchisee. He fronts most of the TV advertising himself for the chain. While this is consistent with the idea of reducing costs and being efficient, it also has high risk for both Harvey and the organisation. If the advertising does not work, Harvey himself is right in the firing line, especially in a mass-market consumer industry such as discount retailing. It would be a lot easier to sit back and let a professional agency do all the work.

Lend Lease has an interesting approach to 'walking the talk'. Its Code of Conduct says:

> We say to our employees that if you are in doubt as to whether anything you are contemplating might breach the Code, apply the following test: "Would I be willing to see what I'm doing or about to do described in detail on the front page of a national newspaper to be read by family and friends?"

> (www.lendlease.com.au)

Be passionate for the cause

We found that the leaders were passionate about their organisations. Time and again we were surprised in interviews by the passion which emerged about the reasons why the organisation existed and why that was so important. The reason for their passion was the existence of a 'cause' – they believe in the value to external parties of what the organisation is doing.

The Telstra archetype research in the early 1990s showed that Australian employees needed to believe in what their organisation was doing – i.e. in the 'cause' of the organisation (see Illustration 6.1 earlier). Illustration 6.2 shows the 'causes' of the winning organisations.

The Salvation Army is the clearest example. Salvation Army officers do not work at the Army for the money or the conditions! (Note however that regular employees are paid the relevant award wage.) Indeed, before you can become an officer there is a long training program to undergo... and the word 'work' is not used – officers 'belong' to the Army. They are drawn to the cause from all walks of life. Some believe they have been chosen for this calling. Salvationists combine work and personal life into an intermingled holistic single way of life. People have to be passionate and determined to stay in the Army and to succeed to leadership. And leaders demonstrate passion for the cause.

But can you really be passionate about digging up resources, working at a bank or a telecommunications company, selling discounted goods, storing records or collecting rubbish? Yes you can! To leaders in winning organisations (and to other people in the organisation too), it is not just a job. There is a cause. This is the real reason for existence – the bigger picture altruism and *raison d'etre* – a cause about which the leaders (and the people) are passionate. Without that passion, a job is just a job.

One executive, commenting on this, said:

> Normal, rational, straightforward people don't build billion-dollar businesses. It takes someone with passion, heart and emotion to do it.

Illustration 6.2 – The 'causes' of winning organisations

Organisation	Cause
Brambles	We undertake boring services that no-one else wants to do better than anyone else and we do it very profitably and have very satisfied customers
Harvey Norman	The chance for individual small business people to share in a national chain with a better range at cheaper prices
Lend Lease	Highest-quality, innovative, large-scale construction
Macquarie Bank	Unique solutions to large-scale customer financial service needs
National Australia Bank	Lower costs and better risk assessment
Qantas	Highest-quality, most reliable flying; representing Australia on the world stage
Rio Tinto	Lowest-cost, highest-quality, environmentally sound mining developments that benefit all stakeholders
The Salvation Army	Save souls, grow saints and serve suffering humanity
Telstra	Building a high-quality communications system for Australia
Westfield	Building and redeveloping the best shopping centres
Woolworths	Getting lower prices for customers

Be decisive

Leaders are expected to make decisions. Of course, through being close to their people, being open to external influences and having good information systems, they are well placed to make good decisions, and make them quickly (adapt rapidly).

A good example is when Westfield was shown a potential development site in its early days in the US:

> When David and Frank Lowy first saw the Westside Pavilion site in Los Angeles in 1980, they took two seconds to visualise its potential and told Richard Green to go ahead and see if the redevelopment they envisaged could be done. (*The Detailed Westfield Story*, p. 90)

Stunned by the speed of their decision-making, Green went ahead, got the approvals and then watched as Westfield produced the necessary $8 million to pay for the land.

We have cited other examples of this speed elsewhere in the book – e.g. Woolworths' change of decision over its first shopping centre tenancy, Qantas' decision to replace its fleet and Westfield's decisions on redevelopment when it purchases existing shopping centres (see Chapter 4).

Have a long-term view

Being decisive is not simply about speed. It is also about commitment. Leaders in winning organisations are not simply short-term-oriented, even when things are not going well. They have long-term views and this provides stability and encourages the pursuit of a clear long-term purpose. Chapter 5, on clear strategy, is about the long term and has several examples.

Rio Tinto toughed out the 1980s in the belief that its long-term view about the value of its resource deposits was correct. It was only after almost 10 years of dogged persistence that it changed its view to a more commercial perspective, when it realised that the industry paradigm had changed fundamentally. The HIsmelt revolutionary iron ore smelting procedure is another example. It has been under development for 20 years and has only just begun to proceed to commercialisation in 2002, providing another demonstration of the organisation's ability to take a long-term view.

Brambles knew the difficulties of expanding CHEP and its other businesses into other countries, especially where it had not been operating before. Yet it announced what it was planning to do, how long it would take... and did it. Westfield has been operating shopping centre developments in the US for almost 20 years and has only grown to become number two in the industry in the 2000s. It has only just entered the UK market with the same concept. Lend Lease's 2000 strategy of a global real estate organisation does not exist anywhere yet... but nor did its earlier concepts of creating a property trust to finance its property management assets, or controlling a financial services firm to capture retail funds for project development.

Communicate, communicate, communicate

Since leaders are captain-coaches on the field and walk the talk, and since the organisations are externally focused, have clear strategies and adapt rapidly, the role of communicating might be assumed. But the ability to communicate and the need for communication is underestimated, while the effectiveness of communications is usually overestimated in most organisations.

What do winning organisations do differently here? Formally, leaders go to great lengths to find different channels in which to communicate frequently. At Macquarie, the CEO has a series of lunches with newly promoted leaders to explain what the role of leadership is. The CEO also attends every 'Camp Macquarie' orientation program for new employees, to present the essence of the Macquarie history, its culture and expectations. Lend Lease uses its annual planning conference to make the leadership team available to a large number of its people and propagate the views of the leadership team. Harvey Norman's conferences for its franchisees are legendary for the passion and commitment generated.

Internal newsletters are an easily available, and frequently used, tool for communicating widely. At Woolworths, which now has over 130,000 employees, the internal newsletter is used as a vehicle to extol both the position of the whole organisation and the virtues of individual successes that have made it possible – role models

165

for others to applaud. Telstra has a daily newspaper for similar purposes. One Telstra executive said:

> Some of our people carry out extraordinary acts that don't get into the public news. But they are appreciated internally. They'll be mentioned in our daily newspaper and they'll often get a personal email from the CEO. That type of reward and recognition means more to them than... being highlighted in an external publication.

Informal communication is undoubtedly more important however. Walking the talk, being available, decreasing internal structural levels, encouraging open (and two-way) communication, social activities, celebrations and casual recognition for a job well done are some of the methods used. We found, however, that while winning organisations understand the importance of communication, there were no consistent individual or unique techniques being used. They just communicated as often, as widely and in as many ways as they could.

Be consistent

Leadership needs to be consistent in its actions and its communications. Walking the talk is a clear way to achieve this. Having leaders who are home grown and having a stable leadership team are key ingredients.

We discussed consistency in some detail in Chapter 3. Consistency implies incremental changes rather than revolutionary changes. So it is not surprising that when there are major changes for an organisation (such as for Qantas and Telstra), or the organisation makes radical changes as a result of its interpretation of its environment (e.g. NAB, Brambles, Rio Tinto and Lend Lease), such changes are difficult to introduce, even for a winning organisation.

The concept of adapting rapidly, which we discussed in Chapter 4, appears to be opposed to consistency... but if the organisation understands the need for speedy change, and the reasons for the change are communicated and understood and the culture is accepting of this, adapting rapidly can be accommodated into a consistency model.

Have few trappings

We were surprised by the relatively modest offices which most of the senior executives we visited had, considering how well their organisations had been performing for such a long time. It must be tempting for winning organisations to stop to 'smell the roses', reward themselves or relax and enjoy their success. But few, if any, seem to have this view.

In many cases, the trappings (or lack of them) reflect the strategic position which the organisation is trying to achieve. For instance, Harvey Norman, Woolworths and Brambles desperately seek to keep head office costs down for fear of the impact any blow out may have on their ability to compete and because they simply hate waste and extravagance.

The organisations attack the issue of trappings in different ways. Because Macquarie is run as a series of small businesses, each of the business leaders is anxious to keep its costs down. Parts of the 'millionaires club' look more like a computer-based sweat shop, which suggests there is little correlation between success and office size, space or furniture.

There were some anomalies here though. One or two of the winning organisations had surprisingly well-appointed head offices that seemed perceptually inconsistent with their stated strategies of low-cost operations. However, each was either changing to a more aligned structure (i.e. lowering the costs of head office) or had a different model of operation (i.e. high quality leads to high productivity) that meant the perceived 'expensive' offices were not in fact so in relation to the model.

Woolworths' history shows that, when it went off the rails in the early 1980s, the top management had become less focused on the business and more focused on themselves. As we mentioned in the 'Walk the talk' section, when Paul Simons came in as Executive

Chair in 1987, one of the first things he did was to get rid of the silver service dining room in the executive office.

Why do we raise this issue of few trappings? Often people are impressed by the luxury of the offices, fittings or accompanying facilities which an organisation possesses. Leaders in many organisations are notorious for the trappings which they encourage or support and 'justify'. Our findings suggest that the quality of trappings is a very poor way to judge how well an organisation is likely to perform. Focus on aspects such as the people, the leadership, the strategy and the ability to execute, not the trappings.

In summary, we found a distinctive set of characteristics marked the leadership teams of winning organisations. Leaders are captain-coach leaders, building the business and grown from within. They are passionate, they walk the talk, are decisive but have a long-term view, they communicate, are consistent in behaviour and actions and don't focus on the trappings of office. These are not the characteristics that we see in our experience of normal Australian organisations, but they should be.

LEADERSHIP RIGHT FOR THE TIME

Consistent with the strategic cycle concept, we found that leadership styles varied according to the particular needs of the time for each organisation. Leaders – and leadership – focus on the issues which the organisation faces at that time. We term this 'leadership right for the time'.

However, the capabilities we have identified here for leadership in winning organisations do not vary across time periods. Only the specific nature of the issues for the particular organisation and the consequent decisions it must make vary. Being decisive, walking the talk, communicating and having a long-term view, for instance, are important regardless of the industry or the time, but the actual decisions made will depend on the specific context.

Illustration 6.3 shows how leadership issues have varied for Rio Tinto over time. Each leader was faced with quite different issues which were successfully managed at the time. In other words, Maurice Mawby's approaches for CRA, which were 'right' in 1960–71, would clearly have been inappropriate for Leon Davis in 1995–2000. Does this mean Mawby did not succeed? Or that Mawby in some way led the organisation inappropriately or incorrectly? No.

We would speculate that any 'Mawby-capable' person would be able to adjust to the needs of the organisation at the time. Indeed, the ability of the leadership and the organisation to adjust rapidly to changing needs is one key characteristic of success. But it does mean that leadership must be 'right for the time'. The issues, skills and needs change.

Another case is Telstra. Prior to commercialisation, Telstra CEOs were public servants who were part of government departments, and their role was to carry out the government policy of getting a phone in every home in Australia. At the time when commercialisation was introduced to Telstra (and other public sector organisations), Mel Ward's role was to develop the commercial skills of the organisation so it could change from a public sector orientation to the idea that activities had to make profits and a return on investment.

As partial privatisation approached, Frank Blount was brought in from outside to focus on improving the quality of customer service and on increasing the commercial focus. In this he succeeded admirably. However, he was fortunate, because during this time the domestic telecommunications environment was rapidly expanding. The industry – and Telstra – grew rapidly, almost regardless of what Blount and his team did!

His successor, Ziggy Switkowski, faced an industry environment where double-digit growth no longer existed... but investor expectations for growth had not changed! Switkowski therefore had to seek new avenues of growth, and to increase margins to maintain profit growth. His international expansion into PCCW, in particular, and his substantial cost-cutting via reducing head count and capital expenditure have been rational responses to a

169

different set of issues. Success for Switkowski's team will come from different avenues than it did for Blount's or Ward's teams.

Years	CEO	Key Issues
Illustration 6.3 – Leadership issues at Rio Tinto over time		
1962–1974	Maurice Mawby	Develop CRA into a strong Australian mining house by discovering and exploiting large, high-grade deposits in Australia. Focus on technical and operational skills.
1974–1986	Rod Carnegie	Become more commercial, more analytical in considering the competitive position and customer needs. Change the nature of the working relationship between management and their people. Diversify into different industries where CRA might be able to grow more quickly and use its capabilities. Create an Australian company competing on the world stage.
1986–1994	John Ralph	Improve profitability. Implement ideas. Make it work.
1994–2000	Leon Davis	Integrate CRA with RTZ into a reunited Rio Tinto. Create a single, profit-oriented global company. Create global product businesses.
2000–	Leigh Clifford	Grow a profitable set of global businesses.

How is 'right' leadership selected?

In each case, we see that leadership and strategy have been adjusted to meet the particular issues and needs for the time. How does this adjustment occur? How are the 'right' leaders selected?

Our research suggests two factors are responsible (see Figure 6.3). First, in winning organisations, new leaders are generally selected from within. Successful organisations have good teams of leaders. They are not dependent on one single leader. As winning organisations are also externally focused and rapid to adapt, they are able to perceive the capabilities needed for the future leaders, understand that these needs are different from those of the current leaders and have a group of good leaders to choose a new CEO from.

Second, the choice of CEO, and sometimes of the other top management, is made by the board. We have noted that there is some commonality across the boards of these winning organisations. We do not think this is coincidence. Good organisations often have good boards. Good board members are desirable. Good companies seek good board members which they find on the boards of other good organisations! So there is overlap between boards of winning organisations. They recognise each other's competence, even if they are in different industries. Interestingly, quite a number of executives would comment to us that 'x' company ought to be in our group... and it was (though this was not revealed to them at the time)!

Figure 6.3 – Selecting leadership right for the time

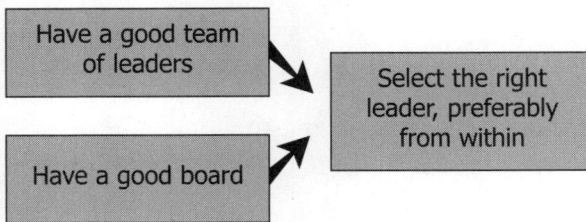

LEADERSHIP PROGRAMS IN WINNING ORGANISATIONS

Recognising the importance of good leadership, most of the winning organisations have formal internal leadership programs and/or models to develop the type of leadership capabilities which they wish to encourage. Illustration 6.4 highlights the current models of some of them, together with our comments. It is important to note that these leadership models do change over

171

time (see 'Leadership Right for the Time'). So these models are more indicative of how the organisations see their future leadership needs than what they may have sought in the past. The variety in these models suggests the different needs of the organisations, the complexities of leadership and the difficulty of developing agreement about what are the specific sets of characteristics and capabilities required. An important aim, however, is to develop home grown and consistent leadership and values.

Illustration 6.4 – Current leadership models from some of the winning organisations

National Australia Bank

- create movement
- display superb balance
- challenge the boundaries
- positive and transparent
- consistently deliver.

Comment: This model highlights the factors of balance, execution and external focus from our framework. 'Create movement' emphasises change, more than our factor of 'alignment'.

Macquarie Bank

- loose/tight management
- sense of identification with team
- take responsibility for results, even where support areas are also responsible
- achieve good levels of profitability and growth
- enhance the productivity, work satisfaction and personal development of other team members
- protect and enhance the bank's reputation and brand name
- enhance the quality of client relationships
- maintain harmonious relations with competitors
- observe limits of authority
- co-operate with other teams

> ### *Illustration 6.4 (cont'd) – Current leadership models from some of the winning organisations*
>
> - be agents of change to improve and develop the bank
> - communicate and promote the goals and values of the bank.
>
> Comment: This model highlights the roles of team, of balance, of entrepreneurship/growth, or managing risk, of external focus, of change and of communication.
>
> **The Salvation Army**
> - live the mission
> - establish pastoral relationships
> - demonstrate spiritual knowledge
> - Christian discipleship
> - build the community
> - develop others
> - lead with firmness and compassion
> - think strategically
> - be personally motivated
> - be adaptable
> - have self-confidence
> - implement plans
> - be tenacious, innovative and have initiative
> - understand the organisation
> - work co-operatively with others
> - have respect for others
> - develop co-operation
> - build networks
> - have professional expertise.
>
> Comment: This model covers a wide range of factors including self-management, relationships with others, building and developing networks, adaptability, walking the talk and personal competence.
>
> **Lend Lease**
> - empowerment
> - delegation

> ### *Illustration 6.4 (cont'd) – Current leadership models from some of the winning organisations*
>
> - autonomy, responsibility and authority
> - feedback, coaching and mentoring
> - strategic interdependencies – inside and outside
> - collaboration.
>
> Comment: This model is focused on structural issues, supporting mechanisms and external networking.

Illustration 6.5 covers another contemporary view of desired leadership styles and needs in Australia. It shows the tremendous variety of perspectives that exist in the leadership area. However, it also provides more evidence for the cause–based, egalitarian model for Australia we mentioned earlier in this chapter. It is also interesting to compare this with Collins' (2001) 'Level 5 leadership', which is related to his work on *Good to Great*. The findings are consistent with his conclusion that powerful leaders possess a paradoxical mixture of professional will and personal humility.

> ### *Illustration 6.5 – Contemporary views of desirable leadership styles for Australia*
>
> Ashkanasy and Trevor-Roberts (2002) participated in a 62-nation Global Leadership and Organisational Behaviour Effectiveness program. Findings for countries varied, with only values-based leadership being found universally valuable and self-protective leadership being found universally negative. The key findings for Australia were:
>
> - Values-based leadership provides vision and inspires people if done tactfully, diplomatically, but in a decisive manner.
> - Leadership must be unselfish and collaborative with friends and workmates – generous, compassionate, group-

> ***Illustration 6.5 (cont'd) – Contemporary views of desirable leadership styles for Australia***
>
> oriented, i.e. egalitarian. The leader should be honest, sincere and modest while building a collaborative team.
> - Leadership should not be individualistic or self-centred.
> - Leadership should not be bureaucratic – formal and needing to follow routines and patterns.
>
> Young (1996) surveyed practising Australian managers looking for the most common descriptors of excellent managers they had seen. He produced the following list. Good managers:
>
> - listen first
> - acknowledge result and effort
> - continuously encourage
> - empower people
> - celebrate even small achievements
> - model appropriate behaviours
> - continuously look to challenge current practices
> - share the vision
> - spend real time in planning
> - learn from everything
> - enjoy their work.
>
> The Mt Eliza Business School leadership model, which is based on local research, is:
>
> - Leadership aligns self, team, organisation and environment towards a preferred future.
> - Leaders are continuous learners who understand their impact.
> - Leaders enable others.
> - Leaders create the future.
> - Leaders interpret and shape the future environment.
>
> While this model is at a very conceptual level, it provides a useful framework for considering the sets of issues which leaders have to be capable in, rather than providing another long list.

A DOMINANT LEADER?

Throughout this chapter we have argued that it is a leadership team, not an individual or charismatic leader, which is needed for success. We have also argued that the issues change over time, so that winning organisations need the 'leadership right for the time'. But the nagging doubt will remain with many readers... wasn't there one single leader who had such an influence on the organisation that that person determined its future fate? This is a very popular view.

Table 6.4 summarises our views of some of the leaders for the winning organisations in terms of this concept of a single dominant leader. It shows that, apart from the possible exceptions of Gerry Harvey at Harvey Norman and Frank Lowy at Westfield, no one leader can be singled out as the person having the dominant effect on the organisation.

Table 6.4 – A dominant leader as driver of winning organisations?

Organisation	Possible Dominant Leader(s)	Comment
Brambles	Oliver Richter	While he was the 'father' of CHEP, Brambles is much more than CHEP.
Harvey Norman	Gerry Harvey	The original establishment of Norman Ross was a partnership, but Harvey has been the dominant figure in Harvey Norman to date.
Lend Lease	Dick Dusseldorp	Certainly established the concepts and ideas behind Lend Lease, but the acquisition of MLC and the later development of a global real estate strategy have been just as significant in Lend Lease's development.

Table 6.4 (cont'd) – A dominant leader as driver of winning organisations?

Organisation	Possible Dominant Leader(s)	Comment
National Australia Bank	Nobby Clark/ Don Argus	Clark was responsible for starting the program of acquisitions that took NAB offshore and Argus carried this on. But the core of NAB had been in existence for many years prior to this and the retreat from the US in 2001 suggests that Clark and Argus have not fundamentally changed NAB.
Macquarie Bank	David Clarke/ Mark Johnson	Established the key elements of the Macquarie 'system', but both acknowledge that Macquarie has developed in businesses and locations which they in no way envisaged.
Qantas	James Strong	Oversaw fundamental changes in Qantas in terms of commercialisation and integration of the domestic airline, but Qantas was a high-service, high-reliability airline for many years before his term in office.
Rio Tinto	Maurice Mawby	In charge when the fundamental large scale discoveries for CRA were made.
	Rod Carnegie	Changed CRA from an excellent Australian miner to a commercial international organisation, but this was an important 'add on' rather than a fundamental change – CRA could not have been successful without its earlier mining excellence.

Table 6.4 (cont'd) – A dominant leader as driver of
winning organisations?

Organisation	Possible Dominant Leader(s)	Comment
Salvation Army	William Booth	Established the Salvation Army in the UK, and provided initial support, but had nothing in particular to do with the success of the Australian church.
	John Gore/ Edward Saunders	Started the Australian church. No particular Australian leaders are credited with determining the future of the Australian organisation's welfare activities.
Telstra	Frank Blount	While he changed the customer service and commercial orientation of the organisation, this work had been in progress for 5 to 10 years previously. Like Qantas, Telstra had a high technical competence which had been in existence for many years.
Westfield	John Saunders	His role in the establishment of Westfield was critical.
	Frank Lowy	He first learnt from, then partnered with, Saunders. Then he led Westfield into overseas markets. To this point he has played a dominant role in the international development of this relatively young organisation.
Woolworths	Percy Christmas	One of the founders and CEO for the first 21 years, when the essence of Woolworths was established.
	Theo Kelly	CEO for 26 years after Christmas and Chair for 17 years till 1980.

Table 6.4 (cont'd) – A dominant leader as driver of winning organisations?

Organisation	Possible Dominant Leader(s)	Comment
Woolworths	Paul Simons	Credited with the recovery of Woolworths from 1987 to 1995. Each played key roles, but none could claim to be behind the key elements of Woolworths, which has always been a team-based organisation.

SUMMARY AND KEY MESSAGES FOR LEADERS

In summary, leadership, not individual leaders, is important in winning organisations. Leadership is team-based behaviour, not about individuals. We found a distinctive set of characteristics marked the leadership teams of winning organisations. Leaders are captain-coach leaders, building the business and grown from within. They are passionate and they walk the talk. They are decisive but have a long-term view. They communicate, are consistent in behaviour and actions and don't focus on the trappings of office. These are not the characteristics that we see in our experience of normal Australian organisations.

Leadership is right for the time. Winning organisations often have internal leadership models and leadership programs, recognising the importance of leadership behaviour to them. The idea that a winning organisation might be entirely due to a single dominant leader is not substantiated.

The key messages for leaders from this chapter are:

* Develop a leadership team.
* Treat the board as part of the team.
* Focus leadership behaviour on building the business.

- Develop captain–coach leader behaviour.
- Ensure that the leadership team is passionate about the business.
- Develop and grow leaders within the business.
- Have a long-term view.
- Make decisive, consistent decisions.
- Communicate widely, formally and informally.
- Recognise that future leadership will face different circumstances and need different skills from those currently used, and select leaders from within that have those skills.

7

LOOKING OUT, LOOKING IN

Externally focused

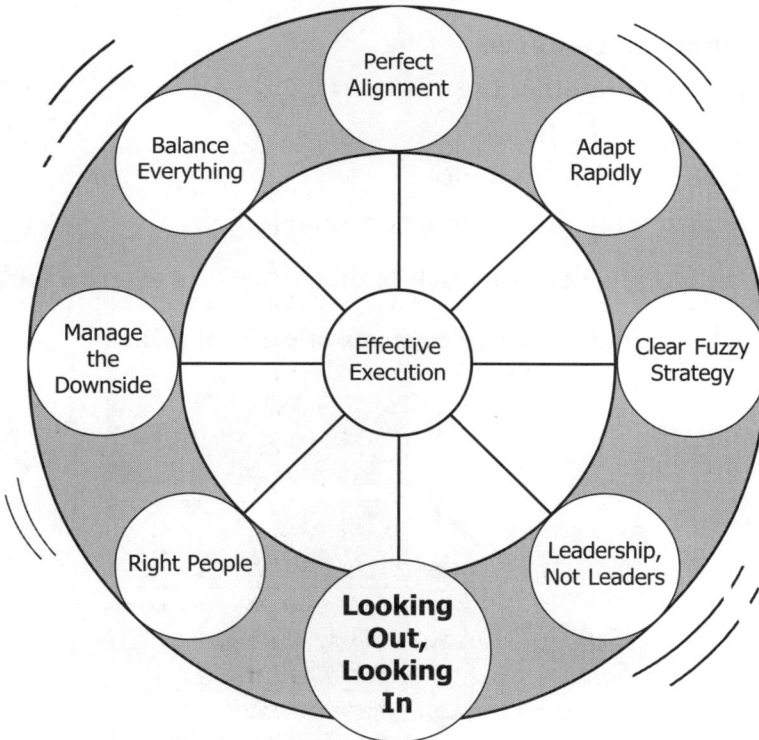

So far, our research has suggested that the essence of winning is internal focus – having a strategy, good leadership, aligning and adapting, in order to execute. Does this mean that winning is simply about extremely good internal focus and execution? Can we ignore what is happening outside the organisation?

Our research found that, while the winning organisations were concerned with aligning all their internal activities, they were also externally focused. They were not simply looking within their own organisations and their own physical environments. They were actively engaged in looking out – exploring what customers wanted, what other organisations were doing, what the community wanted, both in Australia and overseas, now and in the future.

Our research found that this element of looking out, being externally focused while also looking in as we have already shown, demonstrated itself in several specific ways (see Figure 7.1):

- focusing on customers
- working with other organisations
- focusing on the future
- thinking outside Australia
- having a sense of community responsibility.

In this chapter, we explore each of these aspects of external focus.

Figure 7.1 – Key elements of external focus

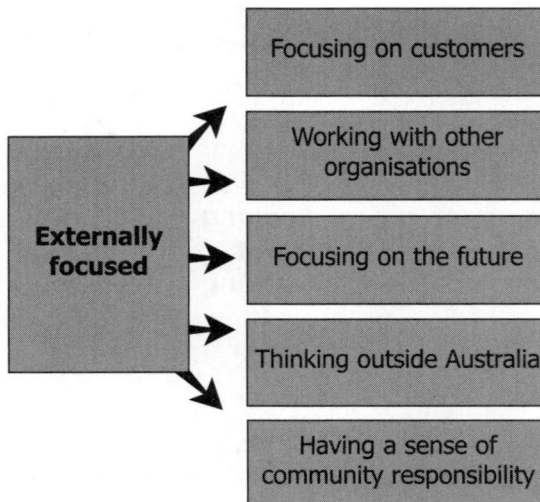

What about shareholders? Aren't they a key part of 'looking out'? We have not included focus on shareholders as a part of external focus. Good results for shareholders, or key stakeholders in the case of non-profit organisations, are a prerequisite for considering an organisation to be successful. All organisations understand that solid shareholder/stakeholder returns are required.

But shareholder/stakeholder returns are an outcome, not a cause of success. We are concerned in this research with the causes of success for winning organisations, from which the outcomes – including shareholder returns – follow. Winning organisations do not think of focusing on shareholders or key stakeholders as a *means* of winning, but as *measures* of winning. The concept of 'effective execution' includes the results for shareholders. Shareholders, then, are not forgotten or omitted by any means! But they are not a key area winning organisations are externally focused on.

In this chapter on 'looking out' we'll look at the roles of customers, working with other organisations, focusing on the future, thinking outside Australia and having a sense of community responsibility. There are many aspects of 'looking out' for winning organisations!

FOCUSING ON CUSTOMERS

It should be no surprise that winning organisations focus on customers. After all, unless customers strongly support the organisation's products and services, how will it succeed? But what is it that winning organisations do to make 'focusing on customers' work? Our research found four factors that winning organisations used (see Figure 7.2). They:

- think 'customer'
- conduct intensive market research
- develop customised products and services
- manage customer relationships.

183

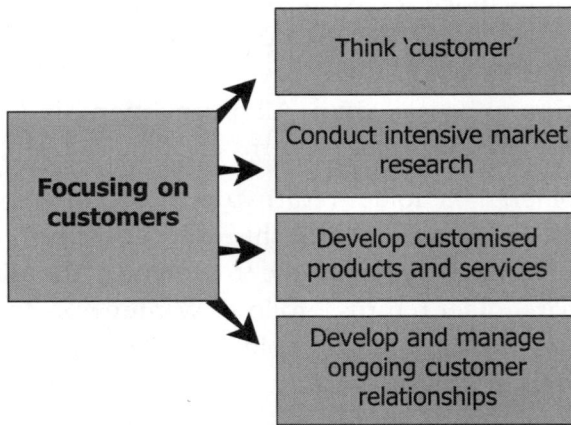

Figure 7.2 – Focusing on customers

Think 'customer'

Perhaps the most important aspect is 'think customer'. Each of the organisations is very clear that its very existence is dependent on satisfying customers. By thinking from the customer's perspective, the organisation can better meet the real needs which customers have.

The Salvation Army provides a very clear example of this. Since the Salvation Army, unlike all the other winning organisations, is a not-for-profit organisation, it has no real reason for existence if its 'customers' (it does not use this word) do not value its services. But there are lots of welfare organisations with which the Salvation Army competes. Most of its services are also provided by other welfare or government organisations.

Why is it, then, that the Salvation Army is so well trusted and supported? One reason is that it really understands the problems which its clients face and produces practical solutions which have as an underlying philosophy the value of the family unit. The services are delivered not by do-gooders, not by government bureaucrats, but by people who are themselves not very well off, are committed and non-judgemental and who can therefore empathise with the issues faced by clients.

'Thank God for the Salvos' is not just a marketing slogan... it is based on the real experience of the Salvation Army as an organisation that faces the issues when sometimes no other organisation does. 'Put your hands together for Sally. She's the only one who cares' – a line from a popular song by Sade – captures this idea. How many organisations are so well loved and respected that they have songs written about them?

Winning 'for-profit' organisations also 'think customer'. Westfield Shoppingtown has developed its 'Ten commandments for customer relations' (see Illustration 7.1) to remind staff of this. In addition, it has a Westfield Shoppingtown promise:

> We promise to keep you smiling each and every time you visit. Our friendly Westfield people are always here for you, with directions, gift suggestions and of course, a friendly smile. If there's anything you need, just let us know. Service with a smile.

Illustration 7.1 – Westfield's ten commandments for customer relations

1. The customer is never an interruption to your work.
2. Greet every customer with a friendly smile.
3. Call customers by name.
4. Remember, you are the company!
5. Never argue with a customer.
6. Never say 'I don't know'.
7. Remember the customer pays your wages.
8. State things in a positive way.
9. Brighten every customer's day!
10. Always go the extra mile!

It also has door decals ('Welcome to our town'; 'You are now leaving our town') which reinforce the same message of friendliness and community. All of this has the same, consistent message –

and yet it is the specific retailers, not Westfield, which these customers are visiting!

Qantas constantly upgrades its service levels, through changing the services given and increasing the quality of the service, to match customer needs, which are identified by doing extensive market research.

Woolworths thinks of itself as a buying agent for the customer, committed to the idea of passing on cost savings in the form of lower prices. The dramatic reductions in milk and egg prices to customers in 2001, achieved by negotiating nationally for lower supply prices, are an example of delivering that result.

Conduct intensive market research

Another way to focus on customers is to undertake extensive market research. This is particularly appropriate in mass markets, where customised products and services may be less feasible. Telstra undertakes continuing major market research studies through its Telecom Customer Attitudes to Service (TELCATS) operation, which it began in 1987. TELCATS enables it to understand customer attitudes and preferences, and hence design products to suit those needs. Since it was partially privatised, the number of products and services offered by Telstra has dramatically expanded to reflect the needs of particular customer segments, often identified through the market research.

Qantas is another that invests heavily in market research, for similar reasons. A selection of passengers is surveyed and passenger comments are encouraged as a stimulus to improving service levels. Woolworths does not focus so much on formal research, but feels it gets a lot of customer feedback through its checkout operators, who are encouraged to gather and summarise it.

There are many other examples. For instance, the Salvation Army carries out extensive market research before deciding to embark on offering a new welfare service. Brambles extensively researches the market before entering a new country with its products and services. Woolworths seeks input from its customers whenever

186

possible and Westfield conducts extensive end-customer surveys to ensure that changes meet customer needs.

Develop customised products and services

A closely related aspect to 'think customer' and conducting market research is designing products and services for particular customers or for particular customer niches. This ensures that the products and services meet the real needs of those particular customers, not customers in general. For Brambles and Lend Lease, this is apparent in the development of unique products and their long-lasting relationships with customers over time. Brambles developed a variety of CHEP pallets to suit different markets and industries. Cleanaway developed a variety of waste containers to suit different types of waste, again based on the needs of particular customers and industries.

Lend Lease sits down with its customers and develops cost-saving sharing plans so that, if certain savings are made, they are shared with customers. This process builds trust and commitment, especially when the savings are actually delivered. It also aligns customer and organisational goals. But it is not easy, or common! Most organisations are concerned about how to charge more to customers and simultaneously give less! And then they don't deliver!

Macquarie seeks out niches where customers are either poorly served or not served at all. It developed the first Cash Management Trust in 1980 for retail investors seeking access to the then-high wholesale investment rates available for their surplus short-term cash balances. Its more recent developments of listed trusts to provide opportunities for retail investors to invest in infrastructure, tourism, telecoms and other utilities are other examples.

NAB's tailored home loan is another example of a customised product which was not imitated for several years. This product enables customers to pay off the loan at a pace that suits their lifestyles and changing ability over time, rather than meet the bank's desire for certainty of repayments. It also enables customers to pay it off faster than a conventional loan, thus providing enormous individual customer value.

187

Developing and managing ongoing customer relationships

Another way to focus on customers is to develop ongoing customer relationships. Customer Relationship Management (CRM) is a developing field of marketing, designed to focus on the whole customer over a period of time, not just on a particular transaction. Because of this relative newness, our research did not find many examples of the use of formal CRM systems. However, developing and managing customer relationships on an ongoing basis is recognised as important by winning organisations.

NAB's Customer Account Management System (CAMS) began in 1988 and was one of the first attempts by a bank to understand and manage customers. It enabled the bank to understand the customer's whole position with the bank, instead of focusing on the results of individual bank products, as was common elsewhere in the industry. As a result, bank staff are able to approach customers with a full picture of their current and past history and use this information to anticipate and meet customers' ongoing, and changing, needs. This proactive approach compares favourably with the usual tactic of waiting to react to a customer enquiry.

Qantas' frequent flyer scheme is another example of developing and managing ongoing customer relationships. Qantas is also a member of the global Oneworld alliance which treats top-tier frequent flyers of one airline in the alliance as frequent flyers of all partners. Though its scheme, introduced in 1990, was not significantly different from that of its close competitor Ansett or other international airline schemes, it gives Qantas a terrific advantage in the restructured domestic airline industry since Ansett's demise. This is due to the inability of the competing Star Alliance to offer a viable product in Australia following Ansett's collapse and the lack of interest in offering a frequent flyer scheme by competitor Virgin Blue, which is focused on low prices.

Other organisations have less formal ways of managing customer relationships. In industrial businesses, relationships with customers are often critical. Lend Lease described the way its relationships with international customers have evolved over time, as follows:

> What is emerging is a series of clients who require a spectrum of services, often starting with consulting and advisory and progressing through to development, project management, finance and structuring. With this range of services come long-term relationships and alliances, and greater security and predictability of revenue and profit. (Lend Lease 2000 annual report)

One example of a long ongoing customer relationship exists between Westfield and Coles Myer. In 1960, Coles wanted to expand into New South Wales, which it did by takeover initially. Westfield approached Coles to persuade it to take space in one of its centres. During the negotiations, Coles mentioned that it was looking for other sites. Westfield staff drove Coles staff around Sydney looking for sites. Coles nominated the sites and Westfield then obtained them:

> Westfield quickly understood exactly what Coles required and deployed scouts to locate sites. In the early 1960s, in a matter of three years, it had built seventeen supermarkets for Coles. (*The Detailed Westfield Story*, p. 33)

It was a mutually beneficial partnership. Westfield played a major role in getting Coles established in New South Wales and Coles contributed to getting Westfield launched in Australia.

Westfield provides a range of extra services to its retailers, including retailing education seminars, skills development, consulting advice and retail study tours in Australia and overseas. In this sense, many of Westfield's customers see it not as a 'landlord' but as a 'business partner', even though it is renowned for being quite hard in its negotiations of rentals with retailers. One retailer said:

> I regard Westfield as a business partner, not a landlord. A landlord is only interested in the rent and sues you when you can't pay. Westfield is different. It cares about your business succeeding. If you are in trouble, it will send in consultants to help. On many occasions I have used this assistance. (Anon, *The Detailed Westfield Story*, p. 129)

189

WORKING WITH OTHER ORGANISATIONS

Focusing on customers is just one way of thinking about external relations. Working with joint venture partners, suppliers and governments are some other ways in which winning organisations think about being externally focused (see Figure 7.3). Winning organisations see other organisations as extensions of their own business. They see the co-operation and co-ordination with other organisations as essential to their own success... so they manage these relationships!

Figure 7.3 – Working with other organisations

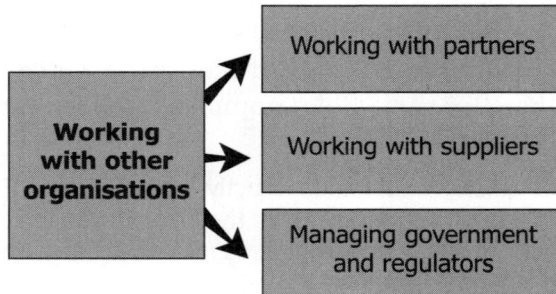

These relationships have several themes in common:

- An ability to reduce an organisation's capital commitment. By working with other organisations, their capital can be used as part of the organisation's own expansion.

- An ability to reduce the risk involved in any activity. Joint venture arrangements not only reduce capital costs but lock in either guaranteed suppliers or customers, reducing the risk of the activity failing.

- An ability to achieve the idea through the resources, capabilities and skills of the other organisation. Other organisations bring their own sets of capabilities, increasing the combined capabilities well beyond those of the organisation itself. Some also share the rewards as the counter to sharing the risk.

- An ability to undertake projects that would not otherwise be feasible. Combining capabilities and capital enables the organisation to undertake projects it would be unable to do by itself.

Working with partners

Our research found that most of the winning organisations are deeply involved in a range of long-term joint venture relationships, particularly as they spread out into new locations and markets. These joint ventures are a clearly chosen style of operation, rather than a set of opportunistically chosen, short-term activities. Working with joint venture partners enables organisations to expand their operations more quickly and access the capabilities of other organisations. However, the loss of control and the need for effective joint venture management means joint activities need to be closely monitored if these approaches are to be successful.

In Qantas' case, working with partner airlines is essential if it is to offer the range of services that customers want. Because airline routes are negotiated between governments, and because many airlines are government-owned, the ability to work with other airlines – competitors in many cases – is essential if Qantas is to offer its desired route structure. Qantas' membership of the eight-partner Oneworld global alliance is one way in which it operates very closely with partner airlines. Codesharing is another, which it uses extensively as well. Achieving common standards and levels of customer service is a key issue for both customers and for partner airlines, to deliver what customers want and expect from such an alliance.

In the Salvation Army's case, government is the biggest source of welfare funds. Coupled with the increasing desire of governments to get out of the actual provisioning of many welfare services, the Salvation Army's ability to work with government – as partner in terms of achieving the objectives of the funding – is critical to its ability to get funds for its desired and required services.

Brambles began its partnership with Guest Keen Nettlefold plc (GKN) in 1972, when it convinced GKN that its (Brambles')

191

idea for introducing CHEP into the UK was economically viable, even though none of the GKN businesses was similar to CHEP. Success in the UK led to GKN partnering Brambles' expansion with CHEP into Europe, and then into North America. The merging of operations of the two organisations in 2001 and the dual listing of the companies is, at the time of writing, the most recent step in the partnership arrangement.

Lend Lease is another organisation which has maintained important relationships with a wide variety of partners. For instance:

- Lend Lease worked with MLC as a major investor in its buildings beginning in 1958. In 1982, Lend Lease acquired 50 per cent of MLC and in 1985 it moved to 100 per cent ownership.
- In 1981, it partnered with the ACTU to develop skills training.
- In 1994, it partnered with IBM to establish Integrated Systems Solutions Corporation Australia (ISSC), a technology outsourcing organisation.
- It has also partnered with:
  - Brambles to enter the airport privatisation market
  - John Lewis and Mirvac in building and construction
  - Prudential in investment
  - Vanguard and Maple–Brown Abbott in funds management.

On any particular project, Lend Lease is also very good at managing partners and suppliers. It is very disciplined upfront in terms of briefs, scoping the project, undertaking all appropriate pre–planning activities, and getting the best people from all over the world to work on the project.

Working with suppliers

In contrast to our findings about working with other organisations and focusing on customers, we were surprised to find that supplier relationships were not regarded as nearly as important to winning organisations as a key for success. The only 'supplier' that was clearly important was people – those who worked for the organisation (see Chapter 8).

However, there are examples of how suppliers are important. Lend Lease and Brambles both have as a philosophy that they wish to work with the best organisations they can find. This is on the basis that the best organisations will be leaders in their fields, pacesetters in industry standards and are likely to have good and professional relationships and practices. Each finds that it works with the same organisations – as supplier, partner or customer – over and over again. This also reduces the degree of marketing needed to 'find' customers for the future.

Woolworths is another which sees suppliers as important. In its annual report in 1995, it said:

> We intend to work closely with our suppliers to improve the supply management chain as part of our commitment to support major branded products. Our suppliers have recognised us as being fair, open and responsive in our dealings and our promotion and development of their own branded products has resulted in the strong growth of product category sales and brand management in our stores...

Westfield and Lend Lease both recognise the importance of suppliers of capital as suppliers. Lend Lease set up General Property Trust – and Westfield followed with Westfield Property Trust – as a source of funds to support the growth of their large-scale property developments.

Nevertheless, these examples were not seen by the winning organisations as key factors in their success. This may well be an area where even winning organisations can develop in the future.

Managing government and regulators

In some industries, managing government agreements or rules is critical for organisational success. Hence, managing governments and their regulation processes can be a critical element for success or failure. This element is often overlooked by organisations which focus only on internal operations, or even on their competitors. Lobbying and public relations skills can be very important, if under-publicised for obvious reasons!

Several of the winning organisations are intimately affected by government rules and regulations. Telstra is perhaps the most affected, since the Federal Government still owns 51 per cent of Telstra in 2002, while it simultaneously controls industry regulation. Telstra's ability to manage the regulatory process, and 'manage down' its 100 per cent pre-deregulation market share to levels that allow sustainable competitors to emerge, has been a major component of its success since its partial privatisation. After almost 10 years of this deregulations process, only Optus and Vodafone have emerged as sustainable competitors, and then only in defined segments of Telstra's total market.

The Federal Government has a major conflict of interest. It receives half of Telstra's annual dividends and has received all of the sale proceeds from the two share sales to date (with more likely to come). Yet, through its regulatory arm – the Australian Competition and Consumer Commission – it is trying to develop a competitive industry, which requires Telstra to 'lose' market share and customers! While its competitors have complained bitterly, the regulators have been unable to enforce quick changes to the industry as Telstra has successfully used the court appeal system to slow the process of change and thus slow the loss of its customers and market share... and profits... which benefit the government!

Telstra has been so successful at this 'managing down' process that in 2002, in the wake of the collapse of several competitors and unsustainable losses by others, the Minister for Communications proposed to deny Telstra the right of appeal to the courts in future. This unprecedented move could dramatically reduce Telstra's power if it is enforced. Another proposal mooted in 2002 was to break Telstra into two – a monopoly infrastructure and a 100 per cent privately owned commercial retail and wholesale unit. Again, it points to Telstra's ability to manage the process so well.

194

For Qantas, also coming from a government-ownership background, managing government and regulators has been similarly important. While there are almost 40 airlines that fly into Australia, some who have sought to enter the international into-Australia market have been denied permission. These denials of new entrants often suited Qantas' wishes – the government-owned Qantas! Of course, governments in other countries have similarly denied Qantas' own requests to expand its routes – in particular the US and Hong Kong. Now, as a completely privately owned airline, Qantas in some ways competes at a disadvantage in country-to-country negotiations where many other airlines are still government-owned.

Rio Tinto deals with a variety of governments (national, regional and local) which approve lease exploration or mining, so that good government relationships are very important. CRA took the extreme tack of becoming 'Australianised' under Foreign Investment Review Board (FIRB) legislation in 1978, so that it could be treated as an Australian company, even though it was majority-owned by UK miner RTZ. CRA committed to work towards majority Australian ownership within a specified time limit and achieved that by 1986. Its highly nationalistic CEO of the time, Rod Carnegie, was convinced of the importance of Australia developing its own international mining companies. He saw the Australianisation process as a way for CRA to succeed at this. It gave CRA greater freedom to pursue projects with more flexibility than if it had been bound by the restrictive provisions of the foreign investment policies of successive federal governments. This step of becoming Australianised shows how CRA was prepared to manage the government relationship for its advantage.

Westfield is another organisation whose management of government relationships – mostly local government in its case – is critical to its success. Westfield's ability to get rapid planning permission for its sites has been outstanding. This ability has been important for getting developments and redevelopments started earlier than competitors would dream imaginable. Occasionally

Westfield has been involved in controversy over its practices but, when challenged, it has always made it clear and open what those practices have been.

The 'battle for Eastgardens' provides an interesting glimpse. In the early 1980s, General Motors–Holden closed its Sydney plant and W.D. & H.O. Wills signalled it was about to do the same with a nearby site. Reluctant to lose more jobs, the NSW Government brought Wills and Westfield together and, after the Government added a piece of Crown land to the package, Wills agreed to stay and expand while Westfield agreed to build a shopping centre – Eastgardens. Protests from all sides came regarding the use of Crown land and sweetheart deals for mates from other retailers who were affected by the new shopping centre. In July 1982, the appeal on the re-zoning was heard in the NSW Land and Environment Court and the future of the development looked shaky. However, the NSW Government intervened and passed an Act of Parliament which ended the proceedings and precluded any appeal.

There are many ways in which relationships with governments and regulators may need to be managed. Winning organisations see this as an important part of their activities for achieving success. The specific issues and approaches will vary from one organisation and industry to another, but government relationships cannot be ignored. They must be managed.

FOCUSING ON THE FUTURE

So far in this chapter we have shown that winning organisations do focus externally and not simply internally. The implication has been that they focus externally on the present. However, we found that winning organisations also focus on the future, not just the present. They are concerned with how their industries and organisations will develop and what the implications of these developments will be. Consequently, they are frequently ahead of their time, or ahead of their industry, in making changes to the way they are run, where they compete and what product and

196

service set they compete with. They are leaders, not followers, in industry and organisational change.

There are two ways in which they focus on the future (see Figure 7.4):

- taking a whole-of-industry view of the future
- focusing on the future of the organisation.

Figure 7.4 – Focusing on the future

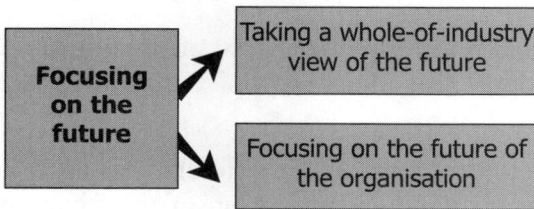

Taking a whole-of-industry view of the future

We frequently observed that winning organisations had a clear view about the nature of their industry and its future development, not just their own organisation. When Brambles decided to go global during the mid-1990s, it was to some extent a repudiation of its past ways of operation as a series of independent small business units focused on local opportunities. Commenting on this, CEO John Fletcher said:

> This is not in any way to say that the old ways were not right... They were fine, but the world has changed... we were always out in front of our competitors, who were by and large 'little guys', and our people were on average better than them. But our competition is no longer the 'little guy' over whom Brambles has an advantage. (Carew, 2000, p. 233)

Qantas is another which has always had a whole-of-industry view. Qantas has always been aggressive about pursuing its position rather than reacting to industry pressure. For instance, whether it has been:

- pursuing its goal of becoming a round-the-world airline in 1958,

- trying to acquire Air New Zealand when it was privatised in 1988,
- seeking $6 billion from the Government for plane fleet expansion in 1989 to ride the wave of tourism growth,
- cutting costs and improving profitability as low-cost airlines became common throughout the world during the late 1990s, or
- seeking to be one of the world's major airlines in what it sees as the coming industry consolidation in the 2000s,

Qantas has had a leading edge view of its industry and its likely future developments and has been proactive about pursuing those views.

In quite different industries, for different reasons, Rio Tinto and NAB both saw the commoditisation of their basic products and services, resulting in them being unable to sustain existing cost levels. Both focused on cost control well before their competitors. For Rio this meant trying to change the nature of workforce management in the mining industry by moving to negotiated individual contracts, rather than accepting industry-wide union-negotiated agreements that reduced opportunities for flexibility, initiative and cost reduction.

For NAB it meant the early recognition that, in a more open regulatory environment, costs were far too high in the industry and low cost operation would be an industry-leading position with competitive advantage. NAB's successful focus on cost control forced its competitors to address their own cost levels explicitly, rather than simply continue with existing industry practices.

Westfield is always concerned with industry developments. When the new Chadstone shopping centre was developed in Melbourne in 1960 – and set the standard for shopping malls in Australia – John Saunders and Frank Lowy were not invited to its opening. Undeterred, Saunders flew to Melbourne, crawled under the protective wire and gate-crashed the opening. He spent most of his time observing in great detail the specifics of the layout of the centre in order to improve his own thinking about the latest developments first-hand, rather than enjoying the celebrations.

Focusing on the future of the organisation

Another approach to considering the future is the narrower way of simply thinking about where the organisation itself is going and what its future is likely to be, regardless of industry developments.

Lend Lease constantly refers to its views of the future in its annual reports (see Illustration 7.2). From its early days Lend Lease held conferences considering external views that might impact the future of the organisation. For instance, in 1981 Lend Lease held its 'Viewpoint 81' conference for 20 of its own leaders and 20 invited distinguished representatives from labour, business and government, to consider the theme of resolution of the conflict between capital and labour. This topic was relevant to how Lend Lease might compete in the future and was highly advanced thinking compared with other industry competitors at the time. It was not for another six years that the Industrial Relations Commission formally allowed enterprise bargaining to begin and thus allowed management and unions to sit down with only the particular enterprise's future, and the future of its particular people, to be taken into account.

Rio Tinto also looks into the future. It is developing the 'Mine of 2020' concept – the idea of a completely ecologically sustainable mine. It sees ecological sustainability as a future trend and wishes to be ahead of that trend, rather than have the concepts forced upon it.

In summary, winning organisations consider their own future and also that of the industry from an external perspective. They are proactive, not reactive, and are leaders in thinking about – and acting on – how they see the future developing.

Illustration 7.2 – Lend Lease forecasts its future

1981
Its future lies in the further development of the group's business in Australia and further expansion in the USA, Asia and the Pacific region.

1983
The successful companies of tomorrow will be those that... become international in outlook. Increasingly, companies compete on a multinational basis... The next five years will be devoted to a consolidation in the USA and Asia... Lend Lease sees the trend from an industrial base to one of services and information.

1987
...objective is to identify and act on trends at least five years before they become evident in the market...

1988
Some years ago we identified financial services as a growth business... We have embarked on providing basic financial services with the ultimate aim of also closing that loop so as to be able to provide all financial services to individuals under one contract throughout their life...

1991
Globalisation also means we can no longer gauge ourselves from a peculiarly rational perspective... A director has also been made responsible for researching and implementing the best environmental practices... An integral part of the change process involves the transformation of Lend Lease into a learning organisation...

1995
Lend Lease's markets will undergo rapid change in the next 10 years... Two major shifts... the emergence of South East Asia... and the impact of technology.

2000
We are now a global company, recently established and largely through acquisitions, but the objective is quite clear – to carry on Lend Lease's traditions and become the most respected real estate organisation in the world...

(Lend Lease Annual Reports)

THINKING OUTSIDE 'AUSTRALIA'

As we have already noted in Chapters 1 and 5, the strategic cycle leads most growing Australian organisations to become 'international' at some point in their lives. As part of being externally focused, we found that winning organisations are very aware of what is going on in their industries outside Australia and are not just focused on the domestic market. We found there were four aspects to this (see Figure 7.5):

1. going overseas early
2. bringing overseas ideas to Australia
3. taking Australian ideas overseas
4. recognising that they are competing in an international market.

This links to our comments on innovation (see Chapter 4) that a great deal of innovation in winning organisations seems to be related to moving ideas across geographical boundaries, rather than developing fundamental 'big bang' new ideas.

Figure 7.5 – Thinking outside 'Australia'

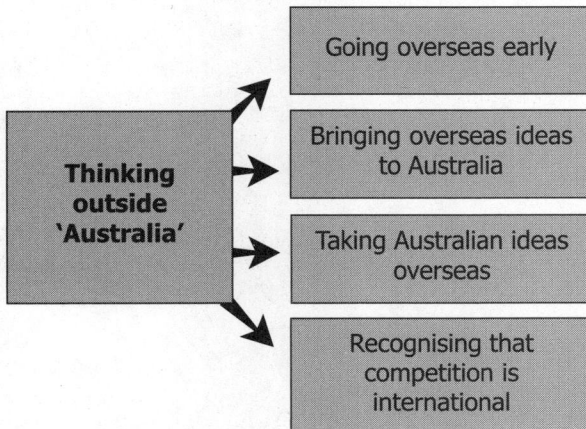

Going overseas early

Many of the winning organisations went overseas early in their lives (see Table 7.1). This move overseas was, generally, ahead of

201

their competitors and was generally dictated by the strategy of the organisation rather than inspired by industry activity or forecasts.

These organisations took it upon themselves to enter international markets. In most cases, the reason was clearly due to the perceived limits of the size of the Australian market for the products and services being produced, e.g. Brambles, Lend Lease, Macquarie, Westfield and NAB. In some cases, it was due to the particular choice of strategy, e.g. Qantas always wanted to be an international airline.

Table 7.1 – Winning organisations go overseas early

Organisation	Year Established	First Overseas Activity	Years of International Experience by 2000
Brambles	1916	1971	30
Harvey Norman	1982	1999	2
Lend Lease	1951	1964	36
Macquarie Bank	1969	1983	17
National Australia Bank	1858	1987	13
Qantas	1920	1935	65
Rio Tinto	1905	Subsidiary of overseas parent	Overseas subsidiary
The Salvation Army	1880	Subsidiary of overseas parent	Overseas parent
Telstra	1901/1975	1985	15
Westfield	1956	1977	23
Woolworths	1924	1929 (but retreated in 1974)	45

Because entering overseas markets is much more difficult than is often anticipated by organisations (see strategic cycle discussion in Chapter 5), the first move is often very minor. But the clear strategic intention of moving into international markets is seen very early. Winning organisations are committed to that move, so they continue to work away at it, seeking sustainable success. Since relatively few Australian organisations operate internationally, this characteristic suggests another way in which winning organisations are different.

Bringing overseas ideas to Australia

In Chapter 4, we noted that bringing overseas ideas back to Australia is a major cause of innovation for winning organisations. Brambles found the bin for Cleanaway overseas. Qantas copied other international airlines in introducing its frequent flyer scheme. Rio Tinto imported Elliott Jaques' ideas on "time span of discretion" from Canada/the UK. Telstra's approved products are mainly from overseas manufacturers. Woolworths' base idea of the discount emporium came from Woolworths overseas. Westfield saw enclosed shopping centres from its visits to the US. NAB's position in the UK/Irish and US markets has given it a window on the world not so easily available to its local competitors.

These examples suggest the importance of this route for 'new ideas' or 'innovation' for Australian organisations. The winning organisations find inspiration for many of the keys to their success by exposing themselves to international ideas and adapting them to the local market. As winning organisations begin to operate overseas, this further exposes them to overseas practices and possible innovations, which they can also 'import' back to their Australian operations.

Taking Australian ideas overseas

The reverse aspect to the practice of importing ideas has been the exporting of some ideas developed locally and the use of them on the international stage. And some of these ideas are improvements of ideas originally brought in from overseas!

While the idea of the CHEP pallet was actually introduced to Australia by US shipping practices during World War II, the Australian government developed the idea of pooling pallets centrally to conserve resources while providing an innovative service. Then Brambles bought the pool, took the idea and developed it into a control and tracking system. It exported the system to the UK, then through Europe, then North America and is, at the time of writing, spreading the system through Asia. It has also done this with the Cleanaway system and with Recall records management.

Westfield has re-exported the mall shopping centre idea to its home – the US! In particular though, Westfield developed skills in redeveloping small-scale shopping centres, branding shopping centres, clustering them, and providing professional asset management and separate asset ownership of the centres through the development of property trusts. It is, at the time of writing, taking these ideas to the UK.

NAB has exported its credit control practices, its tailored home loan package and its ability to market to local communities to the UK, New Zealand, Ireland and Hong Kong (having withdrawn from the US in 2001).

Recognising that the market is international

For some organisations, an important aspect of success is their recognition that they are competing internationally. Regardless of conditions in Australia, particularly on the supply side, these organisations realise they must be internationally competitive, especially regarding customers.

Rio Tinto is an obvious example, since the scale of its Australian operations is such that most of its sales are made to overseas corporations, where prices are set regardless of where the product is sourced from. In 1981, CRA noted in its annual report:

> CRA operates in world markets. We must pay constant attention to costs and operating efficiency... particular attention is being given to service functions and overhead costs... there have been

> 33 major tax policy changes in Australia over the last seven years...
> [compared with] none in Brazil... [Our] competitors are
> strengthening their position.

Macquarie views its main competitors as international players in
investment banking. It realises that to compete, even locally, it
must be better than these international players, since they have
scale, experience and brand reputation beyond what Macquarie
can aspire to. One Macquarie executive said:

> Being the only Australian investment bank but competing against
> the international/global players, everyone is bigger than us. We
> will never win on brand name. We must have a better idea or we
> will lose. We need to do more than just the job... Each time we
> lose, it is because we stuffed up, not because of luck or other
> external reasons.

Increasingly, as organisations proceed through the strategic cycle,
it becomes imperative that they understand international competitive
forces rather than rely on their strong local position for success.
The globalising moves of Brambles and Lend Lease, Qantas'
involvement in the Oneworld alliance, NAB's experience in Europe
and the US, Telstra's linking with Pacific Century Cyber Works,
Westfield's development in the US, and other similar developments
by the winning organisations show that international competitive
forces become more important for organisations over time.

HAVING A SENSE OF COMMUNITY RESPONSIBILITY

A final aspect of external focus for winning organisations is that
they have a sense of community responsibility, rather than a simple
responsibility to maximise returns to shareholders, provide maximum
value to customers, or even optimise returns to key stakeholders.

We do not see this sense of community responsibility as being
particularly different from best practice in this area. Many
organisations have such a sense. But, given the outstanding financial
and market performances which these organisations exhibit, it
may be considered surprising that they are also providing benefits
to the general community and that they see this as a part of their
role and responsibility.

205

One example is Lend Lease's community of interest. It is a deeply held value within Lend Lease that the best organisation performance occurs when all interests are actually aligned, and this includes the interests of the community. In 1996, Lend Lease introduced the idea of encouraging – and paying for – all its employees to undertake a day's work in the community. In its 1997 annual report, it said:

> On 21 November 1996 we requested employees from all Group companies in Australia and overseas to spend a full day working at a community or charitable organisation of their choice... The benefit to our employees as well as to those they worked for was very obvious.

The Salvation Army sees the 'community' as its effective 'customer'. While the Salvation Army helps to improve the lot of individuals and of particular families, it sees the ultimate beneficiary as the whole community. For the Salvation Army, 'sense of community' is what the whole of life is about. 'Community' is not some separate group.

Rio Tinto's exploration and mining activities often disturb the natural environment. This can create a great deal of local community resistance, even though large economic benefits follow this activity for the local community as well as for Rio Tinto. Rio Tinto has enshrined both its environmental policies, and its aim to benefit local communities and respect local community customs and practices as much as possible, in its principles. Part of its statement 'The Way We Work' says:

> Wherever the Group operates, good relations with its neighbours are fundamental to long-term success. Knowing that each local community is different, the policy of Rio Tinto is that every operation shall strive to understand and interact constructively with its local communities and to assist their development in ways which apply the following principles:
>
> • Mutual respect
> • Active partnership
> • Long-term commitment. (p. 8)

This can cause potential economic costs to an organisation. For instance, Rio owns Jabiluka, the third-largest uranium deposit in the world. But it is located within the Kakadu National Park in the Northern Territory and, as well, local Aboriginal communities are strongly opposed to its development. As a result, in 2001, Rio Tinto stated that it would not develop Jabiluka without the full support of the traditional owners.

Westfield is another which places community very highly in its thinking. Westfield has had its 'four objectives' since 1986:

1. to reward its shareholders with maximum benefits
2. to provide its employees with satisfying work opportunities in a progressive enterprise
3. to give its retailers the right environment to maximise sales in its shopping centres
4. to fully meet the expectation of society and the interests of the communities in which Westfield operates.

Westfield shopping centres are different because of the way in which they take account of the community and become community centres, not just shopping centres. They focus on the human side. They are more 'social'. Their initiatives appeal to the mass market, irrespective of social composition.

While these approaches are not unique, our experience is that most organisations do not see community responsibility as a particular part of their business model. Any charitable contributions are idiosyncratic and discontinuous. They are often related to the whims or personal interests of particular individuals in the organisation, with no clear relationship to any defined 'community'. Many organisations eschew this role altogether – 'Our role is to make money for shareholders'.

The experience of the winning organisations suggests that taking a wider view of the role of the organisation and its relationship to its communities may be more important than has previously been perceived. It is another indicator of the importance of balance for winning organisations (see Chapter 10).

SUMMARY AND KEY MESSAGES FOR LEADERS

Winning organisations look out as well as look in. They are externally focused as well as internally focused. Our research found five ways in which this external focus showed out. Winning organisations are focused on customers. They work with other organisations to extend their own boundaries. They are focused on the future, not just the present. They are thinking beyond 'Australia' and beyond their own organisation's situation. And they have a real sense of community responsibility, as well as responsibility to the many other stakeholders.

The key messages for leaders from this chapter are:

- Think 'customer'.
- Develop customised products and services, using intensive market research.
- Develop and manage ongoing customer relationships.
- Work with other organisations on a partnership basis to expand resources and reduce risk.
- Manage governments and regulators as part of normal activity.
- Work with suppliers on an ongoing relationship basis.
- Focus on the future, from a whole-of-industry perspective.
- Think outside Australia.
- Go overseas early.
- Bring overseas ideas home.
- Have a sense of community responsibility as part of the normal activity of the organisation.

8

RIGHT PEOPLE

Committed and proud
People for the cause

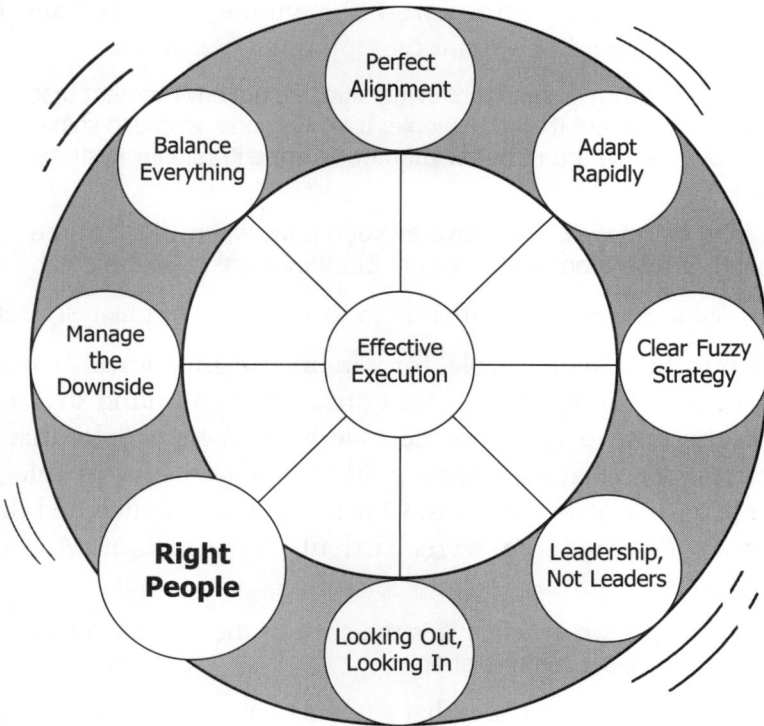

When we were writing the first draft of this chapter, we asked our secretary to get a copy of a recent research study which suggested that CEOs thought people and culture were more important than financial results.

She retorted:

> Everyone knows people are the key. If you get the right people, everything else follows.

Unfortunately, not everyone does 'know' this. Indeed, this important idea of 'right people' is buried in most organisations.

Many organisations state somewhere in their public material, 'People are our greatest asset'. But every time we hear this statement, we cringe. Why? Because we know from experience that most of the organisations that espouse it simply don't really believe it and certainly don't deliver on it.

But this is not what we heard from the winning organisations. In fact, what we heard was quite the opposite. We heard:

> We create an environment of ownership. It's the environment that is more important than the people. It allows good people to shine. No, our people aren't better than our competitors. Our systems are.

> I think our people are above average now, when I look at the other organisations we deal with. But they weren't [in the past].

These statements are very different to 'people are our greatest asset'.

So what is the role of 'people' for winning organisations? As we'll show in this chapter, people are critical. But we found that it is having the right people, not necessarily the best people, that is important. And having people within a system, not people as individuals or as prima donnas. Our research also concluded that the attitudes of people were particularly important. As one interviewee put it:

> In a competitive industry, it is the spirit of the workforce that matters, not the remuneration.

There are two characteristics that seemed common to interviewees across the winning organisations. They are the 'right' people who are committed to the organisation and proud of it and its achievements... but they get embarrassed saying this, and don't want to make much of a fuss about it. It is a quiet and humble proudness. Very egalitarian. Very Australian.

210

In this chapter, we'll first explore what we mean by 'right' people and why these people are rarely the 'best people' that organisations so often talk about. We'll discuss the process of selecting these 'right' people and of investing in them, and discuss other supporting mechanisms that are necessary to ensure right people can produce the results the organisation needs and wants. Then we'll talk about what 'committed and proud' means and how it shows in an organisation (see Figure 8.1).

Figure 8.1 – Right people

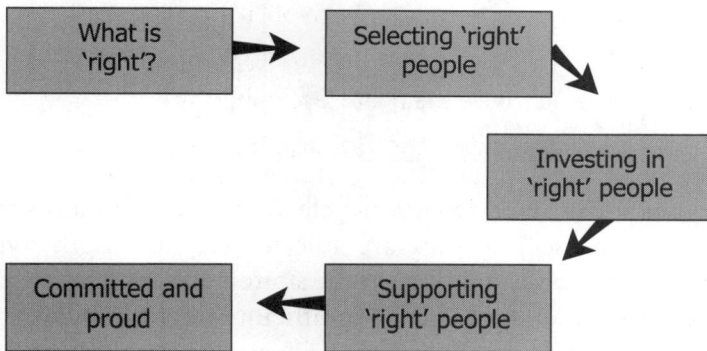

```
[What is 'right'?] → [Selecting 'right' people]
                                    ↓
                          [Investing in 'right' people]
                                    ↓
[Committed and proud] ← [Supporting 'right' people]
```

WHAT IS 'RIGHT'?

So what is it that determines whether or not we have the 'right' people in the organisation? We found that there are two determining features in the winning organisations – people need to fit the culture and the strategy and people need to have the right attitude (see Figure 8.2).

Fitting the culture and strategy

The essence of 'right' is alignment to the culture and strategy of the organisation. What this means is that the 'right' people for one organisation are the 'wrong' people for another, even in the same industry. There is no universal type of person who is ideally suited for every organisation. Different people will be attractive to – and attracted to – different types of organisations.

211

This is encouraging and positive news for organisations... and people! The fact that a person does not 'fit' into one organisation is likely not to be the fault of the individual or the organisation, but more simply that that organisation seeks different types of people for its strategy and culture. Keep on looking!

Figure 8.2 – What makes 'right' people?

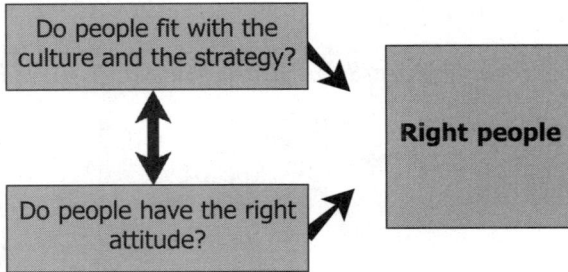

But organisations need to be very clear about what their strategy and culture are, so that they are able to seek the 'right' type of person. Lack of understanding of the strategy or culture, or lack of a clear strategy or culture, makes it difficult to get the right people. It also explains why it is not necessarily appropriate to bring in an apparently successful leader from a very different organisation and expect to achieve the same success. Illustration 8.1 shows the 'right' type of person that might be sought by some of the winning organisations at particular times in their history.

As the situation changes for organisations, the type of person sought would also change. For instance, over time technical skills have become less important at Rio Tinto and Qantas while commercial acumen has become increasingly important. At Brambles, financial and local entrepreneurship skills have become less valuable and having an international perspective and the ability to fit into a global system have become more important.

Right attitude, not formal qualifications

The appropriate formal qualifications for the position were never mentioned as being important in selecting people. What was mentioned was attitude.

Illustration 8.1 – 'Right' types of people at some of the winning organisations

Brambles 'right people'

- are growth-oriented/opportunistic/have a nose for a deal
- are profit-driven
- thrive on challenge/able and willing to grow and learn
- are macho, egalitarian, grass roots, down to earth
- can develop good long lasting customer relationships
- can find creative ways of doing a job efficiently
- are tight with cost control
- know how to 'crunch a quid'.

Qantas 'right people'

- provide great customer service
- epitomise the spirit of Australian people
- are concerned with doing things the right way
- can handle crises
- are able to change quickly/can find creative solutions.

Lend Lease 'right people'

- are entrepreneurial
- are innovative
- value highest quality
- work well with all types of people
- take responsibility
- deliver targeted outcomes
- are young.

The Salvation Army 'right people'

- are practising Christians
- like to help underprivileged people
- are prepared to follow the systems and structures
- get the job done
- are frugal
- are efficient.

Formal qualifications are essentially assumed. They get applicants to the line, but they never get them over the line. Right attitude does. Attitude is a differentiation which winning organisations seek. For instance, half of the top management team at Woolworths in 2002 did not have a degree, enough to disqualify them from even applying for a management position at many organisations. But all of them have the right attitude. It's the same for selecting checkout staff. Woolworths is looking for those with the desire to serve customers, not those with the right qualifications.

Having the appropriate skills is also assumed, at least on entry to the organisation. (As we'll see, winning organisations mostly develop new skills on the job or in-house as people rise through the organisation.) So skills and the ability to carry out the job for which people are being interviewed are also assumed to exist. Interviewees definitely need these, but they won't lead to success in the organisation. But right attitude will.

What is the 'right' attitude? This is really a subset of the 'right' people theme above. Each organisation has a view about the type of attitude it wishes to encourage, and that attitude varies from organisation to organisation. For instance, at Qantas, willingness to give great customer service is a critical element, as it is at Woolworths. At NAB, being conservative, liking hard work and being tough on cost control are key attitudes that are valued. At Brambles, being willing to get dirty through being involved in the operations or being able to 'crunch a quid' were key attitudes desired in its people prior to its move to global businesses.

Best people or not?

While organisations like to argue that their people are the 'best', and that they want to hire only the 'best' people, this saying is just like 'people are our greatest asset'. Few organisations actually hire – or even try to hire – the 'best' people in practice.

Surely though, part of being a winning organisation must be that they hire the 'best' people? Isn't this implicit in 'right' people?

The clear, but uncomfortable answer is, no. Even winning organisations don't hire the best people, unless you take 'best' to mean the narrow view of best fit with the desired culture. Illustration 8.2 shows our analysis of the practices of winning organisations regarding hiring 'best' people and why they choose those practices.

Again we see this as 'good news' for people and also for organisations. You don't have to be the 'best' in any formal academic sense, though you do of course have to have the requisite skills. There are many opportunities in all types of organisations in all types of industries. For personal success, over and above skills what matters is whether you fit the culture which the organisation has or wants and – importantly – whether your attitude matches what the organisation seeks. The right attitude can be a winner – for both individuals and the organisation.

SELECTING THE 'RIGHT' PEOPLE

If we know what 'right people' look like, how do we go about finding them? Selection is obviously the way in which people come into the organisation, while development within the organisation is a way to improve the abilities of those who are hired.

Selection is not the key

In most human resource/management texts, a great fuss is made of selection. An error in selection can be costly, both in getting rid of the wrong hire and then in restarting the selection process... so winning organisations obviously must get their selection processes right. Right? Wrong!

Our research showed that the winning organisations were not particularly good at selection. Not one organisation claimed to have a unique or even a better selection system than its competitors. No winning organisation claimed that its selection processes were a key to its success.

Illustration 8.2 – The 'best' or not the 'best': who is hired?

Hire the 'best'	Why this practice?
Lend Lease	Culture is hire the best, hire young, empower them, support them and reward them, to get high-quality, innovative solutions.
Macquarie	Need the very best people to come up with the innovative ideas needed to succeed against international competitors.
Rio Tinto	Philosophy is that the best people give better ideas, which gives better productivity, which gives low cost.

Don't hire the 'best'	Why this practice?
Brambles	Company has grown from low-skilled areas and relied on 'good blokes' who are financially astute, happy to get dirty and can see opportunities.
Harvey Norman	Main 'people' are franchisees, who see the opportunity to work for themselves through Harvey Norman as an opportunity to move from being a very good salesperson to joining a system and making gains which they could not otherwise aspire to. As franchisees are limited to one franchise, Harvey Norman doesn't want brilliant people with ambitions beyond this level.
National Australia Bank	Has been a 'rise-through-the-ranks' (promotion on seniority) organisation. You have to be a lender to be successful. Entry qualifications are not high.
Qantas	Most jobs are low skilled. Industry has been protected by regulation until recently. Government ownership led to a 'job for life' mentality (assisted by generous travel benefits for employees).

Illustration 8.2 (cont'd) – The 'best' or not the 'best': who is hired?

The Salvation Army	People are 'called' to join, so the organisation does not specifically seek out 'best' people. Remuneration makes it difficult to attract the 'best' people.
Telstra	Government 'job for life' background and low skill requirement of many jobs has not encouraged high-flyers to apply until recently. Government influences still make it difficult to attract the best.
Westfield	Seeks hard-working team players who can fit into a family-led autocracy.
Woolworths	Depends on part-time and casual work force, largely unskilled jobs with a heavy emphasis on youth workers.

One organisation stated that it used scientific psychological testing procedures, which were said to work... but it had quite a high turnover rate soon after people joined. The same organisation offers 'spotter's fees' to its people to find new people who would fit into the organisation. The logic here is that people who work in the organisation are best able to know who might 'fit' with them and the organisation. This approach also puts a large degree of personal responsibility on current people in the hiring process – no-one wants to bring in someone who doesn't fit. This process also implies that people in general may be just as good at judging selection fit as placing ads or using recruitment consultants and psychological tests.

A common characteristic was that winning organisations experienced high turnover early on, i.e. shortly after the selection period. However, they also reported that their overall turnover rate was lower than average for their industry. Figure 8.3 shows this pattern. It is very similar to those of organisations with the 'cult-like cultures' described as a success factor by Collins and Porras – the culture ejects those who don't fit very quickly. Those who do fit are absorbed into the culture... which is effectively reinforced by these hires.

Figure 8.3 – Staff turnover patterns at winning organisations

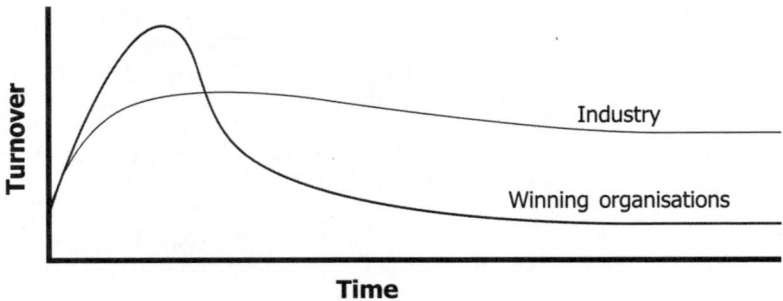

So the overall result for winning organisations is better than competitors... but they don't do particularly well at the start. This implies that, even though they are well aware of their cultures and what type of person they seek, they are not particularly good at selecting such a person.

Surprisingly, winning organisations did not seem particularly concerned about this. There are several reasons why this might be so:

- Their reputations as high-performing organisations means they have more and better people applying to join. A selection error may thus be easily overcome.
- Despite all the work on selection practice, there remains a qualitative component – a 'feel' about the final decision. No mechanical or quantitative process for selection has become accepted across a variety of organisations and industries as definitively better than all the rest. Organisations are still searching for the most effective selection processes.

- The use of systems to provide good feedback and performance measurement and management of people in winning organisations means that selection errors are identified early and the problem is addressed.
- People who think they might fit but find they don't often take themselves out of these high-performance cultures.

Woolworths is an interesting example. It is besieged with applications from school and university students for part-time jobs, particularly in its 24-hour supermarket stores, where all kinds of people can work all kinds of different hours that suit them personally and also fit the needs of the organisation. Students fill out a standard application form. Woolworths interviews people, and most are offered a position. They attend some basic training and an introduction to Woolworths, then they begin to work part-time. Most drop out within a year or two, as their objectives and lifestyles change. A very small number – which Woolworths makes no attempt to identify beforehand or through the selection process – stay. They have particular aptitude... and they like working there! They learn required specific skills on the job and get promoted. But promotion depends on on-the-job performance, not on the selection process, or qualifications.

In summary, selection errors get fixed rapidly at winning organisations. And while they would like better systems, there doesn't seem to be a perfect one, or one which is widely accepted as being most effective.

INVESTING IN PEOPLE

In contrast to the relative failure of their selection processes, winning organisations spend a lot of time investing in their people once they have joined. Several aspects of this investment were clearly followed by winning organisations. They were (see Figure 8.4):

- commitment to training/learning/development
- focus on in-house customised training and development
- support for career development.

Figure 8.4 – Investing in people

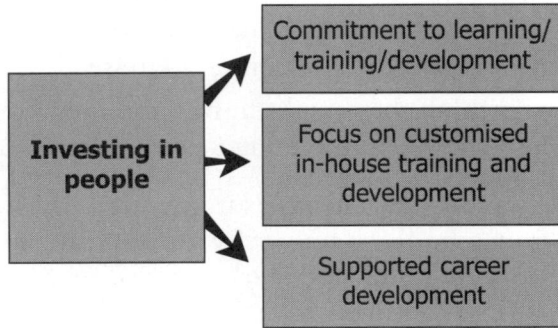

Commitment to learning/
training/development

Investing in
people

Focus on customised
in-house training and
development

Supported career
development

Commitment to training/learning/development

Most of the winning organisations have had a large variety of training programs for all levels of people in the organisation throughout their history. They have been consistently committed to training and development of their people.

In organisations with large volumes of small transactions, training to get details right is essential. So it is no surprise to find organisations like NAB, Qantas, Woolworths and Telstra consistently involved in heavy on-the-job training programs. For instance, when Qantas joined the Oneworld alliance in 1998, it became involved in a training program covering virtually all the 220,000 people involved in the original five partner airlines.

When organisations are involved in major cultural or strategic change programs, large amounts of training with some development is also essential, and we saw this across the winning organisations. For instance, as it prepared for the future through its Vision 2000 program in the late 1980s, Telstra trained more than 10,000 people each year to introduce more commercial skills and a different strategic vision into the organisation. Qantas undertook large amounts of customer service training in the early 1990s as it moved to merge Qantas and Australian, standardise service standards and also improve its customer service levels.

Of course, without such training, these initiatives have no chance of succeeding. This is exactly what does happen in many organisations! The concepts of change in many organisations are often not supported with the training required... and they fail. So, in this sense, what we see here is that winning organisations that undertake major changes do provide the training support necessary for the change agenda to succeed. This is consistent with the emphasis on execution and alignment (see Chapters 2 and 3).

But winning organisations do much more than provide the essential basic or minimal training. CRA (now Rio Tinto) underwent an enormous proactive organisational development program over many years to change the fundamentals of working relationships in the organisation, unit by unit (see Chapter 6 for details). There was no guarantee of success. Indeed, most external analysts would have doubted the chances of success of such a monumental effort. In 1982 it said that it had not reduced education and training despite the severe downturn in its markets and profits, another indication of its view of the importance of training and development. In 1990, CRA reported that it spent the equivalent of 7 per cent of payroll on training activities, much more than most organisations.

In some cases, the winning organisations feel let down by the education system and have become large-scale trainers of apprentices themselves. For instance, Woolworths, now the largest employer of apprentices in New South Wales, recognised shortcomings and worked with the education system to adjust the focus of courses intended to fulfil the needs of large employers who needed skilled staff in non-traditional apprenticeship areas.

Lend Lease has had a major relationship with the ACTU over almost 30 years, training over 21,000 apprentices and creating 50,000 new jobs. The ACTU–Lend Lease Foundation receives a share of the pre-tax profits of Lend Lease to be applied to help young people acquire skills. This program has been taken into other countries, including Indonesia and the UK. In addition, the Dusseldorp Skills Forum developed training for retail and commerce programs as subjects for Year 11 and Year 12 high school students in New South Wales, subjects which are accredited as part of the students' normal study programs.

Other important aspects of training relate to personal development and self development. While no clear pattern emerged about any particular approach, or commonly agreed elements, most organisations encouraged or provided for a lot of this. For the Salvation Army, there is a five-year cadet-in-training program, including a two-year residential program, prior to being 'commissioned' into the Army. Organisations like NAB and Telstra encourage and support vast numbers of their people attending external degree and non-degree training and education courses. Rio Tinto engages all its employees in a variety of general and specific in-house programs, particularly focusing on developing teamwork through experiencing common training and development activities.

A focus on in-house customised training and development

An interesting discovery was that a number of the winning organisations had their own in-house training facilities. Woolworths, Qantas and the Salvation Army all have their own training colleges. Partly this may be justified by the volume of training undertaken by these organisations. Partly it is explained by the desire to have control over premises, both in terms of programming schedules and confidentiality – running programs in company facilities rather than 'shared' venues reduces the risks of information leakage and information can be handled more freely in general conversation outside the formal training sessions.

A more interesting discovery was that a number of the winning organisations undertook the training and development activities using their own staff as teachers and facilitators. Most organisations outsource most of this work to specialist teachers and facilitators. However, some of the winning organisations view training as so important and so specialised for the organisation that it is best done by 'insiders' – managers responsible for day-to-day operations.

Managers in most organisations, if asked to lead training activity, would reply that they do not have time and are not good at it. Organisations whose managers take on this role are sending out an important message: this is an important activity and you are best to learn from the people who understand the situation best.

The reason why so little is known of the CRA (now Rio Tinto) organisational development program, despite its size, duration and major effects, is that it was almost completely taught by in-house managers, using specially designed in-house materials. Few outside the organisation knew what was going on or took part in it.

Since some of the programs took managers out of the organisation for four to six weeks at a stretch, the investment in time as well as money was enormous. CRA spent around $50 million a year on training and development activities during this period.

However, what made this activity really different was that people were expected to deliver on the ideas, not just undergo the training. As one former executive said:

> You went away for training, ideas were implemented and those ideas would be seen in action. Everyone took part in training, implementation and running of systems... Management was committed to embedding it in the organisation. The ideas were connected to the job, not disconnected and they have a continuing life. They developed a common language and common principles.

Many other programs in winning organisations were developed in-house, used in-house materials and were taught by in-house people. Woolworths, Qantas and the Salvation Army, for example, developed their own materials or had customised programs undertaken in their own premises.

Macquarie's CEO attends every orientation program to lay out the history of Macquarie, what Macquarie's philosophy is and, importantly, what Macquarie expects from its new people. Clearly laying out expectations right at the start makes it easy to set up consistent assessment procedures.

Lend Lease's orientation program is similar. Despite Lend Lease having a very supportive employee benefits package and strong mentoring systems, the impact of the orientation program was quite different. One former executive described it:

> They told you that two-thirds of you wouldn't be here in a year's time. It was very tough, even brutal. It was based on performance, but it got the best coming to the top. It was run internally by retired and semi-retired Lend Lease people who could bring real experiences to the program.

These experiences are quite different from the training activities of most organisations. Many operating managers are too busy to even speak to their subordinates who are attending programs, let alone attend the programs themselves or prepare and present them. Most organisations are increasingly turning training and development responsibility over to individual employees – 'this is your responsibility' – yet are not prepared to support them, even if the people pay for it or undertake the work in their own time. Is it any wonder that employees of most organisations are less loyal, less committed and quicker to jump ship now?

Support for career development

In an increasingly uncertain organisational world, career development for the long term is being given less consideration in training and development activities. There is an emphasis on self-learning and the development of a culture of being individually responsible for your own personal learning. We found this was true on the whole for winning organisations too. Yet we found not only some excellent examples of career development activities during the period, but also a sense that career development was still important.

Perhaps the most famous example is the 'white room' which was set up at CRA under then Chief Executive John Ralph. On whiteboards in one room of the head office were arranged the current organisational structure of all the individual units of CRA, with the names of all the managers. Each year, when personal development reviews were done, the senior executives would meet in the white room to consider promotional opportunities and movements that might be made. The beauty of the room was that everyone's name was available for all to see and to discuss simultaneously. (Usually people who are a long way away are forgotten and not considered.) Another important difference is that appointments made were the responsibility of the whole executive team, not the particular manager to whom the appointee would report.

Rio Tinto in Australia also uses a 'two levels down' process whereby managers do annual employee assessments not just of direct reports but also of those two levels down. This forces managers to have an 'eye' for talent and to seek good information on those who are not actually reporting to them. It also takes some of the subjectivity out of the assessment process between manager and direct subordinate, because other opinions are considered.

Lend Lease has a much more informal but equally important mentoring and coaching system. Each manager has a mentor, usually from another part of the organisation. This is part of the support network, essential when managers are given large responsibilities early on. It operates informally, which is consistent with Lend Lease's open communications style.

In summary, winning organisations invest strongly in their people, while simultaneously encouraging them to take responsibility for investing in themselves. However, the specifics of each training/ learning/development program depend on the particular organisation and its situation. No specific techniques or patterns were detected as common in our research.

SUPPORTING PEOPLE

Investing in people is one thing. But what about the environment in which they work? Is it conducive to *using* the results of training and development? How well are people supported?

In each case, our research showed that the supporting environment was aligned and consistent with the people and the training they were receiving. This environment includes the elements of leadership, systems, culture, strategy and structure. Of course, as with other aspects of 'people', each supporting environment varied according to the culture and strategy being followed. But we did find some specific common supporting factors (see Figure 8.5). They are:

- Having a team environment
- Promotion from within
- Measuring performance and providing feedback
- Rewarding performance – financially
- Rewarding performance – non-financially.

Figure 8.5 – Elements supporting the 'right' people

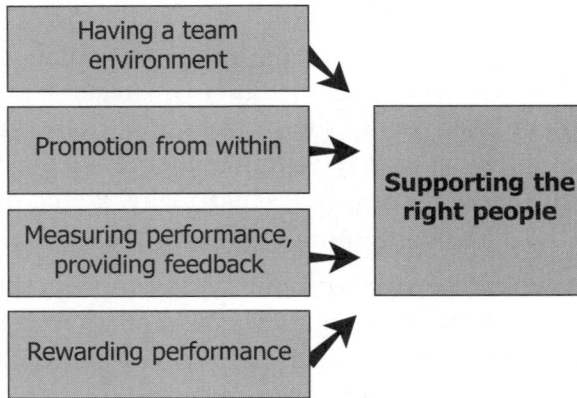

Having a team environment

In Chapter 6, we discussed the idea that leadership was about a team of people, not just an individual. We found this applied to people also. We found the word 'team' was used a lot, even where organisations were clearly wanting individuals to take responsibility. For instance, an executive at Rio Tinto said:

> We are very close, very collegiate. There is not fierce competition between the divisions. If it is a good project it will get funded. We are not competing for a given bucket of money.

Yet Rio Tinto heavily emphasises individual responsibility!

226

At Macquarie, getting into a team is important for individual success. People with ideas 'recruit' people to join the project team needed to make their idea work. Having the right skills – and particularly attitude – is important to be 'recruited' or 'chosen' to form part of one or more teams. At assessment time, co-operativeness and helpfulness are important attributes to be considered alongside individual profits generated, as Macquarie recognises that it takes teams to get ideas implemented.

Westfield and Woolworths are other organisations which are very team-oriented. Throughout the period of analysis, Westfield constantly referred to the role of 'team' in its success:

> The value of the 'Westfield Team' cannot be quantified... [it is] even more important than the assets disclosed in the balance sheet. Fully recognising this value, Westfield actively pursues policies designed to maximise job satisfaction at all levels so that each team member is able to make a full, worthwhile contribution to the development of the company. (1986 Annual Report)

> Our ability to create and maintain such a busy schedule is only possible through the exceptional abilities and enterprise of our staff. (1989 Annual Report)

> ... [We have a] highly focused, dedicated and hard working team that is fully committed to the company's goals. (1995 Annual Report)

> Although [executive] left Westfield 10 years ago, like many other long-serving senior executives he often works as a consultant on special projects. [Executive] was an important member of the team that successfully took Westfield into the UK in 2000. (*The Detailed Westfield Story*, p. 100)

Promotion from within

We have noted previously (see Chapter 6) that leadership tends to be home grown and stable. This also applies to the people as a whole. Each of the winning organisations experienced lower turnover than competitors in its industry and most had a clear expectation that promotions would come from within. Of course, if the people you hire are good, the organisation is doing well and growing, why *would* you hire from outside instead of promote from within?

Promotion from within encourages those who join that there are future prospects for growth and development, not just for the organisation but for individuals. This provides an incentive for people to do well... and to stick around. If training is provided and development encouraged, these are further reasons for remaining and contributing.

The only cases where significant promotions came from outside were when organisations were changing culture. Qantas and Telstra have had to emerge as more commercially oriented organisations from their public sector backgrounds, so significant changes in people have taken place at both. NAB has sought to become less conservative, but very few of those who have been hired in at the top levels have remained – a classic example of the cult-like culture ejecting those who did not fit.

Measuring performance and providing feedback

What the winning organisations do very well is make it very clear what people need to achieve individually and in their teams, measure performance against those targets, provide feedback on that performance and reward based on the results (see Figure 8.6).

Once again, there is nothing magical here... except that winning organisations actually do it (effective execution; delivering results), they don't just talk about it – and that's a big difference.

For instance, NAB measures individual performance quarterly and does it quantitatively. People have only a few key performance indicators which are set and agreed beforehand. There are no more than five areas with no more than three indicators in each. They are all quantifiable, all objective. The question is "How can the manager help you to achieve these?", not "What do I have to achieve by myself?" One executive said:

> In our performance management processes, we agree objectives and have a quarterly conversation about feedback on that.

Personal development plans are encouraged and most people have them. We celebrate simple things to show employees they are valued.

Figure 8.6 – Setting KPIs, measuring performance, providing feedback and rewarding performance

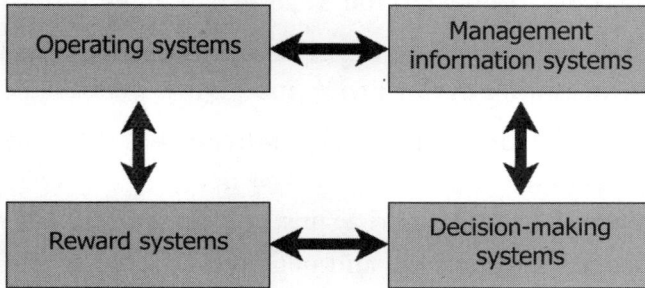

At Lend Lease, the KPIs are very challenging, but there are very big incentives for achieving them. Lend Lease does not tolerate non-success. People will do everything they can to achieve the KPIs, which they have been involved in setting and which have been thoroughly considered in the pre-planning process. One former executive said:

> [My supervisor] didn't muck around. You knew where you stood. You got positive and negative feedback, but the negative was always framed positively.

Another said:

> They don't tolerate non-success. They would review performance, monitor you and coach you, but they will terminate you quickly if necessary.

Macquarie says that it does not have to fire people very often, as most people who are not performing know it very clearly, feel uncomfortable and leave of their own volition if they don't fit. At Macquarie, non-selection of an individual into new teams that are formed to develop new activities is taken into account in performance assessment, and is a good signal that an individual is not valued by peers.

Employee surveys were used frequently in winning organisations and they were taken seriously, with changes being made following their analysis. Organisations said that they received very high rates of response from their people – indicating a keen interest in the issues – and they tended to publicise the findings and indicate what would be/had been done to address the key issues raised.

Overall, several points can be made to summarise the findings regarding measuring performance and giving feedback:

- Performance targets are set for individuals, clearly and quantitatively.
- Performance is measured against the set targets.
- Feedback, both positive and negative, is given to individuals frequently.
- Individuals are expected to respond to the feedback, positive or negative.
- Organisations work with individuals to help improve their performance but, if no performance improvement occurs, they are prepared to take quick action to fire the person.

Rewarding performance – financially

Apart from the Salvation Army, performance is highly rewarded financially by winning organisations, especially at the top. However, several aspects of financial rewards are significant:

- Rewards are highly correlated with individual and/or team performance.
- Individual rewards are highly variable.
- Financial rewards are not the only driver or reason for working at winning organisations – contributing to the 'cause', being in a winning organisation and other non-financial rewards were seen to be important.

In most of the winning organisations, there is a high degree of bonus or profit-sharing or even share-granting in the total remuneration package. As one Macquarie executive said, as we observed his team of people at rows of computers outside his glass-walled office:

> There are people out there earning a million dollars, but the person sitting next to them might be getting only a fraction of that. You wouldn't know from looking at them, or how they behave. It just reflects their relative performance. That's the system. They know it and they accept it.

The process is quite clear and transparent to everyone at Macquarie. A specified percentage of profit goes to the staff, as does a specified percentage of surplus earnings above a targeted ROE. All permanent staff get profit share. The CEO cuts up the pool according to the dollar profit contribution of each division. Each division head then cuts it up on the same basis for groups, whose heads then cut it up for individuals. Each individual's performance is assessed, not only by individual profit created, but also for contributions to the team. Each individual's performance is reviewed and the bonus is linked to the review, which is very frank. Any individual who is not happy with their allocation is free to leave! Macquarie says it has not lost a senior person it wanted to keep in at least 15 years. One Macquarie executive commented on the system:

> We run the division like a business, judged entirely by the P&L statement. We know what our costs are [as a result]. The P&L is our greatest management tool, but others are copying it. We have total autonomy, but we are also totally responsible. There is no great money god in the sky.

Lend Lease has a much more complicated reward structure, primarily because it is more concerned with providing for individual welfare. Lend Lease was one of the first to introduce employee superannuation. It also introduced company-paid employee health plans in 1979 and introduced subcontractor disability insurance cover in 1980 – all far-sighted welfare moves. In 2002, it has a 'cafeteria-style' employee benefits scheme where people can select their own package of desired benefits, confirming that it is still a leader in this area.

231

Like Macquarie, Lend Lease allocates a fixed percentage of profits for employees. This practice was introduced in 1973. However, Lend Lease uses it to buy shares in the company and they are allocated equally to all employees, regardless of position. In addition, senior staff can earn significant bonuses, based on individual performance.

At Harvey Norman, the franchisees are essentially highly incentivised employees. Their remuneration is determined by their sales, less their direct costs and controllable investments, less a fixed formula charge from the head office for its services in taking care of central decisions such as purchasing, advertising and financial control.

Rewarding performance – non-financially

But not all the 'rewards' from working at winning organisations are financial. People don't work at the Salvation Army in the expectation of receiving high salaries. A different type of person works there and receives rewards in quite a different way. The benefits include the satisfaction of helping a great world-renowned charity and, more importantly, of helping individuals in need.

Other organisations are not high payers or rewarders by their industry standards. For instance, those who work at Telstra and Qantas also get a great deal of their satisfaction out of the non-financial returns. At Telstra, it is the opportunity to work with new technology in a rapidly changing industry. Telstra is the only game in town of any size in its industry, so it is the only organisation able to undertake a whole raft of technology-related activities that make organisational life exciting for communications technologists. And being relatively newly listed on the stock exchange adds more colour to working for the organisation.

At Qantas, the 'glamour' of international flying, Qantas' amazing safety record and reputation and the kudos from working at an icon brand for Australia that is highly cherished by Australians, provide excitement, challenge and responsibility. People are proud to work for Qantas.

Non-financial rewards are valued in all the winning organisations. For instance, Lend Lease has its 'Chairman's Awards', Macquarie its 'Macquarie Awards' and Qantas has its 'Service Above And Beyond' Awards to recognise people within the organisation who have done outstanding work which may not be recognised by the formal performance measurement systems. These awards are peer-based and are often regarded as more valuable than any confidential monetary bonus that might be awarded.

COMMITTED AND PROUD

During our interviews, we continually found that the 'culture' of the organisation was a key to success. But, as with 'people', each culture was different, so there was no sense of one common culture which is the 'winning' culture. Each culture had many compelling and internally consistent characteristics, but they were not common across the organisations. Copying any one of these cultures could be achieved... but that might not be the appropriate culture for your organisation.

However, we found that the people we interviewed – and their comments about their colleagues – indicated that all were very committed to the 'cause' which their organisation was pursuing. They were very determined to succeed in achieving that cause or maintaining the success of that cause.

We also found that people were very proud of what their organisation had achieved and was achieving... but they in no sense wanted to brag about it or wave the flag in any patriotic way. In fact 'proudness' came out almost shyly. People were proud but embarrassed to say how proud they were of what their organisation had achieved. This is rather like family pride. People are often proud of their family but they often don't make a fuss of their family members outside the family... and would be embarrassed if their family made a fuss of them.

So we came to the view that two common aspects of all the cultures were that the people were committed and proud. And as we reflected on our other organisational experiences, we realised that these are not attitudes which most people have toward their organisations. Most people would like their organisation to succeed... but they don't feel committed to it, for a wide variety of reasons. Our experience is that most people would like to be proud of their organisations, but when they look at the practices and behaviour of their organisation or its leaders they have feelings ranging from neutral to anger (though they rarely express, or are given the opportunity to express, these negative feelings to their leadership).

Passion again!

As we have previously mentioned, we found interviewees were extremely passionate about their organisations. A number of interviewees wanted to give us the history of their organisation so we would understand why it had done what it had and why it was where it was. But it was a quiet passion we detected, not a table-thumping passion, or a shout-out-loud passion.

'Committed and proud' is an outcome of getting the right people, investing in them, supporting them and making sure they are aligned with the rest of the organisation. There is no single formula for what makes people able to be, or want to be, committed and proud. It depends on the specifics of the organisation and its context. So we give here some examples of how 'committed and proud' came out for several of the winning organisations.

The Telstra experience

At Telstra, one interviewee's eyes lit up when he talked to us about the technological developments that had occurred and would continue to occur in the industry. He was eager to discuss how working at Telstra enabled technically minded people such as himself to be involved in the latest global technologies for the benefit of the whole country.

Another explained to us the egalitarianism that existed at Telstra, that Telstra had been able to develop and operate with a long-term view and that it was focused outwards, all of which made it an exciting organisation to be a part of and contribute to. People felt they could actually make a difference, not only to the organisation, but also to the nation, through how Telstra operated and developed. He said:

> It's nice to know that what you do does actually make a difference to how the country operates.

Another interviewee noted how Telstra was valued by the community:

> Telstra people rise to the needs of the community. There's a great deal of empathy between Telstra workers and the community. The community expects Telstra to be there in emergencies and to help the community in crises. We do it, we volunteer for it, but we don't get much recognition in the media for it.

The Brambles experience

Brambles is a difficult organisation to analyse because, for much of its time, it has been extremely unwilling to be open to the press or other external analysis. Carew said:

> Instead of corporate policy manuals Brambles operates with some rules for survival that include keeping away from politicians and avoiding being quoted in the press. Commenting to mainstream media or business press or to anyone connected, however vaguely, with the sharemarket is regarded as a serious offence. A Brambles staff person is well advised to remain discreet at dinner parties. Hiring of public relations consultants is discouraged... (Carew, 2000, p. 237)

But the degree of commitment at Brambles is clear. Gary Pemberton, chair in 1993, said:

> Brambles' corporate culture strips away a lot of the things people hide behind – a lot of the jargon, the reporting, the structure, a lot of the ceremonies and the committee meetings that go into traditional management. It is aggressively focused on return on investment and its employees are very aware that they are judged primarily on how they perform financially. You deliver or you don't. (Carew, 2000, p. 236)

235

An interviewee, when asked why Brambles was so unwilling to publicise its story, said:

> I really can't understand it. They have so much to be proud of. They are very hard working. They are humble and proud. It is OK to celebrate wins, but more important to know what we [Brambles] can learn or what we have learned from the experience.

The Lend Lease experience

When asked what it was like to work for Lend Lease, two interviewees who no longer worked there gazed into the distance and smiled in admiration as they remembered the experience. One said:

> It's a unique culture – promoting innovation and entrepreneurial behaviour, never standing still. It is very consistent. They treat people fairly and with integrity. They develop people... There is a strong level of personal and professional development... They leave it to you to develop... but you are thrown in, then picked up and supported... They have striking, good quality leadership with the ability to influence people to follow that vision... They don't tolerate non-success...

The other said:

> They have a culture of driving down responsibility. You took pride in your work and you'd do whatever it took to complete it. The leaders knew everything. They were smart, intuitive, good people judges, they digested detail rapidly. The company took care of its employees... As a young person, it was the company to join. You were able to be a decision-maker... It was about opportunities, not pay, about career development. Quality was never stated but the aim was always to 'be the best', to be a role model. They always picked the best option in terms of decisions, projects, people to do business with.

The Qantas experience

Qantas is perhaps the easiest example to see how 'committed and proud' operates, as it is highly visible and has been an international success story for many years. Many individuals have experienced Qantas favourably as customers. One interviewee said:

> We have our own special pride in building a sense of history... Customers love the brand. They are very protective of the brand

and its values. They see Qantas as synonymous with Australian success.

Another said:

Staff are exceptionally proud to work for Qantas. Yes, some [technical staff] do complain, but technical staff are very opinionated and are sure 'their way' is the best... so they complain... but they still like Qantas and don't leave... The Qantas brand took a long time to build. It is built on the pioneering days, staff pride, the pride of Australia and an Australian international success story. Being an icon, it is emotional.

And another said:

The people are personally committed to Qantas... We love the challenges, the diversity, the constant change. Volunteers are easy to get. There is a pride of working here for an Australian global company.

Humble: success is never assumed

In the comments quoted above, there is no real sense of shouting out loud about how good the organisations are. There is no sense of 'We are the best and we're going to let everyone know about it.' Perhaps that is why we don't know in Australia which ones these winning organisations are. Or perhaps it reflects cynicism towards the all-too-frequent PR statements that overhype an organisation.

We found none of this. Only one of the CEOs we interviewed could be described as extrovertedly proud and shouting about it. Yet when we interviewed him, he made it clear that his organisation had not been successful throughout its career. Indeed, he pointed out that, on at least two occasions in its history, it had almost 'gone under'. In his view, success had to be earned and could never be taken for granted. "There are always competitors waiting to eat your lunch if you lose focus or intensity", he said.

Another senior manager was not even sure his organisation belonged in the sample! He felt his organisation was really four different businesses and was not sure its track record justified its inclusion, as it had so many problems and so many issues to address.

These are hardly the attitudes we might expect from proud and successful people in winning organisations. And these are not the attitudes found in lots of short-term high-flying organisations that burn brightly for a few years, then decline, collapse or are taken over and forgotten about. The cases of Enron and One.Tel are typical recent examples at the time of writing.

But they *are* typical attitudes of winning organisations. Collins (2001) calls this attitude 'Level 5 leadership'. He described this as 'the triumph of humility and resolve', noting that this style of leadership exists at all 11 of his 'good to great' US companies. This idea of humility and resolve is very similar to our findings of being committed and proud (but humble).

Are winning organisations patriotic?

There is a hint of patriotic nationalism in the winning organisations. As part of their external focus and wider view of the world, our winning organisations are proud of their 'Australianness' in their achievement. It is most obvious at the ex-government organisations – Telstra and Qantas – where each had a particular role for the nation for most of its life. But it also exists at other organisations.

Table 8.1 considers how each of the winning organisations treat patriotism. From this evidence, we can't conclude that nationalism is important in its own right, but we do see that quite a number of the winning organisations are quietly proud of their success as an Australian organisation taking on the world. However, they clearly don't see this as something that is a cause of their success, nor part of their particular 'cause'. Being Australian is not the reason for their success in any way. We'll return to this theme of how important 'Australia' is in Chapter 11.

SUMMARY AND KEY MESSAGES FOR LEADERS

People are an important element of the framework for winning organisations, but it is getting the 'right' people, not getting the 'best' people, which is important. Selection is not as important as might be expected, as selection errors are fixed rapidly and winning organisations have more and better people to recruit from. Attitude is an underrated component of selection. Winning organisations invest heavily in all their people, focusing on in-house customised training and development. Coupled with a wide variety of supporting mechanisms – a team environment, a policy of promotion from within, strong measurement, feedback and reward systems – people know where they stand and are supported. An outcome of this is that people feel committed to and proud of their organisation and its achievements, regardless of the industry or context. And that's what we would all like to be able to say!

Table 8.1 – How important is patriotism?

Organisation	Is Patriotism Important? How?
Brambles	Yes – showing the Europeans (and now the rest of the world) what Australians can do
Harvey Norman	No – not important
Lend Lease	No – not important
Macquarie	Yes – beating the global competitors and establishing a presence in their major markets
National Australia Bank	No – not important
Qantas	Yes – the only Australian international airline for most of its life
Rio Tinto	Yes – Australianising itself to develop the country for Australia and Australians
The Salvation Army	No – not important
Telstra	Yes – responsible for developing and maintaining the Australian communications system for most of its life
Westfield	Yes – exporting mall developments back to the US – the home of malls
Woolworths	No – not important, but proud of having outlasted the original Woolworths from the US, which has closed down

The key messages for leaders from this chapter are:

- Ensure people fit the culture and strategy.
- Select people whose attitudes fit.
- Invest in people through training and development.
- Focus on in-house, customised training programs which are properly supported by managers and management.
- Support people in their career development.
- Promote from within.
- Set individual and team targets and KPIs, measure performance, provide good feedback and reward performance based on outcomes.
- Reward in both financial and non-financial ways.

9

MANAGE THE DOWNSIDE
Managing Risk

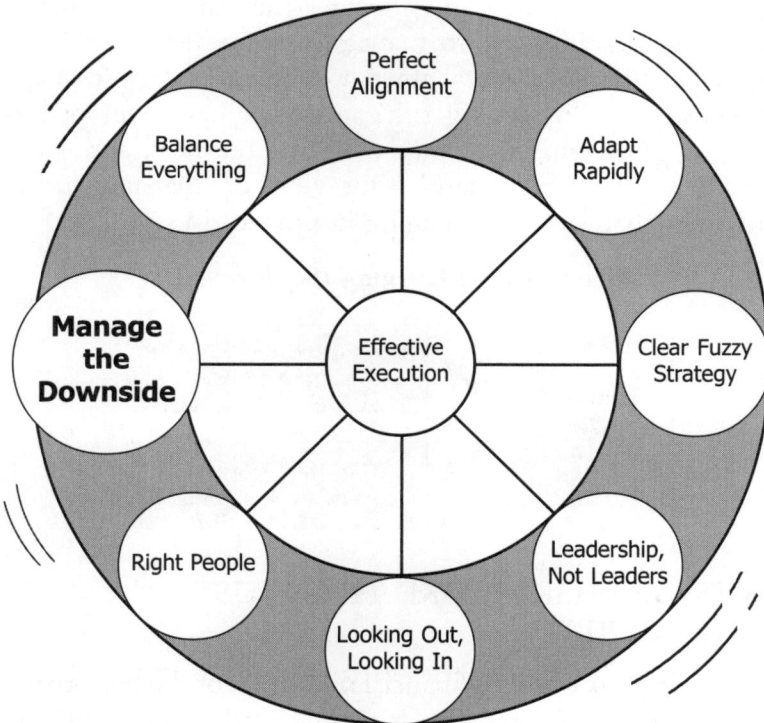

Although the winning organisations have been growing rapidly and entering new fields of activity, they described themselves to us as conservative! At first this surprised us. We did not see them as conservative at all! How could they describe themselves this way? In what ways were they 'conservative'?

Gradually, we came to see that winning organisations are not only conservative financially, but they are also conservative about risk. We came to the view, however, that this conservatism was not about avoiding risk but *managing* risk. Winning organisations are well aware of risk and realise that accepting risk is important if they are to progress, but they wish to manage the risks which they take as best they can. This awareness of and attention to *managing the downside* emerged as an important aspect of their success.

But what is 'risk'? And how do winning organisations manage it? In this chapter we'll investigate the various types of downside risk that need to be managed and consider the range of techniques winning organisations use to manage risk (see Figure 9.1). We also need to distinguish between what we mean *here* by 'managing the downside' or 'managing risk' and what has developed as a function for managing insurance risks in a business, and is often now called 'risk management'. Our view of 'managing risk' is much wider than simply managing insurance risk.

Figure 9.1 – Managing the downside

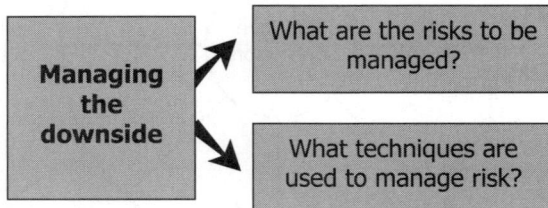

DOWNSIDE 'RISK': MORE THAN JUST FINANCIAL RISK

Many people think of risk as financial risk. In a world where financial results are very important, this is natural, and financial risk *is* an important element of risk. However, winning organisations are concerned with managing many different types of risk (see Figure 9.2). They are:

- strategic risk
- financial risk

- technical risk
- operating risk
- political risk
- legal risk
- reputation risk.

Identification of these risks, and then the management of them, is a key to their success. Let's go on and cover each of these types of risk.

Figure 9.2 – Types of risk to be managed

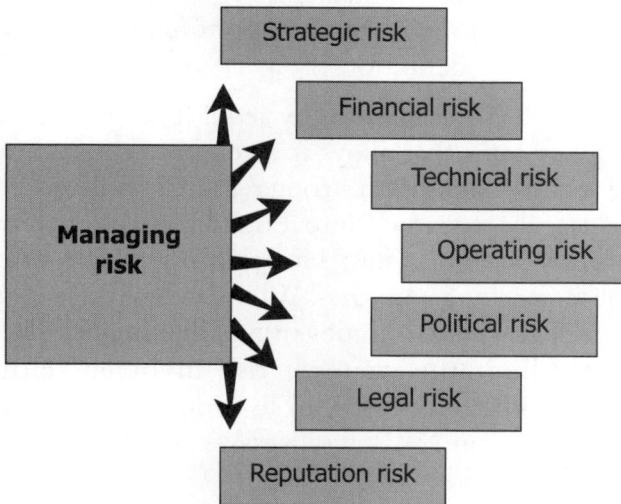

Strategic risk

Strategic risk is the most fundamental risk. When an organisation adds another activity to its business portfolio, even if it is simply expanding its existing business into another geography, it takes on a new risk. This type of risk is rarely given much attention by most organisations. It is simply assumed that the organisation will have the capabilities and resources to overcome any problems that emerge. Even for winning organisations, we see the problem of strategic risk emerge when they go overseas or diversify. At this stage of their strategic cycle, they often struggle to continue to make the gains they have, partly because of taking on new strategic risk which they have not had to cope with before.

This new risk can't be avoided if the organisation wishes to grow its activities in either a product or market sense. But managing the risk is not about avoiding risk. It is about *minimising* risk for a particular outcome or optimising outcomes and risk.

Having a clear strategy is one of the best ways to minimise strategic risk. Having the ability to say 'no' to an opportunity that does not fit the existing strategy is one way of managing risk in this area. For instance, Woolworths sees itself as a high-volume, low-margin retailer. While analysts would like it to go overseas with its existing businesses, it sees enough growth opportunities in Australia within its current business definition.

NAB will only expand overseas by acquisition into countries with robust legal systems that allow it to enforce contract terms, and will only acquire banks with strong regional positions. In the past, NAB has largely expanded into English-speaking countries, but more recently has gone into Hong Kong, Indonesia and other non-English-speaking countries. While both of these requirements severely limit the opportunities in a globalising world, they also significantly limit the strategic risk involved. However, as demonstrated most recently with its Homeside divestment, they certainly don't mean NAB avoids risk.

Financial risk

All the winning organisations are concerned about financial risk, which they regard as the volatility of the financial results that are key outcomes of their operations. For instance, Lend Lease has an aim that only one-third of its profits will be from building activities and two-thirds will come from ongoing revenue streams – building management and rental streams. Macquarie and NAB focus very heavily on financial risk, due to their high gearing ratios, which magnify any negative financial outcomes. Brambles is another which focuses on this type of risk, because its organisational philosophy has been heavily centred on profits and return on investment, and so any misjudgement of financial risk will immediately impact on its fundamental value.

Technical risk

An often overlooked element of risk relates to the technology choices which are made by organisations for their operations. Telstra's position has been heavily influenced not only by its original monopoly but also by the fact that, over time, it has been seen to make the right technology decisions for its (and the country's) telephone infrastructure. Throughout its life, Telstra has received little or no criticism of its technology choices. Had it got them wrong, it would not be able to hold its position so well in a deregulated environment. Note that criticism of Telstra's pay-TV business performance is not related to the technology choice as such, but to the business decisions and outcomes for that business to date.

Rio Tinto is another organisation for which technical risk is critical. It has rejected undertaking several major projects because of the perceived technical risk involved, such as the Wimmera industrial minerals deposit in Victoria.

Major technical risks apply to most organisations. Qantas' choice of plane type and mix, Westfield's choice of mall shopping centre designs and Brambles' choice of business portfolios are some other examples that we tend not to hear about, because the decisions have been wisely made.

Operating risk

Operating risk refers to the soundness of the systems for operating the technological system and the capability of the people to operate them. These are fundamental risks for any organisation – can we do what we say we can, when we say we can?

We should not take operating risk for granted, as it applies to the fundamentals of the business, and generally affects the whole of the business. One of the reasons the winning organisations have been chosen is because they do have these capabilities and are

245

able to execute to deliver expected results. This is not true of all their competitors, and it is certainly not true for most organisations in our experience. Many organisations simply don't deliver what they offer or say they can. Telstra's failure to succeed internationally to date, NAB's withdrawal from the US market, and Westfield's and others' withdrawal from diversifications done during the 1980s illustrate that even winning organisations can be caught out occasionally. (Of course if they are caught out more than rarely, they would cease to be 'winning' organisations...).

Political risk

Another underestimated risk is political risk. Political risk is the risk of failure or underperformance resulting from unfavourable political decisions being made. For some organisations, political risk is the crucial risk to manage. The ability to gain a licence or authority is necessary for many attempts to enter overseas markets (e.g. Qantas for airline routes, Rio Tinto for rights to explore and mine, Telstra and NAB for government approval to operate). Inability to manage political risk can stop the organisation dead in its tracks. Yet very little attention is paid to political risk in normal strategic or operational management considerations. In Australia the political issues of:

- the four pillars banking policy
- digital TV policy
- land rights
- government-to-government airline route negotiations
- Australia's exclusion from ASEAN membership, and
- ACCC views about competition

are just some key issues that impact on individual winning organisations' development and which they must manage successfully.

Legal risk

Closely related to political risk, the law itself must also be managed. Lobbying activity by organisations can affect both political and

246

legal decisions, with Telstra and Westfield being known for aggressively managing the legal system to their advantage. As well, there are of course fundamental legal issues, such as consumer and employee rights, contract law and insurance responsibilities and liabilities, which apply to all organisations. Legal outcomes in cases regarding issues such as smoking, public liability insurance and asbestos are typical of the sorts of decisions that are mostly out of the control of one organisation, but which can create havoc with their futures.

Being aware of these issues, lobbying to change laws and planning for changes in the law are necessary if an organisation is to successfully manage its legal risk.

Reputation risk

Related to political and legal risk is the risk to an organisation's reputation from the consequences of a particular event, where a risk is unforeseen, or where the outcome has much more dramatic consequences than are predicted. An organisation's reputation can even be damaged by the behaviour of a single individual employee.

Lend Lease suggests that, when making judgements about whether activities are appropriate or not, its people consider whether they would be happy if their activities were publicised in the national press. As part of its risk management function, Macquarie specifically considers what the risks to its reputation might be if it engages in particular events or enters a particular transaction. With the increasing public focus on corporate reputation and the beginnings of an industry to measure 'reputation', it seems likely that this risk will be seen as more important in the future.

In summary, there are many significant risks which must be managed if an organisation is to be able to execute and deliver its results. Each individual risk can have a major impact on results, far beyond what would be considered the probable outcome, so each must be analysed and managed.

247

TECHNIQUES FOR MANAGING RISKS

Winning organisations recognise that failure to allow for the various risks can completely overshadow the outcomes of their normal operations. Small omissions can have big consequences.

So how do winning organisations manage risks? Unlike most of the other elements and factors in our winning framework, there appears to be no clear set of techniques which is used by most of the winning organisations to address this important concept. This is probably because of the significant differences in the operations and industries of the winning organisations and the limited development of the concept of managing risk. So we cover here the range of techniques which we observed, while noting that no one winning organisation used them all and no one technique was used by them all.

The range of techniques used are (see Figure 9.3):

- upfront planning
- independent risk assessment
- laying off risks
- being conservative
- project management
- contingency planning
- good reporting and control systems
- quality of people, assets and systems
- being rigorous
- balance sheet management.

Macquarie has developed its risk management function more formally than most. Illustration 9.1 explains how Macquarie goes about managing risk.

Upfront planning

One of the best ways to manage risk is to conduct thorough planning before major activities are undertaken. Good upfront planning improves the chances of effective execution. Rio Tinto, Lend Lease and Westfield emphasise this, as they are very vulnerable to early errors on a project which will have an impact right down the line and may not be easily rectified. Rio's upfront planning includes undertaking several independent studies of the project before approval is given (see the next section, 'Independent risk assessment').

Figure 9.3 – Techniques for managing risks

Upfront planning

Independent risk assessment

Laying off risks

Being conservative

Project management

Managing risks

Contingency planning

Good reporting and control systems

Quality of people, assets and systems

Being rigorous

Balance sheet management

In putting forward a project proposal at Lend Lease, the proposer is expected to have contacted everybody within Lend Lease who might have some knowledge or insight into the issue.

Illustration 9.1 – Macquarie Bank's approach to managing risk

Macquarie has a separate Risk Management Division which reports to the CEO and the board. It has responsibility for oversight of prudential management throughout the organisation.

This approach to risk management is part of Macquarie's 'loose/tight' management philosophy. Central management of risk is part of the 'tight' aspect, to be matched against the 'loose' management of entrepreneurial behaviour within each operating division.

At Macquarie, there is a risk management culture. The Risk Management Division's activity is not a policing function, as it often is in other organisations. The basic approach is that no new deals or businesses are entered into without a full understanding of all the risks involved.

Risk Management considers risk in terms of credit risk, finance risk, market risk, operational risk and legal compliance. Limits are set in conjunction with the businesses and these are taken very seriously. Daily monitoring of credit limits allows for rapid intervention at an early stage on any problem. When problems arise and results do not meet expectations on a particular project, Macquarie goes back and works out what went wrong and what should have been done, usually within a month of discovery of the problem.

The director of the Risk Management Division said:

> Most mistakes in companies are the result of not voicing concerns early enough. I look into the abyss and assume things won't go right. You have to bring this conflict to the surface...
>
> Risk management at Macquarie is not a stone wall or a hurdle. You have a right to respond. It's a deliberation between two parties.
>
> Risk remains with the business in the P&L and bonus pool. You need to keep faith with the cowboys. If we make a bad call, that's not our problem. It is the business' problem.

Of course it is worth doing this well, because financial rewards are tied to performance. It helps focus on where the rewards will be.

The aim is to try to ensure that all issues have been considered and all the knowledge available is brought to bear on the project before the proposal is prepared. This approach forms the basis of the project management which follows.

Lend Lease make it difficult to get a project approved through the planning process. Not only are internal rate of return (IRR) hurdle rates high, the project also needs to demonstrate that Lend Lease has the management and organisational expertise to run it. There also needs to be an exit strategy – what will Lend Lease do if the project goes wrong? This last feature is very unusual. One former executive described how this consideration of an exit strategy reduced the risk involved:

> Due to the policy of waiting until the development is pre-sold or tenants are pre-committed before construction begins, the worst thing that can happen is that the company may be forced to sell off the land which, as Lend Lease only buys prime property, is always in demand.

The Salvation Army is another organisation which does not begin a new project without having first undertaken a thorough investigation. A project could be establishing a new church community or setting up a new service. In each case, the Salvation Army is concerned about whether or not it has the resources to carry out the project, whether the project is really justified and whether other organisations can be brought in to share the resource input (e.g. the government). Before beginning a new service, it carries out extensive market research to see what the real need is and to see how it might best be provided.

Independent risk assessment

A key problem for most organisations that carry out risk assessments prior to beginning a project is that the people carrying them out have a vested interest in whether the project goes ahead or not. Accounting and finance groups that often carry out this work have a vested interest in the project *not* going ahead, to show that they are not just 'rubber stamping' operational activities and to preserve their conservatism principle and image.

Rio Tinto recognises this problem and requires three separate assessments:

- a case by those proposing the project
- a technical assessment of the project
- a financial assessment of the project.

Those who are proposing the project can't be involved as members of an evaluation unit and those in one unit cannot also be in another. As one interviewee said:

> This balances the enthusiasm of the project champions. The internal [evaluation] teams have also been operators so they are experienced in understanding the operations role.
>
> We have time to do this as it now takes about 18 months to undertake the environmental assessment, so that needs can be assessed and reassessed in that time period.

NAB was the first of the major banks to introduce its own separate Credit Assessment Bureau, which provides an independent assessment of major credit proposals. NAB attributes its better bad loan performance through the 1989–92 recession to it having better credit assessment than its competitors. It was more prepared to say 'no', due to the existence of this independent bureau. Interestingly, it was this factor (lower loan losses) that enabled NAB to have the capital to bid for most of its overseas acquisitions at a time when competitors both here and overseas were strapped for cash.

Telstra also has its own Risk Management group. Its aim is to identify future industry and competitive issues and what Telstra's response should be. This allows Telstra to be proactive in trying to shape the industry for its own competitive advantage and to be better placed to react to problem issues when they emerge.

Laying off risks

One way to manage risk in a transaction, new project or new business development is to pass it off to other parties.

There are several ways in which this can be achieved (see Figure 9.4):

- structuring the transaction
- using networks to reduce risks
- sharing the risk with partners
- sharing the risk with customers
- sharing the risk with employees.

Figure 9.4 – Ways to lay off risk

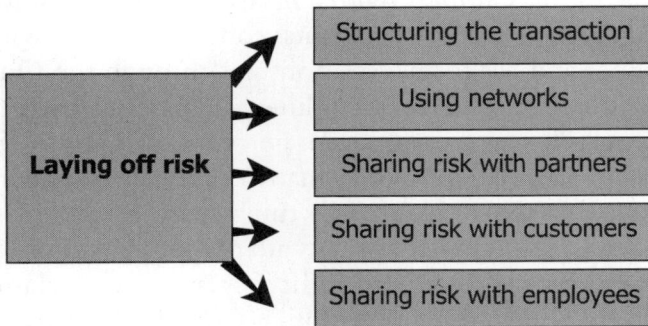

Structuring the transaction is one technique for laying off risk. In building, a key issue is whether there are tenants who will take up the building when it is completed. Wherever possible, both Lend Lease and Westfield pre-tenant a building so that, as soon as it is completed, it is occupied and cash flows from sales or rentals begin. Pre-selling also gives early cash flows before development even starts.

Another way in which they reduce the risk to themselves is to sell the buildings to fund managers who specialise in property ownership. Both have property trusts in which they have long-standing relationships and interests – General Property Trust for Lend Lease and Westfield Property Trust, Westfield America Trust and Westfield America Inc. for Westfield. This moves the asset out of their balance sheets as soon as it is completed, though they do retain a role in managing the building (which improves their financial balance sheet management).

Table 9.1 shows how the process works for Westfield. It shows that Westfield accesses four different types of investors – the public in Australia and in the US, and institutions in both places – and splits its activities in three different ways – design and building, Australian ownership and US ownership. Although the apparently risky activities of development are in the holding company, given the vertical connections the risks are substantially reduced, as a ready market exists for new shopping centres.

Laying off risk by *sharing it with a network* is another solution to risk management. For instance, Qantas codeshares routes with many other airlines and has formal relationships through the Oneworld alliance with seven other major airlines – in particular with British Airways, which owns around 21 per cent of Qantas. Sharing networks enables Qantas to offer many other routes which appear to be its own but which are actually run by partners or codesharers. Westfield has had long partnerships with property investors General Shopping (Luxembourg), Credit Suisse (Switzerland) and Rodamco (Netherlands), and customer Coles Myer, which means it is far easier to raise funds and find anchor customers for its sites.

Sharing risk with partners is another approach to laying off risk. Joint ventures can be used to do this. Brambles used a joint venture with GKN to expand CHEP into Europe and then internationally. Initially this was 80:20 in favour of GKN, but over time it became 50:50. Rio Tinto often enters an exploration or mining activity on a joint venture basis, and often with competitors.

Brambles and Lend Lease lay off risk by agreeing to *share gains with customers*. While this sounds like it is giving up profits, what it actually means is that customers are as interested in cost savings as Brambles and Lend Lease. This alignment of motivations contrasts with the normal buyer/seller conflict... and achieves better results for all, including more satisfied and loyal customers, thus reducing future risks of customer switching.

Table 9.1 – An example of laying off risk in the building industry: Westfield in 1997

	Westfield Holdings	Westfield Property Trust	Westfield America Trust	Westfield America Inc.
Incorporated in	Australia	Australia	Australia	US
Activity	Designs, builds, leases and manages worldwide shopping centres Manages public investment companies	Owns interests in Australian, New Zealand and Asian shopping centres	Owns shares in Westfield America Inc.	Owns interests in US shopping centres
Ownership (approx)				
Lowy family	35 per cent	—	—	—
Australian institutions	30 per cent	75 per cent	—	—
Australian public	35 per cent	25 per cent	75 per cent	—
US institutions	—	—	—	15 per cent
US public	—	—	—	20 per cent
Westfield Holdings	—	—	25 per cent	48 per cent
Westfield America Trust	—	—	—	17 per cent

Source: Adapted from Westfield America case, Harvard Business School, August 1999

A final way to lay off risk is to *share it with employees.* Harvey Norman lays off some of its major risks – of buying the wrong products and of having too much stock – to its franchisees/ employees. Stocks held are owned by the franchisee, not Harvey Norman. Sales people are all employed by the franchisee. Therefore, it is up to the franchisee to deal with non-performers. Harvey Norman charges a fee for generic advertising and for the provision of central services. It also utilises the information from the sales floor, as franchisees and buyers together make better buying decisions than buyers alone – another way in which risk is reduced, with no negative effect on business activity. This system provides much higher motivation for franchisee employees to sell than a normal employment system. This is partly because the risk is with the franchisee and partly because franchisees may potentially receive much larger gains than might be available under a more conventional employee/employer remuneration agreement.

Being conservative

Can entrepreneurial organisations be conservative?? Yes, they can! A very interesting finding was that all the organisations see themselves as conservative in the decisions which they make. Yet they also see themselves as quick to adapt and entrepreneurial! We'll address this contrast in Chapter 10. Suffice to say here that the organisations are indeed conservative. This conservatism showed in three ways. Winning organisations are:

- *Strategically conservative.* They stay with what they have been doing and do not move too far away from that (see Chapter 5). For instance, for very different reasons, NAB, Woolworths and Qantas would be regarded as averse to strategic risk – unwilling to take on big risks by changing their strategies.
- *Operationally conservative.* If business leaders see their business activity as 'my business' they are much more conservative than if they see their funds as the money of a big corporation... so it doesn't really matter what happens

to it or where it comes from. This concept is particularly strong at Macquarie and Brambles. Winning organisations are also averse to operational risk in that they desire to share risk, as we have demonstrated above.

- *Financially conservative.* Winning organisations have a policy of low gearing ratios. Also, most winning organisations are very concerned about costs, e.g. Woolworths, Telstra, Rio Tinto, the Salvation Army, NAB, Harvey Norman and Brambles. They do not wish to be exposed unnecessarily to financial risks.

Project management

Project management is a technique designed to understand the risks and interdependencies in a project and provide a tool for managing them. Project management is useful both in upfront planning and also for ongoing control during the project. It has the highly desirable feature of predicting the date of the completion of the project, thus providing the basis for 'on time and on budget' outcomes.

This technique was first used in building construction and development in Australia by Lend Lease and replicated by Westfield shortly after. It is of great use in this industry, where there is a high risk of delays and failure to complete on time if activities are not co-ordinated. However, it is useful in many other industries. Rio Tinto is another winning organisation which applies it rigorously in the mining construction industry. It also provides a basis for ensuring 'effective execution' occurs.

Contingency planning

Several organisations have very strong contingency planning processes to cope with short-term specifically unpredictable – but generally expected – changes.

Qantas faces daily schedule-matching problems, particularly for international flights where weather conditions across the world are quite different. But it can happen in Australia too, particularly if either Sydney or Melbourne airports are out of action or running behind schedule for any reason. When planes are not on time, passengers miss connections and crew, plane and maintenance schedules are thrown out. In addition, passengers are unreliable in turning up for flights, so Qantas (like other airlines) overbooks, risking the problem of not having enough seats if more than the forecasted number actually turn up. Qantas can't simply throw its hands up and say 'sorry' in these cases. So it mounts extensive contingency plans to ensure that such situations are effectively planned for as much as possible.

Apart from these daily problems, the handling of which rapidly affects − negatively or positively − the reputation of an airline, more major industry disasters can occur, such as the collapse of an airline, a major world political event such as the Gulf War, or even a plane crash at an airport. Through the last few years from the time of writing, the domestic pilots' strike, the collapses of Compass (twice), Impulse, Ansett and its subsidiaries and the suspension of Ansett in peak Christmas and Easter periods have all resulted in huge short-term fluctuations in the demands on Qantas' operating systems and people. Contingency planning greatly assisted in these cases, as did the determination and volunteerism of Qantas' people to help stranded passengers of all airlines complete their journeys.

Telstra is another organisation for which contingency planning is important. Like Qantas, Telstra must cope with daily emergencies − phone outages, partial network failures, extreme weather conditions − yet have a national (and international) system of millions of phones and computers working 24 hours a day, 7 days a week. People and businesses have very little tolerance these days for communication system failures.

More than this though, in a deregulated system Telstra considers carefully what its competitors are likely to do − proactively and reactively − in the marketplace, and simulates what is likely to happen under various conditions. Using this game theory approach, Telstra is able to plan to effectively respond in the best way possible to predicted moves by competitors... and to predict how competitors will likely respond to Telstra's own moves.

Our experience is that this type of gaming approach to competitors is rarely undertaken, though it is well known in theory. Telstra's experience suggests there is considerable value in this approach to forward planning for competitive moves.

The Salvation Army is another which relies on contingency planning. Much of the Salvation Army's work is difficult to plan for – how many emergencies will there be today/this year? Consequently, the Salvation Army has to be prepared to cope with these 'unexpected' emergencies. It copes through the extensive use of hierarchy and detailed and well-tried systems and procedures. Its military structure is highly valuable for these types of situations. For this reason, the Salvation Army is also very helpful in general civil emergencies, such as floods and bushfires, where it can apply the same skills and systems to get the job done.

Good reporting and control systems

When the project or operations are under way, the ability of an organisation to measure what is happening and to use that information to control or change operations is critically undervalued. We have already reported on this under 'effective execution' (see Chapter 2). However, the same systems are valuable in managing risk as well as delivering positive outcomes.

Winning organisations specialise in having excellent reporting and control systems, though each system is necessarily specific to its own situation. Lend Lease was one of the first in Australia to develop exception reporting, enabling it to focus on the outliers rather than being swamped by 'normal' operating information. Harvey Norman receives information from its many individual store franchisees. This enables it to know how the whole range of franchisees are trading on a daily basis. It then provides information back to franchisees that could be used to help them run their businesses more profitably.

Qantas has excellent revenue management systems which enable it to conduct better analysis than its competitors, allowing it to

259

better respond to market changes. Ironically, many of these systems were put in place under Gary Toomey, who left to become CEO of rival Air New Zealand/Ansett, where he found very poor information systems.

Qantas' cost, cash flow and treasury management systems deal with over 100 countries and thousands of agents on a system that is available in real time all the time. Sales need to be reconciled by passenger, by route and by agent. Qantas is sought out by banks and telcos for benchmarking costs, reliability and information quality from its systems. Qantas keeps all customer transaction data for three years and uses that to model its future business.

The Salvation Army is very strong on systems, consistent with its hierarchical structure. Systems cover everything from people management to expansion rules for congregations to training and selection to financial management to emergency planning. They enable it to keep close control of its activities. This is particularly important in an organisation with limited resources.

Quality of people, assets and systems

An interesting approach to reducing risk is to hire quality people, use quality assets and have quality systems for managing operations. The logic is that good people, assets and systems perform better than those of lower quality. Therefore, though the organisation pays more upfront for quality, it receives greater productivity, offsetting the upfront cost. Rio Tinto, Lend Lease and Macquarie use this approach.

However, it is largely untested as a general argument. Rio seeks low-cost outcomes from its mines, whereas Lend Lease and Macquarie seek more innovative, value-creating, high-quality solutions, for which they will be better paid. Each is happy with its outcomes. Interestingly, competitors have not sought to replicate the latter approach. This could be for several reasons. They could believe that this approach does not work, that it would not work for them, that they could not afford it, or that their own approach gives them a satisfactory position.

There does not appear to be any empirical evidence to support or oppose these approaches. Perhaps they are simply the result of the important process of aligning everything (see Chapter 3) and effective execution (see Chapter 2). Aligned systems, albeit starting from different points and with different organisational philosophies, are able to reach similar outcomes if appropriately managed.

Being rigorous

Of course, it is not just having the systems that gives good results, it is using them. Here again, the winning organisations distinguish themselves by their overall rigour in using what systems they have, particularly in the financial area, which is of fundamental importance for ensuring the survival and well-being of the organisation.

The difference from normal organisations is that, in winning organisations, budgets and targets are almost sacrosanct – you are expected to achieve them at a minimum, not a maximum. And significant individual rewards are based heavily on this, reinforcing the importance of the system.

Woolworths not only has rigorous reporting of quantitative and qualitative information, but it also has simple KPIs so that it is easy for individuals to focus. As one interviewee said:

> We are very focused. We have targets and budgets. This is a numbers game. You need to meet the budget... We assess and reward on a variable basis against last year – once you achieve 6 per cent over last year, rewards start and continue to increase.

Brambles is another that focuses on the numbers and is rigorous. Numbers are agreed with individuals who are responsible. They seek to make those numbers, knowing that is what is expected. Lend Lease, Macquarie, NAB and Harvey Norman are similar.

Balance sheet management

One aspect of managing risk which has received less attention than it might is that of balance sheet management. The focus in financials is usually on the profit and loss statement (now officially called the statement of financial performance). However, winning organisations have found that balance sheet management (the balance sheet is now officially called the statement of financial position) is an important tool for managing risks.

We are not suggesting that balance sheet management is a clear distinguishing feature of winning organisations. But there is certainly a suggestion that rigour and financial discipline is increasingly being applied to the balance sheet and not just the profit and loss statement.

For instance, Westfield and Lend Lease 'sell' the properties they build, often to vertically integrated property owners such as General Property Trust (Lend Lease) or Westfield Property Trust (Westfield). These are different organisations whose role is to hold or own the property and receive the rental streams. These cash flow streams are very stable, so returns are very predictable. As a result, investors in these companies are happy to accept lower returns (for lower risk) than are investors in the construction organisations, where risk is perceived to be higher. Consequently, the balance sheets of the total operation are 'split' into component parts. This enables the builders to borrow more cheaply... and not have those borrowings on their balance sheet.

Another approach is to reduce the importance of the size of an investment in assets by generating income streams from services, rather than making profits from holding assets. Lend Lease, Westfield and Macquarie have all sought to achieve this. Woolworths is similarly unbundling its property assets to use the funds more in its core business of retailing. The use of joint ventures to share risks can also have the effect of valuable assets being held by others.

Table 9.2 gives some examples of how various techniques are used to match particular risks.

Table 9.2 – Matching risk management techniques to risks

Risk	Useful Techniques
Strategic	Upfront planning; independent risk assessment; laying off risks; quality of people, assets and systems; being conservative; contingency planning; being rigorous; balance sheet management
Financial	Being conservative; laying off risks; project management; reporting and control systems; rigour and financial discipline; contingency plans; being rigorous; balance sheet management
Technical	Upfront planning; independent risk assessment; project management; contingency planning; quality of people, assets and systems; being rigorous
Operating	Laying off risks; project management; quality of people, assets and systems; reporting and control systems; being rigorous
Political	Upfront planning; contingency plans; laying off risks; balance sheet management
Legal	Upfront planning; contingency plans; being conservative; laying off risks
Reputation	Upfront planning; laying off risks; contingency planning; being conservative; quality of people, assets and systems

SUMMARY – KEY MESSAGES FOR LEADERS

Being conservative in managing downside risk is important for winning organisations. As well as seeking growth and progress, they also seek to reduce the risks involved in those activities. There are a wide variety of downside risks to be managed: strategic, financial, technical, operating, political, legal and reputation risk. A single omission or action by a single individual can be devastating to the normal operating results if risks are not well managed.

There are a variety of techniques used by winning organisations to manage risks. There is less consistency here than in most other chapters, though, because the differences in each industry and situation and the lack of focus in the past on managing risks mean that best practices have not yet developed here.

The key messages for leaders from this chapter are:

- Understand the variety of risks which can critically affect the long-term results of the organisation.
- Use techniques to manage those risks.
- Use upfront planning.
- Allow for independent risk assessment of major projects.
- Lay off risks to others involved in the activity.
- Be conservative in thinking and action.
- Use project management techniques.
- Allow for contingencies in planning.
- Develop and use excellent control and reporting systems.
- Use good-quality people, assets and systems.
- Be rigorous in operations and analysis.
- Manage the balance sheet.

10

BALANCE EVERYTHING
And, And, And

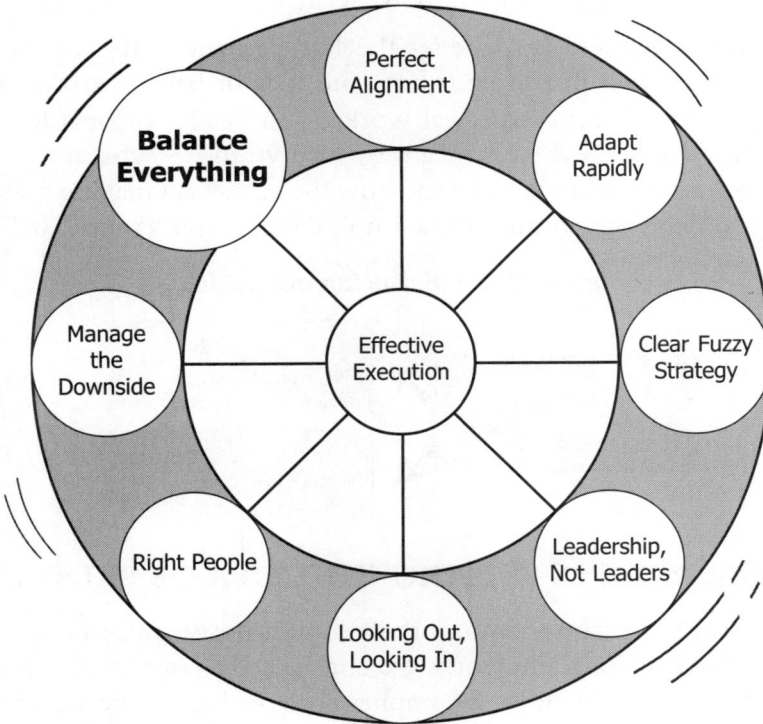

As we analysed each of the winning organisations, it became very clear that there is no simple '1, 2, 3' or 'A leads to B which leads to C' formula for success for any of them. They do many things well. They are not choosing to focus on only a small number of issues or variables. They focus on many items... and yet they each have a clear focus.

This seems paradoxical. Yet the more we looked, the more consistent this paradoxical picture was. And you will be aware of this phenomenon from reading earlier examples and chapters. Winning organisations seem to balance everything in their world. It is not a case of A or B but A *and* B... *and* C *and* D and so on. So we came to the view that 'balance' was a key element in the 'winning framework' of winning organisations. And it was a case of balancing many things – 'and, and, and' – not a case of balancing a few things. To capture this idea, we termed it '*balance everything*'.

In this chapter, which addresses the last element of the winning framework, we'll first look at how the idea of balance occurs in other empirical and theoretical work on successful organisations. Then we'll address what is meant by 'everything' – what it is that winning organisations balance and how they go about making good, balanced decisions in this very complex world (see Figure 10.1).

Figure 10.1 – Balancing everything

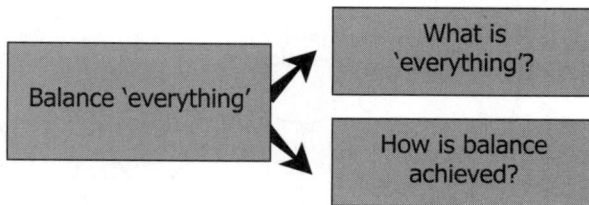

OTHER MODELS SUPPORT THE IDEA OF BALANCE

The idea that 'balance' is important should not surprise us. Each of the other major frameworks we considered in our foundations for this research includes or implies 'balance' as a key element (see Chapter 3 for a brief discussion of each of these frameworks).

Built to Last and balance

Collins and Porras explicitly include 'balance' in their *Built to Last* framework under the heading 'No "Tyranny of the Or" (Embrace the "Genius of the And")'.

They say:

> You'll notice... that we use the yin/yang symbol from Chinese dualist philosophy. We've consciously selected this symbol to represent a key aspect of highly visionary companies: They do not oppress themselves with what we call the 'Tyranny of the OR' – the rational view that cannot easily accept paradox, that cannot live with two seemingly contradictory forces or ideas at the same time...
>
> ...highly visionary companies liberate themselves with the 'Genius of the AND'...
>
> ...a highly visionary company doesn't want to blend yin and yang into a gray, indistinguishable circle... it aims to be distinctly yin *and* distinctly yang – *both* at the same time, all the time.
>
> Irrational? Perhaps. Rare? Yes. Difficult? Absolutely. But... "The test of a first-rate intelligence is the ability to hold two opposed ideas in the mind at the same time, and still retain the ability to function." (pp. 43–45)

They also use this concept of balance or 'and' elsewhere in their framework. For instance, the ideas of:

- 'preserve the core/stimulate progress',
- 'more than profit', and
- 'try a lot of stuff and see what works'

are all about doing both or doing several things at once and concentrating on them both/all.

In Search of Excellence/7S and balance

Peters and Waterman also make it clear that balance is important in their 7S model for excellent companies in *In Search of Excellence*. They make it clear that each of the Ss affects all the others, that all are important and that all need to be aligned. In their model, it is a case of balancing all seven of the elements to become an 'excellent' organisation. So, even though 'balance' is not a specific idea in the model itself, it is implied by the framework and is implicit in the words used.

The E-S-C gap analysis and implementation framework and balance

Hubbard's (2000) E-S-C gap analysis and implementation framework (see Chapter 3) also implies the concept of balance. In this framework, not only does the organisation need to align its strategy with the requirements of its external environment and its internal capabilities, but the elements of the framework used to align the strategy – leadership, people, culture, systems and structure – all need to be aligned. To be effective the organisation has to balance (and align) all these elements to deliver the strategy and get the outcomes required.

The balanced scorecard and balance

It's obvious just from the name that Kaplan and Norton's (1996) framework for measuring performance expects a 'balanced' approach to organisational activity. The balanced scorecard implies that financial, customer and employee stakeholder interests all need to be served. It also demands that both a short-term and a long-term perspective are considered for the 'growth and learning' measures of the scorecard to be achieved. Such a balanced measurement approach can only make sense if the underlying activities of the organisation are planned to be balanced.

So we see that there is very strong empirical and theoretical support for the concept of 'balance' and its importance. Even more, the idea of balancing many elements, not just one or two items of key focus, is brought out consistently through these frameworks. However, we also see from Collins and Porras' comments earlier that doing this, executing this is considered to be extremely difficult. It is easy to talk about and even conceptualise, but difficult to make happen. But that is exactly the challenge, and that is what winning organisations manage to do! This is one of the key elements that makes an organisation a winning one.

WHAT IS 'EVERYTHING'? AND, AND, AND

The idea of 'everything' conjures up impossibilities – how can we possibly focus on 'everything'? What does 'everything' mean? Everything really just means the 'many' things an organisation has to balance if it is to succeed over the long term. Achieving this balance is complex and difficult. We use the word 'everything' to convey this complexity.

We do not have a list of 'everything'. Clearly it will vary from one industry to another, one organisation to another, one level in an organisation to another. We summarise here what our research shows are the key factors which the winning organisations address. We have grouped these into a number of themes, below (see Figure 10.2). Organisations must:

- balance perspectives
- balance philosophies
- balance organisation levels
- balance operations/activities/functions
- achieve an overall balance.

Figure 10.2 – Balancing 'everything'

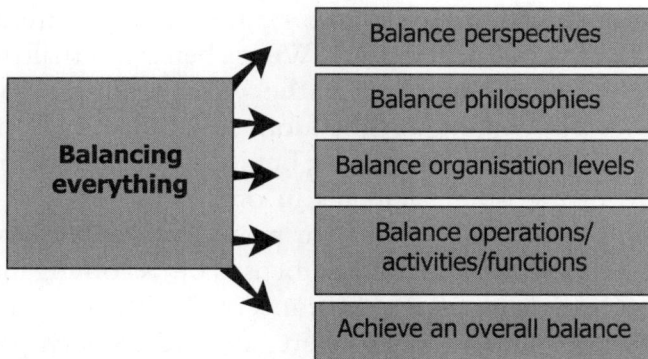

Balance perspectives

Many organisations tend to have only one perspective or to primarily focus on only one perspective about what is important to the organisation. This makes it easier to focus on what to do

269

and often reflects the (possibly erroneous) beliefs of the CEO or top management team about what is important.

However, our research did not find that organisational life was so simple! Instead, we found that winning organisations know that they must balance several different perspectives simultaneously if they are to succeed (see Figure 10.3). These include balancing external and internal perspectives, stakeholder and shareholder perspectives and short-term and long-term perspectives. A focus on one *or* other of each of these pairs of perspectives leads to an unbalanced view, unbalanced actions and possibly disaster sometime in the future.

Figure 10.3 – Balancing perspectives

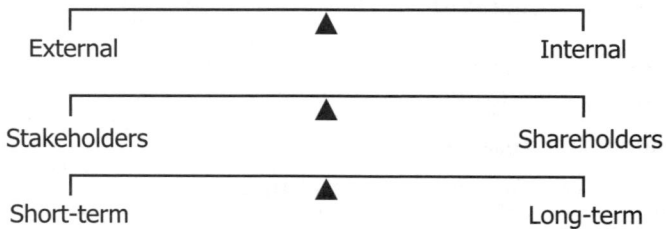

External	▲	Internal
Stakeholders	▲	Shareholders
Short-term	▲	Long-term

External and *internal perspectives*

Winning organisations are able to simultaneously consider both external and internal perspectives. We see being externally focused as one of the key elements in the winning framework (see Chapter 7). But winning organisations are not externally focused *instead* of having an internal focus, but incorporate both views. In fact, most of the other elements in our framework are heavily internally oriented. The point we made in Chapter 7 was that winning organisations are not just focused on becoming internally aligned and efficient, but are also concerned with fitting into their external world. They are very aware of that external world. That awareness and linking to the external world is quite different from the orientation of many normal organisations.

For instance, Woolworths is very concerned about its internal logistics management, but it is also aware of what new products consumers are interested in and what other forms of retailing are emerging. Qantas is very concerned about efficient scheduling of its planes, but it is also concerned about what services are being offered to passengers by other airlines and what new technology developments are occurring.

We can think of 'external' and 'internal' in other ways too. Winning organisations are aware of the national market, which might be seen as the 'internal' market, but they are also very aware of what is going on in international or overseas markets, even when they are not international themselves. The Salvation Army is aware of other solutions being proposed in the world for social problems. Woolworths is very aware of how Wal–Mart, the global leader in discount operations, is developing. NAB uses its overseas experiences to bring knowledge back into its Australian operations.

Stakeholder and *shareholder perspectives*

One of the biggest debates about organisations is where their 'responsibilities' lie. No-one denies that financial performance is important or that shareholders deserve a reasonable return on their investment. No-one denies that, without at least minimal financial performance, an organisation dies. However, it often dies from lack of cash flow, not lack of profits. This can occur regardless of how other stakeholders are being served.

Nevertheless, empirical evidence clearly shows that winning organisations balance a variety of perspectives and are not focused on financial returns alone. For instance, while Brambles argued throughout most of its life that it was heavily driven by financial returns ('crunch a quid'), we also know that Brambles:

- carefully chooses the organisations it wants to partner with
- seeks to develop strong customer relationships over time
- seeks to develop specially customised products for its customers
- has its top managers spend a lot of time with the regular people in the organisation, knowing that it is their performance which determines the outcome for the whole company.

271

Brambles does not seek to 'rip off' its customers to increase its shareholder returns. It does not seek to exploit its people just to increase financial returns. So 'financial returns' or 'financial focus' is just one perspective (albeit a very important one in Brambles' case). Even for Brambles, by itself it does not accurately represent the required or desired behaviour.

The evidence that winning organisations use a stakeholder approach – a balanced scorecard approach to performance, not just a financial approach as is often advocated – is overwhelming. Table 10.1 provides examples of how winning organisations balance other stakeholders.

A variation on this stakeholder and shareholder theme is that winning organisations are concerned with both financial and non-financial measures and outcomes. It could be argued that keeping stakeholders happy ultimately serves the bottom line. For instance, perhaps Macquarie and Harvey Norman focus on their people and pay them high rewards simply because 'it is all about money'. But even this is still a narrow argument. Macquarie people certainly do receive a lot of money for their efforts, but the solutions they come up with for customers have been equally valuable, or even more so, for them. Macquarie people only benefit if customers benefit.

Another variation on the theme occurs through the gain–sharing concept, whereby future targeted gains are agreed to be shared with customers, employees, suppliers or partners. A shareholder-oriented organisation would keep all the gains for itself. A financially focused organisation would do the same. Gain–sharing represents a way of linking the interests of more than one stakeholder group... and, whatever the short-term results, the long-term ones are likely to be beneficial, and beneficial to all! Lend Lease, Qantas, Brambles and Woolworths are some of the winning organisations that use gain–sharing approaches with stakeholders.

In summary, of course shareholders are important... but they are just one of several stakeholders. Winning organisations balance the interests of them all according to their particular circumstances and situation.

Table 10.1 – Examples of stakeholders other than shareholders that are important to winning organisations

Organisation	Other Important Stakeholders
Brambles	Customers, partners, people
Harvey Norman	Franchisees
Lend Lease	People, customers, partners, community
Macquarie	People
NAB	Customers
Qantas	Customers, partners, people, Australian people
Rio Tinto	Local communities, people
Salvation Army	Clients, church, governments, people
Telstra	Government, Australian community
Westfield	End customers, customers, community
Woolworths	Customers, suppliers

Short-term and *long-term perspectives*

Another classic debate, especially for public companies, is the argument that, since the sharemarket is very focused on short-term results, listed companies need to focus on the short term and not on the long term. Despite the fact that finance research does not actually support it, this argument is put forward with increasing intensity. However, it is usually put by CEOs and organisations whose performance is poor, rather than by those whose performance is good.

Winning organisations don't have this view at all. They see that both a short-term and a long-term perspective is required. Both short-term and long-term results must be achieved. Consider these examples:

- Brambles spent 20 years getting CHEP established throughout Europe... yet it is said to have a short–term focus on this year's performance.

273

- Woolworths measures its performance weekly... yet its Project Refresh continuous improvement project is expected to run for more than 10 years.
- Westfield is continually redeveloping its shopping centres... but most of them continue to trade through the redevelopment so that the year's sales and profit targets can be reached.

In summary, winning organisations don't choose to focus on the internal *or* the external, shareholders *or* stakeholders, short term *or* long term. They focus on *all* of these, in order to produce a balanced result overall.

Balance philosophies

Winning organisations also balance a variety of different philosophies about the essential nature of what an organisation ought to be. There are endless possible philosophies that might be used. Our research found that winning organisations balanced entrepreneurial and conservative, stable and changing, loose and tight, clear and fuzzy and objective and subjective philosophies (see Figure 10.4).

Figure 10.4 – Balancing philosophies

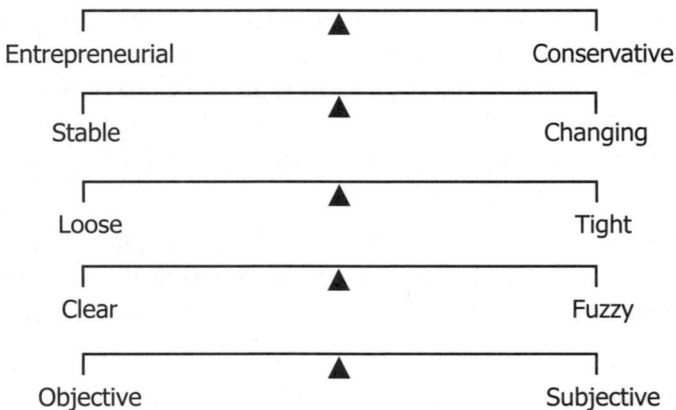

Entrepreneurial	▲	Conservative
Stable	▲	Changing
Loose	▲	Tight
Clear	▲	Fuzzy
Objective	▲	Subjective

Entrepreneurial and *conservative*

While the winning organisations have all been entrepreneurial in their development to some degree, even the most entrepreneurial and opportunistic also regards itself as conservative! We reconciled this issue in Chapter 9 (managing the downside) but, for most organisations, this is a classic 'either/or' choice – they believe that the organisation should be one or the other.

What we see for the winning organisations is that they are entrepreneurial in the sense of seeking new ideas, considering new opportunities, taking advantage of short-term events, developing new products and services and moving into new geographies. However, we also see that they do this within clearly defined strategies, laying off risks whenever they can, being conservative financially and being sure that they have the capabilities to undertake the new activities.

Telstra has invested billions of dollars to enter Asian markets, particularly the Chinese market, which represents highly risky strategy for an organisation with limited international experience and success. It reduced its risk by investing on a joint venture basis with local partners which had good relationships in the Chinese markets, and also by structuring the deals to allow for a series of options to increase or decrease its investments, based on certain outcomes. Simultaneously, in its home market, Telstra has been conservative in resisting change to protect its strong positions in various market segments.

Stable and *changing*

Another paradox is that winning organisations are very stable in some ways... yet they are also constantly changing in others. Organisations tend to want to be stable around:

- what their strategy is
- who their people and leaders are
- what their culture is.

On the other hand, they are constantly seeking new opportunities which, if undertaken, will require change. They are constantly seeking:

- continuous improvement... which requires change
- to innovate
- to grow
- to expand product and service ranges.

Collins and Porras refer to the need to 'preserve the core/stimulate progress'. This is what we see here – the need to preserve, or hold stable, the core of the organisation while simultaneously seeking change in its activities and the methods of operation it uses. Winning organisations achieve both! Together! They have few CEOs and make few changes to their basic strategy, but they are constantly changing their organisational structures and their product and service ranges, the way they deliver the strategy and what markets they deliver it to.

Qantas maintains its high-quality service international profile, but seeks to reduce costs on domestic routes in the face of a low-cost competitor, Virgin Blue. It is also developing a new brand – Australian Airlines – to capitalise on the increasing number of tourists seeking low-cost airfares to a wide variety of destinations that Qantas cannot economically service with its high-quality service/high-cost model.

Loose and tight philosophies

The term 'loose/tight' originates in the Peters and Waterman study. While only Macquarie uses this as a formal part of the wording of its values, 'loose/tight' is a highly appropriate descriptor of the behaviour of most of the winning organisations. The centre focuses on a small number of critically important variables ('tight'). The units, on the other hand, have the ability to innovate and experiment ('loose'), provided they meet the organisation's requirements on those items which are centrally controlled.

Most of the organisations push responsibility down the line. One example of this is autonomous business units which are not cross-subsidised and can largely determine their own future development (entrepreneurial) and make their own decisions (empowered, responsible). Macquarie, for instance, has over 40 separate business units... but the public sees it as one investment bank.

On the other hand, organisations retain central control of a small number of key items. For the banks it is credit control and risk management. For entrepreneurial organisations it is budget and targets (which must be met). For all organisations it is culture and values. Units can be autonomous, but they need to conduct their activities within the value system of the whole organisation.

Clear and *fuzzy*

A variation on 'loose/tight' is 'clear and fuzzy', which we used to describe the strategies of the winning organisations (see Chapter 5). We don't see completely clear strategies, as might be expected in textbook solutions. The lack of plain and simple vision and mission statements supports this view. Yet the strategies are quite clear in practice and, as they unfold over time, strategic change is incremental in virtually every case. The fuzziness is in the details of the variations and small increments. For instance, is a new business really related? How exactly does new business fit?

We see that there is an element of freedom (fuzziness) in strategic development, but within a constrained (clear) existing framework of current strategy and position. This is a deliberate choice, not an accident. Winning organisations want to be clear at the core and fuzzy at the edge.

Objective and *subjective*

Neither a coldly objective analytical philosophy nor a hot-blooded passionate one are enough by themselves. Both are needed for winning organisations. Cold, objective organisations can be right in their analysis and activities... but they are no fun and so who cares what they do? Passionate organisations are exciting and motivating, but may be badly organised and run out of money without proper analysis. Head and heart are *both* required.

Winning organisations are clear-headed and objective. Gathering 'facts' is critical for proper evaluation and assessment of their position or for a new proposal. But winning organisations also have fun and are passionate about what they do. As one Telstra executive said to us:

> People around here work very hard. But we also know how to have fun.

Brambles' waste management division might not be considered a lot of fun to work in. But Carew disagrees:

> Waste services, says Pemberton, was staffed by 'bright young things who went places... we were very cheeky young larrikins who enjoyed the excitement of it, the intellectual challenge of creating something new'. (Carew, 2000, p. 107)

People in winning organisations are committed and proud (see Chapter 8). They want a cause. Leaders in winning organisations are passionate about the cause of the organisation (see Chapter 6) and engage their people.

In summary, it is not a case of choosing a single focus for the organisational philosophy. A wholistic philosophy is necessary – entrepreneurial and conservative, stable and changing, loose and tight, clear and fuzzy, objective and subjective. All balanced together. It's a hard order to fill.

Balance levels

Winning organisations also balance the importance of the different levels of the organisation. Careful consideration of the different levels and balancing of the information, activities and concerns at each level is necessary. Otherwise, the organisation can quickly become remote from its customers and make incorrect decisions due to acting on a biased sample of information. The levels which winning organisations balance include top and bottom, individual and team and small business and large business (see Figure 10.5).

Figure 10.5 – Balancing levels

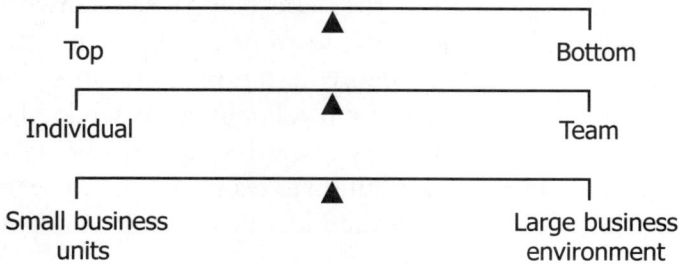

Top · Bottom

Individual · Team

Small business units · · · · · · · · · · · Large business environment

Top and *bottom*

There are many levels within an organisation – usually five to ten or more from CEO to shop floor. Most people are involved at only one or two levels in the organisation and so that is their perspective on it. But the view from the top of the mountain is quite different from the views from the bottom. The organisation must be aligned and work at all levels for best results. Does the view at the top (the leadership group) really understand the views at the bottom (and in the middle)?

For most organisations, there is a dramatic difference in how different levels perceive it and its performance. Leadership is often out of touch with customer-facing and operational people. This means the analysis and consequent solutions proposed at the top may not be appropriate and therefore may not work, as they may not address the real issues that exist.

Winning organisations have mechanisms for ensuring that the levels of the organisation are connected and mixed. Leadership walks around, it communicates, it listens, it acts on what it hears, it provides channels from the bottom to the top and it reduces the levels of hierarchy to decrease this top/bottom issue.

Individual and *team*

At most organisations, there is either an individual or a team approach to the way the organisation behaves. Individual initiative can be frustrated in team-based organisations, while it can be difficult to get co-ordination in individually oriented organisations.

While winning organisations emphasise the role of the individual and individual responsibility, they also emphasise teamwork! And both individual performance and team performance are rewarded! High-quality individuals are desired... but prima donnas who can't work with or in a team need not apply. For instance, while Macquarie heavily rewards individuals, its reward structure also takes into account the individual's contribution to teams. Failure to be included in teams will, of course, limit the individual's ability to contribute.

This focus on both individuals and teams partly explains why the structure of the organisation constantly changes. As an individual moves from one position in the structure to another, it is not just that person's tasks as an individual which have to be covered – it is also their role in the various teams they are in.

Small business units and *a large business environment*

Not only do winning organisations encourage the development of autonomous business units (see Chapter 2), they also seek to develop a small business philosophy... but within the environment, and with the benefits, of a large business framework.

We see a clear focus on business units at:

* Macquarie, Brambles, Lend Lease, Harvey Norman, Woolworths (each store)
* Westfield (each shopping centre must succeed)
* the Salvation Army (each church community is its own unit).

Over the last five years, Qantas and Telstra have also moved towards a business unit focus. Brambles and Lend Lease have, since their globalisation strategies were introduced, moved towards global businesses rather than their previous more individual unit focus.

Yet the organisations also see that their large size has advantages – for instance, through:

* buying power (Harvey Norman, Telstra, Woolworths)
* ability to replicate or improve (Westfield, Rio Tinto)

- ability to provide customer benefits (Qantas, Macquarie, NAB, Telstra, the Salvation Army)
- scale (Rio Tinto, Lend Lease, Brambles).

Balance operations/activities/functions

Another way in which balance occurs is between the variety of different operations, activities and functions that exist or take place within the organisation. Many normal organisations are predominantly focused on or dominated by a single function (e.g. marketing, accounting, or production), or they are dominated by a particular business or business unit. This often makes it very difficult for them to accurately evaluate information and opportunities which come from the dominated operations, activities or functions.

Winning organisations are able to avoid these problems. They seek balance across areas. For instance, Macquarie's risk management function is neither policeman nor supporter of the more entrepreneurial business units. It has a role and it plays its part. Lend Lease seeks to balance the streams of income it receives from its variety of business units, to avoid becoming too dependent on one unit or one business stream.

Overall balance

In the discussions above, we have given examples of particular situations that describe the specifics of an approach. However, more important than the individual items is the concept of overall balance, of balancing 'everything'. Balance is not simply A or B, or C or D. It is A and B and C and D... and E and F and more!

Fred Hilmer gave his views as a non-executive director of how Westfield operates. His overwhelming impression is that of balance – balance of many things: and, and, and. He said:

> According to an old saying, 'When presented with a choice between two good alternatives, take both!' (*The Detailed Westfield Story*, 2000, p. 131)

281

Westfield's success, and the spirit behind it, is a perfect example of 'taking both', of being able to combine seemingly opposite approaches to develop its own unique Westfield way. This entails being both:

- adventurous *and* careful
- big picture *and* detailed
- fast *and* measured
- here and now *and* in the future
- demanding *and* paternalistic
- exacting *and* expedient
- public *and* private
- extravagant *and* frugal
- firm *and* flexible.

When asked why other organisations didn't copy its approach to business, one Rio Tinto executive said:

> Others can copy parts of what we do but not the whole set.

In responding to the same question, a Macquarie executive said:

> There are a number of pieces that would have to be put into place simultaneously... [We are] similar to other investment banks. The difference we perceive is that we take it further and enforce it more rigidly. We articulate it, write it down and apply it more rigidly with very formal processes.

When we analyse organisations like the Salvation Army, Telstra, NAB and Qantas, they epitomise to us this concept of 'overall balance'. One could be very critical and say they are not 'best' at much... but what comes through for each of them – and for the other winning organisations – is a comprehensive, solid performance in all areas, over long periods of time. They have managed to get the balance right... and that, as Collins and Porras said in the quote given at the start of this chapter, is an extremely difficult thing to do. That's why they are winning organisations!

HOW IS BALANCE ACHIEVED?

It's all very well to read about being 'balanced' and what to balance, but how is it achieved? What do winning organisations do to balance their perspectives, philosophies and levels of operations to get a balanced set of outcomes?

We found several important factors in winning organisations that addressed how balance is achieved (see Figure 10.6). They are having:

- a culture that supports diversity of views
- an information system that provides diverse information
- leadership that values information
- a humble, self-critical leadership that is willing to admit mistakes
- the ability to make decisions and deliver results.

Figure 10.6 – How is balance achieved?

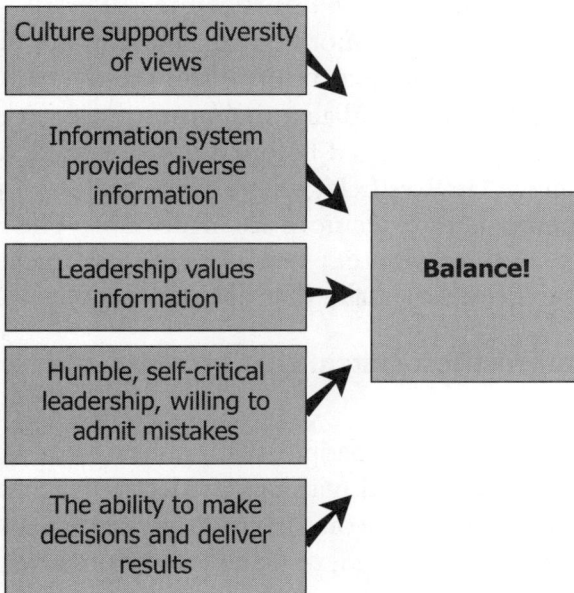

Have a culture that supports diversity of views

To make balanced decisions, a variety of perspectives, ideas and information must be available and must be discussed. The chance of any one individual or group being able to 'represent' this diversity is zero. One of the biggest issues for most cultures, especially 'cult-like cultures' is the difficulty of allowing different views to exist. So we have another paradox: the culture must be tight, but it must support a diversity of views. More than just allowing different views, the culture must value and support them, since without that support they will wither and die.

In most organisations that fail, or even those that decline, the pointers to decline or failure are there well before the decline is recognised. Why aren't these pointers seen? Examinations after organisational failures show that weak signals that go against the prevailing orthodoxy are assumed to be wrong or are ignored... until they become strong signals, at which point the decline is well under way.

Most organisations simply don't value diversity of views. Consequently, diversity cannot flourish. But it is not diversity for diversity's sake. Effective execution is still the overriding theme. Decisions must be made and alignment must occur. Yet a variety of views must be encouraged before a decision is made. We see this, for instance, at Westfield, where wide groups of people are brought together before decisions are made. Everyone is expected to speak up and contribute... but a decision is made and then everyone is expected to make that decision happen.

Have an information system that provides diverse information

Many organisations have people with diverse views, but often those views are not backed with any evidence. Decision-making where people simply decide on their own 'gut feel', personal values or prejudice may well consider a wide variety of views, but many of these views will be ill-informed.

In our experience few organisations in Australia really have good information about their markets, industries, competitors, environments or the future trends likely to affect them. It takes time and effort to develop such information. The information needs to be systematically collected. Neither of these conditions usually exists.

In practice, it is difficult to get appropriate and reliable information in Australia. We do not have a culture that values freedom of information. Much information is not made publicly available and many organisations are not listed and thus not required to provide useful information to the public arena. As a result, even if the culture supports a diversity of views, much of the information required in most organisations for making decisions is simply not there, so the basis for good decisions is extremely shaky.

Information can be built up. It can be collected. It takes time and effort... which of course means costs and responsibility. Macquarie set up its own economic research database in the 1980s, for its own internal use. Such was the paucity of good information, even on such basic issues as macroeconomic statistics, that, being entrepreneurial, Macquarie found that it could sell the data to others.

Internally, the use of the balanced scorecard is a way in which a diverse set of information can be encouraged and used to balance the set of issues which an organisation has to respond to.

Have a leadership that values information

One of the reasons why such information is not gathered in many organisations is that leaders in Australia have preferred the 'she'll be right, mate', gut feel, intuitive approach to decision-making rather than the considered analysis of factual, quantitative data.

In addition, information is power. In many organisations, depriving people of information means they cannot challenge the leadership (often of a single, autocratic leader). In such cases, leaders don't *want* information to be collected, as it may undermine their past decisions and give power to others. Use of this information by others can be personally embarrassing... so it is easier to avoid the risk by not having information widely available! You can't manage what you can't or don't measure.

In winning organisations, information is valued. It is used for decision-making and it is shared widely, so that many people are able to use it and provide different – and informed – perspectives.

Have a leadership which is humble, self-critical and willing to admit mistakes

These characteristics are not associated with many leaders, though we did highlight them in Chapter 6 (leadership, not leaders) as important aspects of leadership in winning organisations. In our experience, many leaders and leadership teams enjoy power. They believe that past successes are due to them and them alone. They believe they have 'earned' the perks which are available at the top of the organisation, either by past service or through simply being in the important positions they now hold. They quickly become remote from their people and how their organisations actually run. They forget how they got where they are.

These beliefs and attitudes are far removed from those of the humble leaders we encountered in our interviews in the winning organisations and in other material in our research. And their descriptions of previous leaders and leadership styles suggested that, for the most part, the same attitudes were held in the past (although there were exceptions!).

We were surprised by the degree to which:

- the leaders admitted errors made
- they were critical of themselves and their predecessors
- they appeared to be willing to learn from past mistakes.

These qualities are critical if the organisation is going to be able to objectively assess the position it is in, learn from it and use that knowledge to go forward. This humble attitude enables leaders to objectively consider information from other sources. Others' ideas can be accepted. Not everything has to be invented here or be the idea of the CEO to succeed.

Simple though these ideas sound, in practice their combination is rare in our experience. Most leaders (and people) are threatened by assessment, by evaluation, by external critique. Many organisational leaders want to defend their past decisions and present positions, rather than accept new evidence. Many leaders don't consider the possibility that 'luck' or external factors might have caused success... even when these factors are often listed as the cause of 'failures' under their leadership.

Have the ability to make decisions and deliver results

Diversity is important but results are what organisations are about. Moving from diverse views through making decisions to getting those decisions accepted and, most importantly, getting the results from those decisions 'on time and on budget' (or better) is what the game is about.

And this brings us back to our winning framework! Winning organisations need to balance 'everything' and the nine elements of our framework are further evidence of the variety of issues that need to be balanced.

Winning organisations need:

- good leadership,
- coupled with the right people, committed to the organisation,
- who are following a clear strategy which is flexible at the margin,
- and focused externally as well as internally,
- who are managing the risks,
- adapting rapidly to changes,
- aligning everything,
- balancing everything, and
- executing effectively to deliver results.

That's a lot of things to balance!

SUMMARY AND KEY MESSAGES FOR LEADERS

The last element in our winning framework is balance. Winning organisations balance everything. They have a variety of perspectives, a variety of philosophies, a variety of organisation levels and a variety of operations, activities and functions to balance in order to 'balance everything'. They do it by having a culture that supports diverse views, an information system that collects diverse information and a leadership that values that information and is willing to admit mistakes.

The key messages for leaders are:

- Balance external and internal views.
- Balance shareholders and stakeholders.
- Balance the short term and long term.
- Balance entrepreneurialism and conservatism.
- Balance stability and change.
- Balance loose and tight policies.
- Balance clear and fuzzy strategy.
- Balance the objective and subjective.
- Balance the top and bottom of the organisation.
- Balance the individual and team.
- Balance small business units and the large business environment.
- Balance operations, activities and functions.
- Have a culture that supports diversity of views.
- Have an information system that provides diverse information.
- Value information.
- Be humble and self-critical.
- Be willing to admit mistakes.

11

HOW DOES 'AUSTRALIA' MAKE IT DIFFERENT?

A key reason for undertaking our study was to answer the question:

Is good business practice global, or is there something unique about business practice and context in Australia that makes succeeding here different?

The answer to this question is both 'yes' and 'no'. Good practice is largely the same. This study would have been useful if all it achieved was to pinpoint which are the winning organisations in Australia and show that they were using the same practices as winning organisations overseas.

However, there are some differences. In this chapter, we address the factors unique to the Australian business context which impact on how to operate, if an organisation wants to be successful. These differences are (see also Figure 11.1):

- the specific comparative advantages which Australia has
- the immaturity of organisations' exposure to local and international competition
- the different motivations of Australians for working in organisations
- the consequent different leadership styles that are necessary for leading successful organisations in Australia

289

- the small market size of Australia
- the use of ideas from overseas
- the role and influence of government in developing organisations in the business environment.

Figure 11.1 – Differences in the Australian business landscape

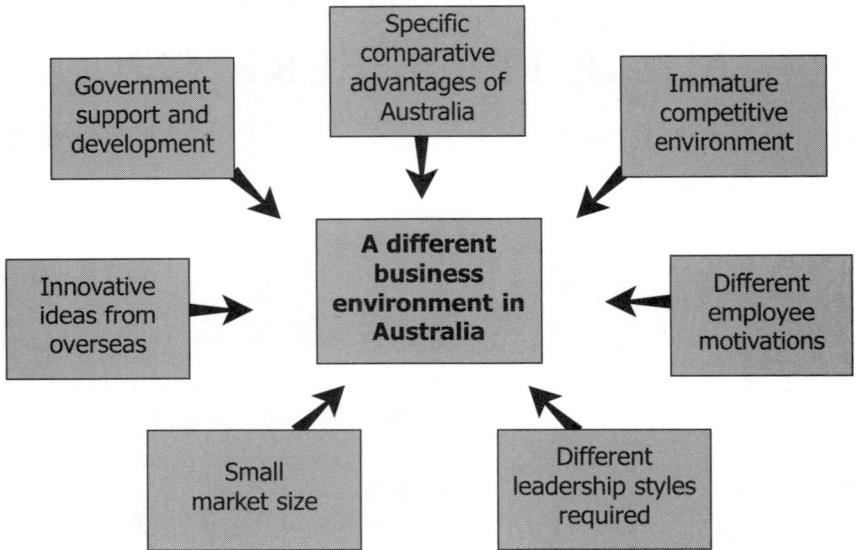

SPECIFIC COMPARATIVE ADVANTAGES OF AUSTRALIA

The nature of the Australian economy and the opportunities it presents obviously influence the types of businesses which develop here. Our large resource and agricultural base provides a natural foundation for the development of major Australian industries and organisations, whereas many of the developed economies do not have similar bases.

For many years, agricultural and mining industries have been the major source of exports for Australia and Australia is known as being a major international supplier of many such products. It is strange, therefore, that apart from CRA – the subsidiary of the international mining firm RTZ – no other winning organisation comes from this background. A possible reason for this is that much agriculture has been small scale, with monopoly co-operatives, sometimes government-owned, being used to market the products overseas. The rapid changes that are occurring in primary industries through industry deregulation and privatisation may yet produce winning organisations in the future, as some organisations emerge with scale. However, this has not been the case for our study.

THE IMMATURE AUSTRALIAN BUSINESS ENVIRONMENT

The 'two organisation' concept: pre- and post-1980

When we were analysing each of the winning organisations, time after time in our interviews we were told that we were really dealing with two organisations. The 'two organisations' idea relates to the changes that have occurred in the business landscape since the 1970s, and particularly over the last 20 years, that have revolutionised winning Australian organisations' way of thinking. This is most obvious at Telstra and Qantas, which moved from being public sector organisations to privately listed companies. However, it also applies at Rio Tinto (through the Australianisation process) and NAB and Macquarie (through banking deregulation), and we are sure it affects many organisations competing in Australia.

These changes over the last 20 to 30 years followed a 30-year stable period from 1945 to 1972, when economic growth and prosperity were the norm and the economy was protected economically, socially and geographically from major disruptive change. This is a very short time period in the history of a country, and even in the history of an organisation. Interviewees often felt that we should only be looking at their organisation from around 1987–90 onwards. The period before this related to a completely different era in their view.

Illustration 11.1 covers some of the main changes that have occurred in the Australian business landscape, to give a quick view

291

of the magnitude of these changes. Although each of these changes – while major in itself – seems absorbable, Illustration 11.1 shows how dramatic the cumulative change has been. It is ironic to note that most of these major changes have been made by Labor governments, not the assumed-to-be-more-business-oriented Liberal governments.

Illustration 11.1 – Major changes to the business landscape in Australia

Year	Event
1971	Bretton Woods pegged exchange rates agreement collapse. $A linked to $US instead of UK pound.
1972	Conciliation and Arbitration Commission grants equal pay.
1973	25 per cent across-the-board tariff cut. Tariff Board replaced by philosophically different Industries Assistance Commission.
1974	Trade Practices Act introduced, which outlawed collusion, price fixing, cartels and other anti-competitive behaviours which were widespread, and particularly addressed the lack of competition across state boundaries. This Act led to subsequent competition reviews and regulation over the period through the establishment of organisations such as the Prices Justification Tribunal, Prices Surveillance Authority, Trade Practices Commission, National Competition Council and the Australian Competition & Consumer Commission.
1975	Jackson Committee Report on Manufacturing Industry Policy. This recommended the reduction of tariffs and quotas and encouragement of the development of a more efficient manufacturing industry.
1976	Coombs Royal Commission Report. This recommended drastic changes to the public service to make it more efficient and more attractive to potential employees.

Illustration 11.1 (cont'd) – Major changes to the business landscape in Australia

1981   Campbell Committee Enquiry into the Australian financial system. This recommended dramatic deregulation of the financial system and opening it to international systems.

1983   Abandoning of currency controls and floating of the Australian dollar. This meant currency risk was introduced as an element to be managed. It also opened up the ability for organisations to invest overseas, not just in Australia.

1983   Government/ACTU Accord introduced. The Government agreed to consult with the ACTU on an agreed wages policy for the country which they would jointly take to the Conciliation and Arbitration Commission, to facilitate wage negotiations and reduce industrial disputes.

1984   New foreign exchange licences granted. Forty new licences made foreign exchange accessible and competitive.

1985   Banking system opened up. The granting of 16 new banking licences (10 were expected in the original 1983 announcement) allowed international banks from overseas and credit unions and building societies from within Australia to enter the banking system.

1985   Government/ACTU Accord Mark II. This traded off wages for increases in superannuation for most employees. It led to the first industrial awards that included superannuation as part of remuneration.

1986   Human Rights and Equal Opportunity Act and Affirmative Action (Equal Opportunity for Women) Act passed.

1987   Introduction of the option of Enterprise Bargaining Agreements – the first time individual organisations were encouraged to bargain with their employees for a deal which was different from that of their

Illustration 11.1 (cont'd) – Major changes to the business landscape in Australia

1987   competitors. This forced managers to be responsible for managing their workforce to rules which they negotiated directly with them, rather than to rules imposed by the courts. This led to big increases in employment flexibility and changes in employment practices.

1987 onwards   The beginning of the government commercialisation and privatisation movement. This has resulted in the sale of many government assets and organisations to private owners and the adoption of commercial principles by most others.

1991   Industry Statement: all tariffs to be reduced to 5 per cent by 2000. This increased the urgency for change in most manufacturing industries.

1991 onwards   Floating of government and mutual organisations on to the stock market. Beginning with the Commonwealth Bank first tranche in 1991 and Qantas first stage in 1993, this eventually made Australia the country with the largest proportion of individuals who own shares.

1993   Hilmer Report. It recommended that the principles of competition be applied in all areas, and highlighted areas such as government monopolies, governments and professional services where price competition or price justification was needed.

1993   Government/ACTU Accord Mark VII: Enterprise bargaining introduced as the standard. This meant governments and unions accepted that bargaining should be the norm at the enterprise level rather than the exception.

1990s   Rapid increase in compulsory superannuation payments as a proportion of payroll – resulting in people developing a sense of personal responsibility for their economic futures, and a rapid increase in interest in financial sophistication by working people.

> ### Illustration 11.1 (cont'd) – Major changes to the business landscape in Australia
>
> **1995**   Australian Competition & Consumer Commission established. This merged the Trade Practices Commission and the Prices Surveillance Authority.
>
> **1996**   Industry Commission becomes the Productivity Commission. This occurred when it absorbed the Bureau of Industry Economics and the Economic Planning Advisory Commission.
>
> **mid-90s** Emergence of the internet – providing the basis for
> **onwards** fundamental changes in business practices, business models and rapid globalisation of ideas and information. This has had a bigger effect on Australia than on some other nations, firstly because Australians are very quick to adopt new technologies and secondly because it dramatically decreased the time within which new ideas became available to what was previously a country made remote by distance.
>
> **1997**   First stage of Telstra privatisation. Sale of airports begins. Wallis Committee Enquiry into the Financial System report.
>
> **2000**   Goods and services tax replaces varying sales and wholesale taxes.
>
> Source: Adapted from a compilation by Ray Cotsell, Mt Eliza Business School, personal communication, July 2002.

Lack of local competition

Locally, most industries in Australia have few major national competitors. Combined with the small market size, limited appeal to overseas companies, the legacy of state-based competitors and the agreed pricing regimes of 30 years ago (some of which still exist in practice), this has meant the typical Australian organisation has limited real experience of a competitive environment. We are only beginning to have truly mature local competitors prepared to use the gamut of competitive tools and techniques available.

The long local boom from around 1994 to 2000 which completed the period of our analysis has benefited those organisations which were able to adapt to these fundamental changes both in their visions of their futures and also in their organisational practices. Even the largest Australian organisations are no longer 'too big' to be acquired. Previously size per se has been seen as a preventative of acquisition. Local size is no longer a relevant benchmark in a globalising economy.

Rapid opening up to international competition

These changes have occurred both incrementally and quickly. Many organisations have still not really adjusted their thinking to where their future lies (international markets), what their future is dependent on (international issues and events) and what their people want (commitment, economic gain–sharing and social relevance).

Since the 1980s, the Australian business context has had an 'awakening' to international forces. Some of these forces are very advantageous (e.g. the growth of Asia as a market) while others are very disadvantageous (e.g. the closure of large areas of manufacturing unable to compete with low–cost Asian competitors).

This reveals the very limited experience which Australian organisations have generally had with international markets. Consequently, we see a lot of 'work in progress' or 'consolidation' in Australian organisations. However, it is notable that our winning organisations generally do have much more international experience than this. Qantas went overseas in 1935, Lend Lease in 1964, Brambles in 1971, Westfield in 1977, NAB in 1987 and several of the others have always had overseas connections.

By 2010, the exposure of the Australian business environment to international markets will have virtually doubled! The winning organisations of the future will need to succeed in these markets. This will undoubtedly make a difference for most organisations in the future, but it highlights how little experience currently exists and, consequently, how immature the Australian business environment is to competition experience.

DIFFERENT MOTIVATIONS: THE NEED FOR A 'CAUSE', NOT A BHAG

The Telstra Cultural Archetype study identified Australians' need to identify a 'cause' in working for their organisations. This contrasts with the American desire to take up a challenge, as seen in the importance of Big Hairy Audacious Goals (BHAGs), which Collins and Porras found to be one of the drivers of their 'visionary organisations'.

As we mentioned in Chapter 1, to Australians, a BHAG is seen as confronting, not encouraging – a challenge which invites the possibility not of success but of failure! According to the Cultural Archetype study, Australians want to feel that what their organisation is doing is worth doing, is achievable and that their leaders can show them how it can be achieved.

This concept of a 'cause' has been discussed extensively in previous chapters (particularly Chapters 5 and 6). We have seen that the concept of a 'cause' can be quite wide (see Illustration 6.2). From our study, it seems likely that it is possible to develop a 'cause' in most or all industries. It depends on the ability of the leadership group to couch the idea, generate emotion around the value of that idea and coach their people towards achieving it.

The absence of vision and mission statements in the winning organisations and the general disdain we heard expressed towards these statements – despite, in our view, their validity as a tool of strategy – may be consistent with the idea of needing a cause. People don't believe vision or mission statements. Organisations are often unable to get their people to identify with the vision or mission.

Whatever the reason, the idea of having a 'cause' which people identify with is a different Australian cultural perspective. Motivating people is a critical part of success for winning organisations: having a cause is an important underlying component for that success.

DIFFERENT LEADERSHIP STYLES: CAPTAIN-COACH LEADERSHIP

The same study which identified the need for a cause also identified that the style of leadership required was also different in Australia. Captain-coach leadership is required – leadership on the field with the troops rather than leadership from on high (see Chapter 6).

This finding is also backed up by other work on Australian leadership (see Illustration 6.5). The Karpin Report into Australian management skills reported that the key strengths were perceived to be:

- hard-working (68 per cent agreed)
- flexible and adaptable (48 per cent)
- innovative/inventive (41 per cent)
- technically sound (31 per cent)
- egalitarian (31 per cent).

On the other hand, the key weaknesses were seen to be:

- having a short-term view (49 per cent)
- a lack of strategic perspective (41 per cent)
- being inflexible/rigid (43 per cent)
- complacency (42 per cent)
- poor teamwork and empowerment (40 per cent)
- the inability to cope with differences (40 per cent)
- poor people skills (37 per cent).

Captain-coach style is quite different both from US BHAG-style leadership and, importantly, from what is experienced at many large organisations in Australia, which is represented by the Karpin Report strengths and weaknesses above. In addition, our experience is that leadership is often remote, perceives itself as all-knowing and all-powerful and is unwilling to share information with the people. All this means there is a very large gap between the desired style for Australia and both the actual style often used and the desired style for US organisations.

For winning organisations, we identified several organisational characteristics that link into the general Australian psyche, and are different and require a different style of leadership. These are all consistent with a 'captain-coach' leadership style, where leaders and followers are similar in their aims and endeavours. While we discuss each idea separately below, they are in many ways integrally linked. They are (see Figure 11.2):

- the 'have a go' attitude
- challenging/changing the rules
- the 'can do'/Aussie battler attitude
- the idea of pioneering for Australia
- being determined/tenacious
- having a team orientation.

Figure 11.2 – Organisational characteristics that link to captain-coach leadership

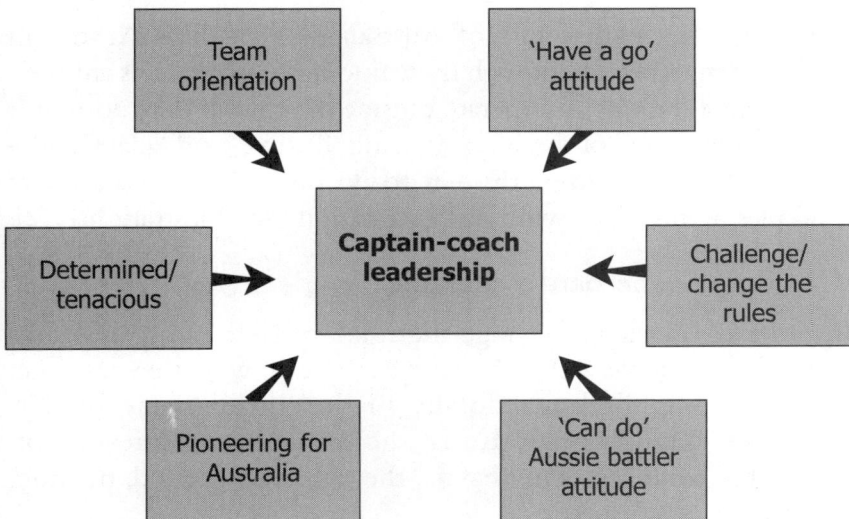

'Have a go' attitude

Most often observed in the cricketing cry to stolid batsmen, "ave a go, yer mug', this attitude of Australians reflects the idea that being defensive has low value. Better to try and fail than not to try. Trying and making a fool of yourself is better than not trying at all.

We see this in Brambles' entry into the 'garbos' field of waste management. We also see it in the willingness of Harvey Norman, Lend Lease, Macquarie, the Salvation Army and Westfield to take on new challenges that neither they nor others have tried.

Along with the desire to try comes the need to be flexible and adaptable, which results from the small market size of Australia. In this sense, having a go is often necessary, as help from large-scale organisations is unlikely to be available.

Challenging/changing the rules

The Karpin Report found that two of the three key strengths identified for Australian management were being flexible and adaptable and being innovative/inventive. Honesty and high ethical standards were seen as low on the 'strength' list and – notably – low on the list of the characteristics of the 'ideal' manager.

Our anecdotal experience of Australians as well as Australian management is consistent with these findings – Australians are keen to challenge the rules or operate outside the rules if they don't suit them. (In fact, one of the ways of being 'flexible' and 'adaptable' – two identified key strengths – is to do just this!) We see many examples of this in the winning organisations (see Illustration 11.2).

'Can do'/Aussie battler attitude

In order to 'challenge/change the rules', people in organisations have to have the view that they can actually do what they propose. This is exemplified anecdotally in the 'little Aussie battler' stereotype. The idea here is that the 'battler' can achieve a lot, despite the handicap of not having the right background, training, equipment or resources.

Illustration 11.2 – Examples of winning organisations challenging or changing the rules

Brambles
Establishing Cleanaway required rethinking of how garbage was handled – from being a unique, one-off, small-scale action to being a standardised, repetitive, large-scale activity.

Harvey Norman
Introducing a new method of contracting with 'employees' as franchisees, which changed the rules about how 'employees' would behave and what they would be responsible – and rewarded – for.

Lend Lease
Introducing the 'community of interest' concept, which changed the aim from building the building for a profit to building a building that would satisfy a wide variety of stakeholder groups.

Macquarie
Developing new financial products, e.g. Infrastructure Trusts. These products package up assets which have previously been seen as requiring large-scale, wholesale financing, not retail financing.

NAB
Establishing flexible home loans when fixed loans were the only alternative.

Qantas
As an Australian retail organisation, focusing on high-quality international-class customer service when this is not the norm for these types of organisations in Australia.

Rio Tinto
Establishing individual contracts with employees when all competitors were using industry-based, court-arbitrated awards.

Salvation Army
Establishing new methods of treating social problems by being prepared to ignore political correctness or social norms and address real issues.

Telstra
Challenging competitors in the courts to slow the pace of market share loss, as required by the privatisation of the monopoly.

Illustration 11.2 (cont'd) – Examples of winning organisations challenging or changing the rules

Westfield   Branding shopping centres rather than relying on branded retailers.

Woolworths Establishing 'fresh food' as a point of difference, rather than packaged groceries.

Many Australian organisations feel this way when confronted with the might of European or North American or Japanese (and increasingly Chinese) organisations as competitors. There is a belief, exemplified in our sports stars and sporting success, that Australians 'can do' it. This attitude by itself can assist us 'punching above our weight'. Intriguingly, organisations such as the giant News Corporation and Macquarie Bank see themselves as 'little Aussie battlers' in their competition with global corporations.

Pioneering for Australia

An idea that kept arising in our study was that, though the organisations were seeking their own success, there was also a degree of patriotism involved, a sense of 'doing it for Australia' (see Illustration 11.3) and in some cases a sense of leading the way for Australia. This idea is of course consistent with those mentioned above. Part of the 'cause' in some cases was 'doing it for Australia'. Part of the leadership style was demonstrating that Australians could do it. Having the ability to change the rules so that they suit Australian needs and the idea of the little Aussie battler are reinforced by this 'pioneering' ideal. Illustration 11.3 gives some examples of this idea.

Illustration 11.3 – Examples of 'pioneering' for Australia

Brambles	Establishing CHEP pallet control and tracking system.
Harvey Norman	Large volume electrical and other product discount stores that are profitable.
Lend Lease	Establishment of property trusts, strata titles, project management and control systems.
Macquarie	An investment bank that specialises in Australia but competes internationally.
NAB	Flexible home loans; cost control.
Qantas	Qantas as a brand representing 'Australia'.
Rio Tinto	Developing large-scale resource deposits for global export.
Salvation Army	Forming business alliances for welfare objectives.
Telstra	Developing Australia's telecommunications infrastructure.
Westfield	Branding shopping centres.
Woolworths	Establishing 'fresh food' as a point of difference.

Determined/tenacious

In order to 'do' the task, to carry out the 'cause', to be successful despite being from a small country, these organisations have had to be very determined and very tenacious. This characteristic is often understated by 'success stories'.

Organisations which are recognised as successes are often assumed to have suddenly arrived, suddenly succeeded. In fact, as we demonstrate in the strategic cycle, particularly through the consolidation stage, winning organisations work very hard for long periods with often little to show for it. They do not start as 'successes'. Indeed, they often start with handicaps! Illustration 11.4

303

lists some of the barriers that the winning organisations have had to overcome. Not one of them was guaranteed success when it began. All have had many barriers to overcome. Success in each case has taken many years.

Illustration 11.4 – Barriers overcome to achieve success by the winning organisations

Brambles	Starting as a small family business in Newcastle; introduced the pallet control system into Europe and the US.
Harvey Norman	Harvey and Norman were sacked by Alan Bond when Norman Ross was taken over in 1982, so they had to start again.
Lend Lease	Started up as a subsidiary of a Dutch building contractor.
Macquarie	As a foreign-owned merchant bank, it had to get a banking licence, of which there were very few.
NAB	Acquiring and managing international banks.
Qantas	Sold business to the government in 1947 when could not raise capital to expand fleet.
Rio Tinto	Survived long resources depression in 1980s and large-scale industrial action as it endeavoured to change the basis of employment.
Salvation Army	Limited resources: reliance on donations from non-Salvation Army members.
Telstra	Developing commercial skills to compete in a competitive world.
Westfield	Lowy and Saunders started as penniless immigrants in Sydney in the early 1950s.
Woolworths	Shareholders refused to support further in 1925; merger proposal with Coles in 1936.

Team orientation

A final aspect that affects leadership in an Australian winning organisation – and a driver for captain-coach leadership – is the desire for a team orientation. Mateship and egalitarianism are alive and well. Australians want to be part of a team – ideally a team of 'mates' – rather than be individuals working for themselves, taking chances for themselves and taking responsibility on themselves.

AUSTRALIA'S SMALL MARKET SIZE AND SPREAD

Another feature which makes being in Australia different from operating in large economies such as the US, Germany, Japan, the European Union and China is the size of market available. The Australian market is miniscule compared with any of the major economies. Further, it is extremely spread out – a factor which non–Australians never really understand until they actually visit the country. Even though much of the population lives in what seems a small number of cities on the eastern seaboard, these cities are far apart compared with their equivalents elsewhere. Finally, unlike some successful small economies (e.g. Singapore, Sweden, Switzerland and South Korea), it does not have a major market on its physical doorstep. Asia is hardly 'close' physically, even if its market size is rapidly expanding.

This small market size means that economies of scale are limited in Australia when compared with those available to international competitors in their home markets. This impacts on many aspects of business operations, including the ability to conduct research and development economically, product run lengths, customer segmentation, physical operating plant size (e.g. one car plant could probably provide all the cars we need in Australia... but which plant, and what about the need for choice?).

When markets were protected up until the mid–1980s, small market size was of little importance. Competitors could not enter and international cost comparisons were therefore of little relevance. In an open international market, this issue is of utmost importance. To be unable to operate at close to world cost levels leaves an Australian organisation vulnerable to significant cost differentials, as we have seen through the closing of a great deal of manufacturing in Australia over the last 10 to 15 years.

But Australia and its organisations cannot retreat to the past 'good times'. The rest of the world is not going backwards! So the future for Australian organisations is not in economies of scale. The future is in finding overseas markets, international niches and competing on differentiation, not cost.

This is quite different from being an organisation in a large economy, where competing on low cost is a viable strategic option and where there are many niches available.

Many Australian organisations are still focused on the local market. Even some of the winning organisations have not yet made the transition to being international (e.g. Woolworths and Harvey Norman), while NAB's recent retreat towards Australia is unsettling and Telstra is struggling to find overseas success. Regardless of the rate at which the Australian market grows, it will never be a large-scale global market, so success for Australia's future winning organisations will not come about by being successful only in Australia.

In the future, being international will be essential to be a winning organisation. In order to be successful, winning organisations will have to compete with international competitors both overseas and in Australia. The element we identified in our winning framework of 'looking out' or being externally focused will grow in importance over time.

BIG OVERSEAS INFLUENCES ON AUSTRALIAN ORGANISATION DEVELOPMENT

Because relatively little research and development is affordable in Australia, many 'innovative ideas' are actually borrowed from overseas and brought back to Australia (see Chapter 4). This is quite different from organisations in major economies, where R&D

is an important function and can be afforded due to product run lengths and scale economies.

Consistent with comments made above, we do not see this changing. Overseas influences – from anywhere and everywhere – will be an increasing factor in the future. The reduction in trade barriers, the inherently small scale of the Australian market and the increasing use of the internet to transfer ideas rapidly around the globe all suggest this.

If Australian organisations are to be winners, they will need to be externally focused and able to rapidly adopt or adapt ideas from overseas. While being externally focused is also of increasing importance for organisations in large economies, the size of the home market available to these organisations will continue to provide them with opportunities to specialise domestically.

THE SIGNIFICANT GOVERNMENT ROLE IN DEVELOPING WINNING ORGANISATIONS

When we began this work, we sought nominations for winning organisations for all types of organisations, specifically including government enterprises and departments. We received very few nominations in this category and no organisation received sufficient to be included in the final group for analysis. Of course, this does not necessarily mean they are not 'winning' – just that, if they are, not enough senior people seem to know about it and recognise it.

Intellectually, it was surprising and disappointing not to have a wider range of organisations to analyse. We are sure it does not mean that listed organisations necessarily make up the overwhelming proportion of winning organisations. What it does mean, as might be presumed from our final group, is that the performance of organisations outside that group are not well enough known for us to identify winners there.

However, reflecting on the 11 winning organisations, we find that government influence is much more significant than it appears (see Illustration 11.5). Not only are two of them direct privatisations

307

from the government, but the government pallet pool which was 'privatised' after World War II formed the core of what is now a much more diversified Brambles. Also, Lend Lease and Westfield directly benefited from the government-sponsored Snowy Mountains Hydroelectricity Scheme.

Illustration 11.5 – Government development of winning organisations now and in the future?

Brambles	Bought the government pallet pool, which formed the basis for CHEP.
Lend Lease	Started work as a contractor to the government Snowy Mountains Hydroelectric Scheme.
Qantas	Most of its life has been a government-owned airline.
Rio Tinto	Benefited from being 'Australianised' by the government.
Salvation Army	50 per cent of its revenue comes from government contracts.
Telstra	Owned by the government for its whole organisational life until recent partial privatisation.
Westfield	Started out serving the needs of immigrants brought to Sydney to work on the Snowy Mountains Hydroelectric Scheme.
Commonwealth Bank?	Has performed very well since being privatised in the mid-1990s and is developing a very good reputation.
CSL?	Has grown dramatically and is now a major international player in niche areas of medical supplies, such as blood.
Medical organisations?	Australian research organisations are well regarded internationally and Australian hospitals are considered to have very high standards.

Illustration 11.5 (cont'd) – Government development of winning organisations now and in the future?

Agricultural organis- ations?	Australia is a significant international supplier of many agricultural products.
Educational institutions?	Education is now one of Australia's major export industries and Australia has a high reputation for quality in some areas.
Arts organis- ations?	Several Australian organisations are world-renowned (e.g. Sydney Dance Theatre, Australian Ballet) and performers and directors are regularly in demand overseas.
Utilities?	This gradually nationalising industry may produce a leading player.

In addition, other recently privatised government organisations, such as the Commonwealth Bank and Commonwealth Serum Laboratories (CSL), have performed extremely well since their privatisations. Due to having quite a short public history, they had little chance of being included in the study when we sought nominations in 1999. Also, Australia Post has dramatically improved its performance over the last 10 years. Though it is not scheduled for privatisation, more public scrutiny may identify Post as a potential winner in the longer term. The commercialisation and privatisation of utilities in Australia seems likely, in the longer run, to identify one or more organisations as these industries settle and consolidate over time.

These examples are probably only the tip of the iceberg, as it is difficult to identify, assess and compare government organisations. Some of those which have not been privatised may also be 'winning' in their sectors. Hospitals and universities are some obvious examples of Australian organisations which have great reputations internationally... but they were not nominated by CEOs for our study.

In summary, organisations which originate in the government sector – and probably many which remain there – have been identified as winning organisations. Just because an organisation is in the public sector does not mean it is not doing a great job, as is assumed by many business people. Naturally, government organisations focus more on the quality of what they produce and on the specific (political) needs of their masters, but it does seem that this starting background provides an excellent foundation for commercial success if they are privatised.

This is different from larger economy countries, where the role of government is less intrusive and support is less important. The role of government is likely to continue to be important for developing industries in Australia and providing the context for organisations in those industries to succeed – or not – internationally. Industries such as agriculture, medicine, universities, film and media are some other areas with significant government support where Australian organisations have developed international reputations. We do not see that continuing in the future without ongoing government support. Given the small market size of Australia, government support provides a way of making the local market 'bigger' and improving its chances of international success. Indeed, the danger is that the government will see 'success' as a reason for withdrawing support.

SUMMARY AND KEY MESSAGES FOR LEADERS

There are several differences in the Australian context that make slavish adoption of international 'success formulas' likely to have limited success. 'Leadership' is not the same in every country. 'Right people', 'looking out' and 'manage the downside' will also have different specific meanings and require different actions, even if the same terms are included in frameworks across different countries.

310

Understanding the basis of these differences is critical for studying success in the Australian market and, ultimately, in the international market coming from a background in Australia.

The key messages for leaders of organisations in Australia from this chapter are:

- Being a winning organisation in the future will be dependent on international success.
- There is very little experience of international business and international success in Australian business history to date.
- Success in Australia does not guarantee success overseas, due to the differences in the Australian business landscape.
- Different leadership styles are required for success in Australia.
- Employees have different motivations in Australia.
- Organisations in the government sector may be just as well placed to become 'winning' as those in the private sector.

12

COMPARING OUR FINDINGS
TO OTHER STUDIES

What we have tried to do in this study is to identify some of Australia's winning organisations and the practices which they use – as a group – that seem to be the key causes of their high performance. In this chapter we try to see how those causes are similar or different to those identified in other studies that have been performed.

As we have seen in Chapter 11, there are context differences in Australia that make operating in this country different, so we would expect some differences in practices for winning organisations here compared to overseas. However, the principles of success seem likely to be very similar across the world – everyone wants to grow, to be profitable, to have happy customers and employees, to have efficient processes, etc. So we would also expect a large degree of similarity in the principles identified.

Throughout the book we have referred to other work which has been done to identify high-performing organisations and the practices which they use. In this chapter we'll compare our findings with theirs. What commonalities exist? What are the differences? And why might this be so?

We focus on the three major studies which have identified specific organisations as winners – *In Search of Excellence, Built to Last* and *Good to Great*. We'll also consider how the issues highlighted for 'winning' organisations and the pursuit of success link to the general issues that must be managed in running any organisation.

OTHER STUDIES OF 'WINNING' ORGANISATIONS

Two US studies have been the forerunners and inspirations for our work. Since our research began in 1999, another US study has been published using a similar methodology. The three studies are:

- *In Search of Excellence* (1982) – Peters and Waterman
- *Built to Last* (1994) – Collins and Porras
- *Good to Great* (2001) – Collins.

These studies have each had a major impact on the business community, for several reasons:

- Their use of business community experience and expertise to identify winning organisations.
- The use of hard quantitative analysis and rigorous assessment to support intuitive sense.
- Their findings accord with what experienced business people think and feel makes 'sense' for successful business practice – but which they could not and cannot prove.
- In identifying specific organisations and their specific practices, they have provided role models to observe and discuss.
- These role model organisations are well known in the community, so that business people are not dependent simply on what 'experts' say is good practice. They can assess it for themselves.

The first study: *In Search of Excellence*

In Search of Excellence was the first study to seek out winning organisations and identify them and their collective practices. Prior to this, business literature was heavily dependent on individual – and independent – case studies.

In Search of Excellence was initiated because of dissatisfaction at US consulting firm McKinsey & Co. with the 'problems of management effectiveness'. At the time, the oil crisis was in full flow and many industries and organisations were struggling to find a model of how to cope with the quite different circumstances which they faced (i.e. low or negative growth, high inflation, high capital costs and dislocated cost structures). McKinsey set up project teams to consider the issues. They talked to many people and found that:

> All were uncomfortable with the limitations of the usual structural solutions... skeptical about the usefulness of any known tools, doubting they were up to the task of revitalizing and redirecting billion-dollar-giants. (Peters and Waterman, 1982, p. 4)

The practices which were identified in this seminal study were instrumental in changing US thinking about how to compete, in the face of the invasion of Japanese companies competing with what appeared to be a different – and superior – model. The essentials of the study are given in Illustration 12.1.

This study publicised the now famous McKinsey 7S technique of analysis as well as the eight key findings. The study has been criticised for focusing too much on high-technology companies, for not making its methodology clear enough and because some of these companies have had trouble since being identified.

However, more than 20 years on, it is notable that many of these companies are still going strongly and have remained high performers for long periods. Of the 14 highlighted, 11 are ranked in the Top 200 in the Fortune 500 in 2002. These companies are all well known and generally admired, though each has naturally endured challenges over such a long period.

The key limiting feature has been the purely US focus of the work. Do its findings also apply in other countries? Which are the best organisations in other countries? The study stimulated the 'excellent' consulting industry which, for at least the next 10 years, focused on trying to apply these techniques to organisations which wished to become 'excellent'.

314

Illustration 12.1 – In Search of Excellence

Study Date: 1977–1979

Methodology:

Asked an informed group of observers of the business scene to identify good companies.

Limited industries studied, for convenience. Excluded 13 European firms.

Applied six quantitative financial tests for a 20-year period – company had to be in the top half of its industry in at least four of six growth and returns measures over a 20-year period.

Used an expert rating of innovativeness over the 20-year period.

Found 43 companies that passed the tests. Interviewed 21 in depth.

Surveyed 25 years of literature prior to the survey period for each company.

Findings focused on 14 that exemplified the eight traits identified.

Key Findings:

- A bias for action
- (Be) Close to the customer
- (Foster) Autonomy and entrepreneurship
- Productivity through people
- Hands-on, value driven
- Stick to the knitting
- Simple (structural) form, lean (head office) staff
- Simultaneous loose/tight properties (decentralised and centralised).

Excellent Companies (top 14 out of 43 in total):

Bechtel	Fluor
Boeing	Hewlett-Packard
Caterpillar Tractor	IBM
Dana	Johnson & Johnson
Delta Airlines	McDonald's
Digital Equipment	Procter & Gamble
Emerson Electric	3M

Visonary companies: *Built to Last*

This study was stimulated when two Stanford University academics, Collins and Porras, wanted to explore what was meant by 'vision' and 'visionary companies'. They had two primary objectives:

1. To identify the underlying characteristics and dynamics common to highly visionary companies (and that distinguish them from other companies) and to translate those findings into a useful conceptual framework.
2. To effectively communicate these findings and concepts so that they influence the practice of management and prove beneficial to people who want to help create, build and maintain visionary companies.

(Collins and Porras, 1994, p. 12)

Built to Last (BTL) had a more 'academic' feel about its research than does *In Search of Excellence*. This study lays out its methodology very clearly at the back of the book, perhaps reflecting the university origins of its researchers. It also has the very strong methodological advantage of using comparison companies, which maximises the chance of focusing on differences, rather than simply 'good' practices.

The *In Search of Excellence* study is not mentioned in *Built to Last* until near the end of the book, where a very brief comparison is made. This is surprising, since the interest and debate generated by the earlier book must certainly have encouraged the research for *Built to Last*.

Like *In Search of Excellence*, its findings begin with business opinion, but a clearly structured approach was used. The study focused on the complete history of the company, rather than the recent period. There were no interviews with the companies. Illustration 12.2 outlines the essentials of the study.

Like *In Search of Excellence*, *Built to Last* is heavily US-centric. There is considerable overlap between the two studies, with 10 of the 17 US companies being in both studies. The overlap would have been greater except that some companies did not qualify for both. For instance, *In Search of Excellence* limited the industries it studied, while *Built to Last* eliminated companies started after 1950.

316

Illustration 12.2 – Built to Last

Study Date: 1988–1994

Methodology:

Surveyed a representative sample of 700 US CEOs seeking five nominations of organisations which were 'highly visionary'.

Identified the 20 most frequently mentioned.

Eliminated those founded since 1950, reasoning that their 'vision' might be due to a single great idea or a single leader. Left with 18 companies.

Selected a good comparison company for each company.

Studied both firms since their inception to understand their evolution and to understand the difference between the good and the visionary company.

Identified nine key factors.

Key Findings:

- Clock building, not time telling (i.e. build the organisation, don't focus on what to do with it)
- No 'tyranny of the or'
- (Success is) More than profits
- Preserve the core/stimulate progress
- Big Hairy Audacious Goals (BHAGs)
- Cult-like cultures
- Try a lot of stuff and keep what works
- Home-grown management
- Good enough never is.

Excellent Companies:

American Express	Merck
Boeing*	Motorola
Citicorp	Nordstrom
Ford	Philip Morris*
General Electric*	Procter & Gamble*
Hewlett-Packard*	Sony
IBM*	Wal-Mart
Johnson & Johnson*	Walt Disney*
Marriott*	3M*

(* = also included in the *In Search of Excellence* sample)

Whereas *In Search of Excellence* was focused on innovative, growing and profitable organisations, *Built to Last* was focused on 'visionary' organisations. These organisations also turned out to be very good stock market performers, though this was not a criterion for choosing them.

A prequel: *Good to Great*

Collins' most recent work, *Good to Great* (GTG), was triggered by concern that the 'great' companies in *Built to Last* were always great:

> ...the vast majority of good companies remain just that – good, but not great... Can a good company become a great company and, if so, how? Or is the disease of 'just being good' incurable? (Collins, 2001, p. 3)

Good to Great was published well after our study was under way. Collins says that this study is essentially a prequel to *Built to Last*, since it identifies companies which had not being doing well but which have been able to turn their performance around. The authors describe these companies as 'nondescript, even dowdy companies, in unglamorous industries'. Illustration 12.3 outlines the essentials of this study. The principles as described are difficult to understand, so we have 'translated' them.

Once again, a key limitation of the study is its total US focus. The approach here is quite different from the other two studies, as the sample was chosen by quantitative analysis of stock market returns with no input from executives at the start.

Good to Great companies may well be of relevance to Australia, since, as we have seen, there is limited 'vision' identified in our winning organisations. While Australian companies seek a 'cause', they do not have 'Big Hairy Audacious Goals' which provide visionary challenges.

OTHER STUDIES

A variety of other studies have also sought to identify winning practices, but they have not identified the organisations from which

318

these practices are drawn, nor have they identified how those organisations were chosen or what their performance was. See Appendix B for details.

Illustration 12.3 – Good to Great

Study Date: 1996–2000

Methodology:

Analysis of Fortune 500 companies from 1965 to 1995.

Looking for companies which had nondescript stock returns for 15 years, followed by at least 15 years in which stock returns outperformed the market by three times.

Sought comparison companies where possible.

Key Findings:

- Level 5 leadership (self-effacing, quiet, reserved, shy leadership)
- First who, then what (get the people right first, then decide on strategy)
- (Be committed and) Confront the brutal facts (yet never lose faith)
- The hedgehog concept (focus on one thing that people are passionate about)
- Culture of discipline (disciplined people don't need a hierarchy)
- Technology accelerators (pioneer selected technologies)
- The flywheel and the doom loop (grand restructures and dramatic change programs will not give the leap required – continuous incremental change is needed).

Excellent Companies:

Abbott Laboratories	Nucor
Circuit City	Pitney Bowes
Fannie Mae	Philip Morris
Gillette	Walgreens
Kimberley-Clark	Wells Fargo
Kroger	

HOW DO OUR FINDINGS ON BUSINESS PRACTICES COMPARE WITH OTHERS?

So how do our findings compare with these others on winning business practice? Let's look at how our study compares to the three American works, first individually and then contrasting all four studies' findings together.

The First XI versus In Search of Excellence

Table 12.1 shows the findings of each study. The two studies agree on the importance of people, of strategy (having a clear one), of customers and of focusing on execution to deliver results.

Strangely, *In Search of Excellence* omits leadership from its list. We think this is an oversight, as everything within the study implies that leadership is important. There is a strong emphasis on the 'strong, charismatic, dominant leader' as the driver of the organisation, which is different from our findings. Peters and Waterman said:

> We must admit that our bias at the beginning was to discount the role of leadership heavily... Unfortunately what we found was that associated with almost every excellent company was a strong leader (or two) who seemed to have had a lot to do with making the company excellent in the first place. (p. 26)

Our study highlights managing risk and the concept of 'everything' more than *In Search of Excellence* does. Our study also has a wider focus on 'external' than merely the customer concept of *In Search of Excellence*. *In Search of Excellence*, on the other hand, includes a finding about structure, whereas we find structure not to be particularly important. Perhaps this reflects the fact that a trigger for the *In Search of Excellence* study was dissatisfaction with current structural solutions.

Overall, apart from the leadership oversight, there is nothing our findings conflict with in a major way in the *In Search of Excellence* study. There is very considerable agreement between the findings.

Given the 20-year time difference between the studies, this is itself interesting and encouraging.

Table 12.1 – The First XI versus *In Search of Excellence*

The First XI	In Search of Excellence
Effective execution	A bias for action Hands-on, (value driven)
Perfect alignment	(Hands-on), value driven
Adapt rapidly	Encouraging autonomy and entrepreneurship
Clear fuzzy strategy	Stick to the knitting
Leadership, not leaders	—
Looking out, looking in	Close to the customer
Right people	Productivity through people
Manage the downside	—
Balance everything	Loose/tight
—	Simple form, lean staff

The First XI versus Built to Last

Table 12.2 compares these two studies. The studies agree on the role of leadership, a clear and fuzzy strategy, rapid adaptation, balance, alignment and execution. Strangely, *Built to Last* omits the role of people; yet, again, everything in the study implies the importance of people.

Our study includes 'looking out' and 'manage the downside', which are not covered by *Built to Last*. It itself includes BHAGs, which we found to be culturally inappropriate.

Overall, apart from BHAGs and the apparent 'people' oversight, there is a very large degree of agreement between the two studies and nothing else in conflict with *Built to Last*.

Table 12.2 – The First XI versus Built to Last

The First XI	Built to Last
Effective execution	Try a lot of stuff and keep what works More than profits
Perfect alignment	Cult-like cultures
Adapt rapidly	Try a lot of stuff and keep what works Good enough never is
Clear fuzzy strategy	Preserve the core/stimulate progress
Leadership, not leaders	Clock building, not time telling Home grown management
Looking out, looking in	—
Right people	—
Manage the downside	—
Balance everything	No 'tyranny of the or' More than profits
—	Big Hairy Audacious Goals (BHAGs)

The First XI versus Good to Great

Table 12.3 compares these two studies. The studies agree on the importance of leadership, of people, of strategy, of alignment and of delivering results.

Our study's factors of 'manage the downside', 'looking out', 'adapt rapidly' and 'balance' are not covered by *Good to Great*. In contrast, there is nothing in that study which is not covered by our work, though the role of technology is a specific issue raised which we do not particularly address (but we do agree that technology per se is not critical).

Table 12.3 – The First XI versus Good to Great

The First XI	Good to Great
Effective execution	A culture of discipline
Perfect alignment	The flywheel and the doom loop
Adapt rapidly	Technology accelerators
Clear fuzzy strategy	The hedgehog concept (First who), then what
Leadership, not leaders	Level 5 leadership
Looking out, looking in	Confront the brutal facts (yet never lose faith)
Right people	First who, (then what)
Manage the downside	—
Balance everything	—

Once again, overall there is little disagreement, though this study highlights fewer and rather unusual factors. This may simply be due to the fact that it is seeking a different type of company and using a different process from the other three studies. The findings may be more relevant for improving organisations rather than identifying 'winning' ones.

The First XI versus all three studies

While we have done a one-to-one comparison above for each major study, comparing all four simultaneously may make it clearer where the differences are.

Table 12.4 shows the findings of all four studies. It shows:

- The agreement on leadership, on people and on strategy. We would have been shocked if these studies did not have anything to say about these three elements (though we see the omission of leadership and people from one set of findings as an 'oversight', based on the actual words in the analysis).

- Agreement around the concepts of adapting rapidly, alignment, balance and execution.
- That our concept of managing risk is new, as it is not present in any of the other studies.
- Our emphasis on 'looking out' rather than simply focusing on customers is a wider external perspective.
- Anything which is not in our findings is not common across any other two studies, so our work does not appear to have missed any major elements.

Table 12.4 – The First XI versus all three studies

The First XI	In Search of Excellence	Built to Last	Good to Great
Effective execution	A bias for action Hands-on (value driven)	Try a lot of stuff and keep what works More than profits	A culture of discipline Confront the brutal facts (yet never lose faith)
Perfect alignment	(Hands-on), value driven	Cult-like cultures	The flywheel and the doom loop
Adapt rapidly	Encouraging autonomy and entrepreneur-ship	Try a lot of stuff and keep what works Good enough never is	Technology accelerators
Clear fuzzy strategy	Stick to the knitting	Preserve core/ stimulate progress	The hedgehog concept First who, then what

Table 12.4 (cont'd) – The First XI
versus all three studies

The First XI	In Search of Excellence	Built to Last	Good to Great
Leadership, not leaders	—	Clock building, not time telling Home grown management	Level 5 leadership
Looking out, looking in	Close to the customer	—	Confront the brutal facts (yet never lose faith)
Right people	Productivity through people	—	First who, then what
Manage the downside	—	—	—
Balance everything	Loose/tight	No 'tyranny of the or' More than profits	—
—	Simple form, lean staff	Big Hairy Audacious Goals (BHAGs)	—

WINNING CRITERIA VERSUS CRITERIA FOR MANAGING ANY ORGANISATION

Our analysis above compares those factors that have been found for winning organisations. We should not confuse those with the factors that are needed to be managed for all organisations.

What the winning framework provides is the issues which differentiate long-term high-performing organisations from their competitors. There are many factors which need to be managed well, but only some of those make the difference between good organisations – those which do most things well – and winning organisations – those which are noted by their peers as being the best organisations in the country (see Figure 12.1).

Figure 12.1 – Issues for Organisations at Different Positions of Competence

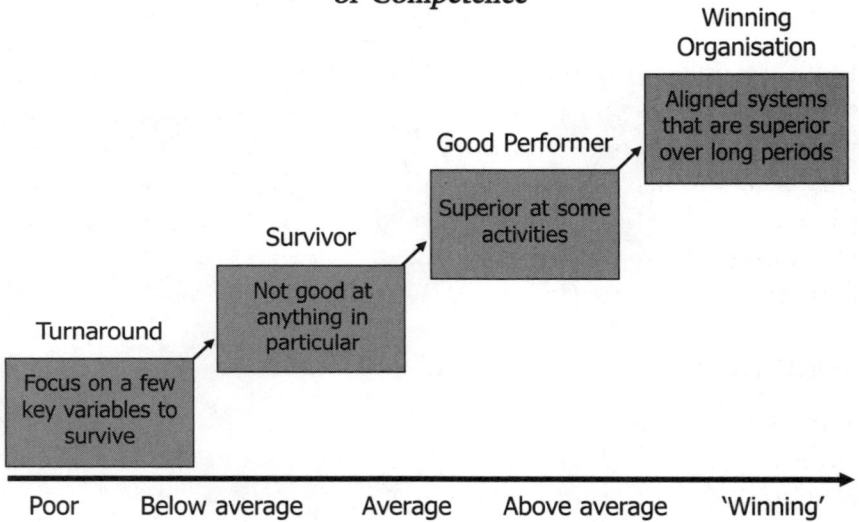

To begin the task of improvement, organisations need to have a comprehensive understanding of what their strategy is, how their business runs and operates and what key capabilities it has which can be used to create competitive advantage in the marketplace.

Frameworks such as the Environment-Strategy-Capability gap analysis and implementation model (Hubbard, 2000, see Chapter 3, Figure 3.2) cover all the factors that need to be managed for all organisations. Taking a strategic approach, Hubbard provides a series of worksheets for assessing the organisation's overall position and deciding what needs to be done to align all the elements. This is a highly integrated qualitative approach, though it is based on the analysis and assessment of objective data.

There are of course many approaches to general organisational analysis. The Australian Business Excellence Framework (ABEF), the source of the Australian Quality Awards, is more process/quality-oriented than strategic. It uses a checklist format and has a quantitative scoring system for those organisations which are quantitatively oriented. Bell (2002) has a variation on the ABEF framework which is also easily accessible. Samson and Challis (1999) also have a checklist approach, based on their experiences with excellent world organisations.

Unfortunately, while these checklists are very useful, none of these sources identifies the organisations on whose practices they are based or gives examples of how the items in the checklist might appear in practice. However, not surprisingly, there is significant overlap on the items of importance. This reflects both the increasing focus on factors for success, and the degree to which a common consensus is emerging about those factors.

SUMMARY

The elements found across the variety of studies assessed here have a large degree of consistency. This is not surprising! The elements of running successful organisations are known. They just aren't practised.

However, our findings, being the most recent and being specifically for the Australian context, build on the others and provide subtle but important variations. Winning organisations need:

- To execute effectively in a disciplined way to deliver the results that they target.
- To perfectly align everything they do to their strategy and to do so consistently.
- To adapt rapidly over time by trying a lot of things and empowering people to take action.
- Clear strategy, which is fuzzy at the edges to enable them to take advantage of relevant opportunities.
- Good leadership, not a good individual leader – leadership that provides a cause for the people to work for.

327

- To be looking out, to be externally focused on the wide world around them.
- The right people for the organisation's strategy and values, people who are committed to the organisation and proud to work for it.
- To manage downside risk, to be conservative.
- To balance everything, using both tight and loose controls.

We think this book provides you with the elements to enable your organisation to become a 'winning' organisation in Australia, *and* with examples of Australian operating organisations that follow these practices. Now it is up to you! 'Winning' is hard work, but it is rewarding. Will your organisation be nominated by your peers for inclusion in this book in 10 years' time?

Appendix A

WINNING ORGANISATION BRIEF BIOGRAPHIES

BRAMBLES

Year and place founded

1916, Newcastle, NSW

CEOs

1916	Walter Bramble
1941	Alan Bramble
1946	Milton Bramble
1948	Tom Price
1962	Warwick Holcroft
1981	Oliver Richter
1983	Gary Pemberton
1993	John Fletcher
2001	Sir CK Chow

Founding concept

Walter Bramble started as a Newcastle butcher and developed a carrying business as a feeder service to the railway terminal.

Key events

1916   W. E. Bramble & Sons established as Walter's three
       sons were now in the business

1917   Motor vehicle distribution added to list of activities

1920   First contract outside Newcastle district to haul rabbits

1925   Motor distributorships extended to Essex, Hudson and
       Rolls Royce cars

1937   Diversified to Port Kembla to excavate blast furnace site

1954   Public listing

1956   Together with Heckett Engineering (US), provided a
       unique service to recover metallic slag for BHP at Port
       Kembla

1958   Acquired Commonwealth Handling Equipment Pool
       (CHEP) from the federal government

1959   Moved head office to Sydney

1969   CHEP split into pallets, containers and equipment
       divisions; acquired Truran Earthmovers and Southern
       Plant Hire

1970   Won Bougainville Copper cartage project; acquired
       Fenwick, Purle Waste Disposals and Industrial Waste
       Collections

1971   Acquired M & W Chard (PNG) and Goroka Toad
       Transport (PNG)

1972   Acquired Port Jackson & Manly Steamship, Armoured
       Escorts and Broman Divers

1973   Acquired Industrial Waste Collection; joint venture
       with Oceaneering International into deep-sea diving;
       sold Steelmark and Manly ferries

1974   CHEP UK 20:80 joint venture established with Guest
       Keen & Nettlefold, a diversified UK manufacturer

1978   CHEP Benelux launched with Groupe CAIB; CHEP
       Europe established

1979   CHEP Canada formed with Canadian Pacific

1980   Bought Redland Purle (UK) with Guest Keen & Nettlefold

1983   Acquired Grace Bros Transport Group

1984   Acquired 49.9 per cent of Groupe CAIB

1986   Increased ownership in Groupe CAIB to 90 per cent; Cleanaway's 10-year contract with Greater London Council began; acquired American Pallet Systems

1988   Acquired Metransa (Spain – transport)

1989   GKN-Brambles Enterprises began – GKN acquired 50 per cent of CHEP Canada and American Pallet Systems; reorganised into regional businesses; entered the US waste management industry by initial purchases in Ensco; bought Choctaw (US crane rental), Sky Reach (US equipment rental), Wreckair (Australian equipment rental), United Transport (Australia – transport), Gardner Perrott (Australia – transport) and TMF (France – transport)

1990   Bought FMS (France – forklifts), Fostrans/Cochez (France – cranes), Lastra (Holland – cranes), Econofreight (UK – heavy freight), Toman (Austria – cranes)

1992   Acquired Ensco, Security Archives (UK)

1994   Acquired NILO (Netherlands – industrial services) and Leto Recycling (Netherlands); started records management in Canada and acquired more businesses in the US

1995   Wrote off Ensco; sold Grace Removals and Wallace Tugs; started operations in Taiwan, Malaysia and Singapore; acquired more US records businesses; established CHEP in Mexico and Chile

1996   Sold Australian general freight; sold Oceaneering, Fostrans and Cochez

1997   Cleanaway acquired Mabeg (Germany)

1998   Cleanaway acquired SKP (Germany); CHEP acquired Gespalets (Spain); Industrial Services acquired Cockburn Corporation (Australia), Recall Records management acquired Eco-Arc (France), CTD (Spain) and Arcavia and Serint (Italy); CHEP set up in Greece, Brazil and Hong Kong; sold Cargowaggon, Atlantic Waste and Seroul

1999   Recall established as global brand

2001   Merger of businesses with GKN under a dual-listed structure.

HARVEY NORMAN

Year and place founded

1961, Sydney, NSW

CEOs

1961	Gerry Harvey and Ian Norman
1982	Gerry Harvey
1994	Michael Harvey
1998	Katie Page

Founding concept

Norman Ross Discounts was a discount electrical retailer which expanded to 42 stores in New South Wales and Queensland. Harvey Norman was begun immediately after the takeover of Norman Ross. The concept of Harvey Norman was owner-operated stores where the owner's expertise and dedication to personal service is backed up by the financial muscle, buying power and management services ability of a larger organisation. The concept expanded from electrical goods to a wide range of household goods including lighting, manchester and bedding, furniture, computers, bathroom hardware, carpet and flooring and home improvement.

Key events

1972	Norman Ross listed on the stock exchange
1982	Norman Ross acquired by Waltons Bond and Gerry Harvey and Ian Ross had their positions terminated. They immediately started up Harvey Norman in opposition, using the new franchise concept
1987	Harvey Norman listed on the stock exchange
1988	Entered Queensland
1992	Entered the ACT
1993	First computer superstore; entered Victoria

1997   Entered New Zealand and Western Australia
1998   Acquired Vox chain of stores, the Loughran Group (Tasmania) and the Joyce Mayne Group (NSW)
1999   Entered South Australia and Tasmania; acquired a minority interest in Pertama, a listed electrical retailer in Singapore
2000   Acquisition of 22 Vox stores
2001   Acquired Rebel Sport.

LEND LEASE

Year and place founded

1951, Sydney, NSW

CEOs

1951	Dick Dusseldorp
1978	Stuart Hornery
1994	John Morschel
1995	David Higgins

Founding concept

Civil & Civic was sponsored by its Netherlands parent, Bredero's United Companies, a significant building organisation, to seek building opportunities in Australia, with a focus on project management, design, engineering and construction.

Key events

1950	Dick Dusseldorp visited Australia to assess the market opportunities
1951	Civil & Civic contractors formed
1958	Lend Lease Corporation formed with Civil & Civic as largest shareholder. MLC encouraged the formation of the new company and provided funding for Lend Lease's first project, North Shore Medical Centre; first productivity agreement established with the Building Trades' Union in New South Wales and the Australian Capital Territory; Lend Lease listed
1959	First (unlisted) National Buildings Trust established; Lend Lease Development formed
1961	Acquired Civil & Civic from Bredero's
1962	Opened in Perth and first project in Adelaide commenced

1963   Employee presentations of results commenced;
        Australian wages staff superannuation commenced
        20 years before the rest of the industry

1964   Operations commenced in New Zealand

1965   First project in Tasmania

1970   Operations extended to the US

1971   General Property Trust formed and the first public trust
        in Australia floated

1972   Memorandum of Understanding signed with Australia
        Council of Trade Unions (ACTU) extending the 1958
        productivity agreement Australia-wide

1973   Commenced operations in Singapore; formation of
        Prime Property Fund, one of the first commingled real
        estate accounts for US pension funds; profit-sharing for
        Lend Lease Australian employees introduced

1977   International Income Property (IIP) launched in the US

1981   ACTU/Lend Lease Foundation set up to encourage
        people to acquire skills

1982   Successful (50 per cent) partial takeover of MLC

1983   Lend Lease Foundation established to promote the
        'well-being of Lend Lease employees and their families'

1984   IIP listed on Australian stock exchanges; Lend Lease
        Association, Lend Lease Youth Council and Lend Lease
        Apprentice Council formed; Work Skill Australia
        formed with Lend Lease as an inaugural sponsor

1985   MLC became wholly owned; Lend Lease Interiors
        began

1986   Equal Opportunity management program introduced;
        MLC multi-manager, multi-style investment
        philosophy introduced

1987   Childcare facilities introduced for Sydney employees

1988   Dusseldorp Skills Forum formed; Australian Trust
        launched

1989   Australian Prime Property Fund (APPF) commenced

1990   All Australian employees received profit-share; Capita
        Group merged with MLC; Mayne Nickless Payroll
        Services acquired

1991   Commenced operations in Europe; Board committee
        for Environment and Occupations Health and Safety set
        up; Australian Water Services formed

1992   First global property fund launched

1993   Yarmouth acquired in the US; Thailand and Jakarta
        offices opened

1994   Integrated Systems Solutions Corporation Australia
        (ISSC) information technology joint venture formed
        with IBM; Sinar Mas joint ventures signed in Indonesia

1995   Hong Kong office opened

1997   MLC sold its building society; acquired ERE and
        merged with the Yarmouth Group

1998   SITEL Asia Pacific launched (joint venture between
        Lend Lease and the SITEL Group); acquisition of
        Southern European retail services company, Larry
        Smith Group; acquisition of 50 per cent of Kiwi
        Property Group (Kiwi Income Property Trust and Kiwi
        Development Trust); Plum Financial Services launched
        (joint venture between MLC and The Vanguard
        Group)

1999   Acquired Boston Financial Group, acquisition of five
        AMRESCO businesses; Lend Lease Projects and Bovis
        merged to form Bovis Lend Lease

2000   Formation of European real estate securities firm –
        Lend Lease Houlihan Rovers; launch of Lend Lease
        Diversified Real Estate Fund; sale of MLC

2001   Lend Lease Real Estate Investments introduces mutual
        fund for US-based investors to invest in European real
        estate.

MACQUARIE BANK

Year and place founded

1969, Sydney, NSW

CEOs

1969   Christopher Castleman
1971   David Clarke and Mark Johnson (joint)
1977   David Clarke
1983   Tony Berg
1993   Allan Moss

Founding concept

Originally Hill Samuel Australia, the Australian arm of an English merchant bank, providing a range of financial services and products of the highest quality in terms of service, knowledge and skill.

Key events

1969   Hill Samuel Australia established
1978   First Australian project finance division set up
1978   Authorised as a foreign exchange dealer
1980   Introduced Australia's first cash management account
1983   First international office opened in New Zealand
1985   Granted a trading bank licence; changed name to Macquarie Bank
1989   Opened offices in London and Munich
1991   Opened US office in Denver
1995   Established offices in Hong Kong
1995   Offices in China established
1996   Funds management joint venture with Arab-Malaysian merchant bank Berhad in Malaysia
1996   Listed on Australian stock exchange
1996   Opened Singapore office

338

1997   Advisory services joint venture with Goldman Sachs in New Zealand
1998   Alliance with Standard Bank in South Africa
1999   Joint ventures with JBWere (equities clearing), Sanham Ltd (South Africa – fund manager), Kookmin Bank (Korea); opened office in Canada
2000   Acquired Bankers Trust (Australia); opened office in Brazil; joint venture with Industrial Bank of Japan.

NATIONAL AUSTRALIA BANK

Year and place founded

1858, Melbourne, Vic.

CEOs

1979   J. D. Booth
1985   Nobby Clark
1990   Don Argus
1999   Frank Cicutto

Founding concept

To service the banking needs arising from the Victorian gold rush in the 1850s.

Key events

1918   Acquired Colonial Bank of Australasia
1922   Acquired Bank of Queensland
1947   Acquired Queensland National Bank
1954   Diversified into non–banking with a 40 per cent shareholding in Custom Credit (finance)
1955   Acquired Ballarat Banking Group
1962   Commenced savings bank operations
1969   Established Chase–NBA Group with Chase Manhattan Overseas Banking Corporation
1971   Acquired control of Custom Credit
1973   Entered insurance business through establishment of National and General Insurance; acquired 100 per cent of Custom Credit
1974   Established Bank of South Pacific for PNG
1981   Merged with Commercial Banking Company of Sydney
1984   Acquired 50 per cent of AC Goode (stockbroking) and 100 per cent of Chase–NBA (merchant banking)

1985   National Australia Financial Management (personal financial services) established; listed on Tokyo stock exchange; established merchant bank in New Zealand; acquired a finance company in NZ

1987   Acquired three subsidiaries of Midland Bank plc – Clydesdale Bank of Scotland, Northern Bank (Northern Ireland) and Northern Bank (Ireland – renamed the National Irish Bank)

1990   Acquired Yorkshire Bank plc; closed AC Goode

1992   Acquired Bank of New Zealand

1995   Acquired Michigan National

1997   Acquired County Natwest Investment Management; acquired Homeside (US residential mortgage loan originator)

2000   Acquired MLC (funds management) and transferred National Australia Funds Management operations into MLC

2001   Sold Michigan National

2002   Sold Homeside.

QANTAS

Year and place founded

1920, Winton, Qld

CEOs

1952	Cedric Turner
1966	R. J. Ritchie
1975	Keith Hamilton
1984	R. J. Yates
1985	John Menadue
1989	John Ward
1993	James Strong
2000	Geoff Dixon

Founding concept

Queensland and Northern Territory Aerial Services Ltd was established by Paul McGinness and Wilmot Hudson Fysh, who purchased a plane to service the outback of northern Queensland and the Northern Territory.

Key events

1921	Headquarters moved to Longreach
1922	First flight from Charleville to Cloncurry
1929	Outback network extended to Brisbane
1930	Headquarters moved to Brisbane
1934	Name changed to Qantas Empire Airways
1935	First overseas flight from Brisbane to Singapore, carrying mail
1938	Headquarters moved to Sydney
1946	Network extended to India, New Guinea and Pacific Islands

1947   Sold out to Commonwealth Government as could not raise capital to compete in an environment where all airlines were government owned and controlled; Government designated Qantas Australia's overseas flag-carrier and it began services to London and Japan

1949   Domestic airline services handed over to government-owned Trans Australian Airlines

1954   Started service to San Francisco and Vancouver

1958   Services extended to New York to establish an around-the-world airline

1967   Name changed to Qantas Airways

1979   Boeing 707s phased out and became world's only all-747 airline; introduced world's first business class

1989   Acquired 19.9 per cent of Air New Zealand

1992   Acquired Australian Airlines

1993   25 per cent of Qantas sold to British Airways

1995   Privatisation sale completed

1997   Sold out of Air New Zealand

1999   Joined Oneworld global airline alliance

2000   Acquired Impulse Airlines

2002   Launched new international subsidiary airline, Australian Airlines.

RIO TINTO

Year and place founded

1905, Broken Hill, NSW

CEOs

1962   Maurice Mawby

1974   Rod Carnegie

1986   John Ralph

1994   Leon Davis

2000   Leigh Clifford

Founding concept

As Zinc Corporation in 1905, applying new technology to treat previously useless tailings at Broken Hill. As CRA in 1961, the exploration for and development of Australian resources.

Key events

1905   Zinc Corporation formed

1911   Head office moved to London

1949   Merged with Imperial Smelting to form Consolidated Zinc, with a subsidiary designed to explore for minerals in Australia

1955   Weipa bauxite reserves discovered

1960   Kaiser Aluminum and Chemical became a partner to develop Comalco as an integrated aluminium smelter

1961   Merged with Rio Tinto to form Conzinc Riotinto of Australia (CRA) for the Australian interests and RTZ for the non-Australian interests

1962   Mount Tom Price iron ore reserves discovered; Hamersley Holdings formed in partnership with Kaiser Steel

1964   Bougainville copper reserves discovered

1966   Hamersley Holdings floated (10 per cent available to the public)

1971   Bougainville Mining floated (10 per cent available to the public)

1972   Hamersley's second mine – Paraburdoo – began production

1978   Australian government policy of 'naturalisation' accepted by CRA; sold alumina production to Comalco and acquired Comalco's 50 per cent interest in Dampier Salt

1979   Acquired Kaiser Steel out of Hamersley; hostile takeover of Broken Hill South began – CRA finished up with Kembla Coal & Coke, Cobar Mines (gold), Electrolytical Refining and Smelting (silver, lead and zinc), Kanmantoo Mines (copper) and Metal Manufactures (steel – minority interest)

1981   Acquired Biotechnology Australia; closed Mary Kathleen Uranium

1982   Discovered heavy industrial minerals at Horsham

1985   Purchased Martin Marietta US aluminium facilities

1986   Became majority Australian-owned

1987   Discovered gold at Kelian (Indonesia) and coal at East Kalimantan (Indonesia)

1988   Started aluminium wheel plant at Bell Bay, Tasmania; merged lead and zinc assets with those of North Broken Hill into a new company, Pasminco; sold Metal Manufactures

1989   Bougainville shut down through militant attacks; Channar iron ore mine began; purchased BP's coking coal assets

1990   Discovered Century zinc deposit; acquired Kalimantan Gold (Indonesia); finalised research work on HIsmelt iron ore process

1993   Sold An Mau Steel, manufacturing investments in Asia; acquired control of Coal and Allied

1995   Merged with RTZ

1996   Renamed Rio Tinto and restructured along six global business lines – iron ore, industrial minerals, copper, Comalco, energy and gold and other minerals – with many acquisitions and divestments

THE SALVATION ARMY

Year and place founded

1880, Adelaide, SA

CEOs

1977	Arthur Linnett
1982	Eva Burrows
1986	Donald Campbell
1989	Bramwell Tillsely
1991	Dinsdale Pender
1993	John Clinch
1996	Norman Howe
1998	Douglas Davis

Founding concept

The Salvation Army was founded by a Methodist Minister, William Booth, and his wife Catherine in 1865 to provide the poor of the East End of London with a church in which they would feel welcome. This soon saw the introduction of feeding, accommodation and other social services. It quickly became a London-wide 'Christian Mission' and then became popular throughout the UK. In 1878 it was renamed 'The Salvation Army', doctrines were written, a flag designed and the first brass band introduced as 'a walking organ'. Women were accepted as ministers of religion from the beginning and the decision not to incorporate the sacraments was made.

Key events

1880	The Salvation Army in Australia commences in Botanic Gardens, Adelaide
1882	Majors James and Alice Barker arrive in Melbourne
1883	First social institution commenced in Carlton for released prisoners from Melbourne Gaol

1891   First free labour exchange in Australia introduced

1900   The Salvation Army 'Limelight' department produces a film of the Federation ceremonies

1915   Red Shield welfare officers go with Australian troops to the front lines

1921   The Salvation Army in Australia divides into two territories

1939   General George Carpenter, an Australian, elected as the world leader

1945   Flying Padre services introduced in the Northern Territory and Queensland

1969   The first Red Shield Appeal using national publicity launched

1983   First Employment 2000 agency opened in Western Australia; later spreads throughout Australia to assist the long-term unemployed

1986   General Eva Burrows elected as General (second Australian and second woman general)

1995   Employment Plus is launched as part of the government's 'Job Network' program

1996   Assistance given to one million people

2000   Cost for the provision of services passes $250 million; Red Shield Welfare Officers go with Australian peacekeeping troops to East Timor (100 years of Salvo/troop services celebrated)

2002   Red Shield Appeal passes $50 million for first time and 'wills and bequests' passes $40 million for the first time.

TELSTRA
Year and place founded
1901, Melbourne, Vic.

CEOs
1975   John Curtis
1981   William Pollock
1986   Mel Ward
1992   Frank Blount
1999   Ziggy Switkowski

Founding concept
The Postmaster–General's Department was established by the Commonwealth government in 1901 to plan, establish, maintain and operate the telephone system for Australia.

Key events
1901   At Federation, control of the telephone system was vested in the new Commonwealth Government and exercised via the Postmaster General's Department
1912   First public automatic telephone exchange in Australia opened at Geelong
1930   First overseas calls available
1954   Telex services opened between Melbourne and Sydney
1956   Subscriber trunk dialling (STD) first introduced between Dandenong and Melbourne
1959   First broadband microwave system opened between Melbourne and Bendigo
1969   Datel service introduced to provide data transmission
1975   Telecommunications Act established the Australian Telecommunications Commission as a separate body from the Post Office

1981   First mobile phones introduced

1989   Telecommunications market deregulation began with
       deregulation of telecommunications equipment sales

1991   Deregulation of the national long distance and
       international telephone call markets

1992   Acquired the Overseas Telecommunications
       Corporation; mobile market opened to competition

1993   Name changed to Telstra

1994   Pay-TV services commenced

1997   Market fully opened to competition; government floats
       one-third of Telstra

1999   Government floats more shares, reducing government
       ownership to 51 per cent

2001   Joint venture with Pacific Century Cyber Works to
       enter the Asian market.

WESTFIELD

Year and place founded

1956, Sydney, NSW

CEOs

1958   Frank Lowy and John Saunders (joint)
1987   Frank Lowy
1987   David Lowy
1997   Stephen, Peter and David Lowy (joint)

Founding concept

Commercial property development leading to specialisation in the creation, development and management of retail shopping centres.

Key events

1956   Westfield Investments founded
1959   Westfield Place opens in Blacktown, Sydney, with one supermarket, two department stores and 12 shops
1960   Westfield Development Corporation listed on Sydney stock exchange
1961   Shore Motel opened
1966   Burwood (Sydney) opened – the first centre to be branded 'Westfield Shoppingtown'
1967   First centre in Queensland opened
1969   Opened first centre in Victoria
1977   Entered US shopping mall market with acquisition of Trumbull Shopping Park, Connecticut
1979   Westfield Holdings and Westfield Property Trust formed and listed
1987   Westfield Capital Corporation listed on Australian stock exchange

1988   Westfield Holdings split into Westfield Australia and Westfield International; Westfield International listed on London stock exchange

1989   Westfield International privatised

1994   Acquired CenterMark shopping centre portfolio in the US – 19 regional and super-regional malls

1995   Entered Malaysia with a joint venture with Rodamco NV

1996   Westfield America Trust listed on the Australian stock exchange

1997   Appointed manager of St Lukes Group, New Zealand's premier shopping centre company

1997   Westfield America listed on the New York stock exchange

1998   Westfield America acquired major shopping centre portfolio of TrizecHahn in US

1998   Westfield Trust acquired major share in St Lukes Group

2000   Entered UK through joint ventures with Hermes and MEPC

2000   Westfield Trust and St Lukes Group amalgamated.

WOOLWORTHS

Year and place founded

1924, Sydney, NSW

CEOs

1924	Percy Christmas
1929	Percy Christmas and George Creed (joint)
1930	Percy Christmas
1945	Theo Kelly
1971	Owen Price
1974	Bill Dean and Paul Simons (joint)
1981	Tony Harding
1988	Harry Watts
1993	Reg Clairs
1998	Roger Corbett

Founding concept

When a business opportunity opened up in the basement of Percy Christmas and Stanley Chatterton's S. E. Chatterton frock salon in Sydney, they decided to use the new open display method of selling to establish a cash and carry store modelled on the American Woolworth company.

Key events

1924	Opened first Sydney store
1927	Opened Brisbane store
1928	Opened Perth store
1929	Established the London buying office; opened in New Zealand
1933	Opened Melbourne store; had 23 stores in Australia and eight in New Zealand

1955   First self-service store; 200 stores in Australia and 55 in
        New Zealand

1958   Entered the food market by acquiring 32 BCC stores in
        Queensland

1960   First Woolworths supermarket; first retailer to operate
        Australia-wide by entering the Northern Territory

1961   Expansion into apparel by acquisition of 70 Rockman's
        stores

1964   First regional shopping centre at Newcastle, including
        first Big W store

1965   Acquired Fitzpatrick's Food Supplies, a leading
        Singapore retail/wholesale organisation

1967   Acquired Cox Bros and Foys department stores

1969   Acquired 26 Nancarrows food stores

1970   Acquired 75 Crofts Food Stores

1978   Sold New Zealand interests

1981   Acquired Dick Smiths (electronics), Philip Leong,
        Purity Group and Roelf Vos group (supermarkets)

1985   Acquired 126 Australian Safeway Stores to become the
        largest food retailer in Australia; acquired 59 Chandlers
        electrical stores; opened Dick Smith in the US; closed
        Homemakers chain of 12 stores

1989   Industrial Equity acquired Woolworths (it had had a
        minority interest since 1986)

1993   Woolworths refloated on the stock exchange

1996   Acquired Cannons Group, including Australian
        Independent Wholesalers; opened first Marketplace
        shopping centre development; introduced petrol
        retailing

1997   First Metro stores

1998   Alliance with Commonwealth Bank to provide
        co-branded financial services; acquired Dan Murphy
        liquor stores.

354

Appendix B

MINOR STUDIES

INTERNATIONAL STUDIES

Many other studies (apart from *In Search of Excellence, Built to Last* and *Good to Great)* have attempted to identify winning practices. However, they have not sought to unveil specific examples of winning organisations, nor have they identified the selection criteria for such organisations.

Dertouzos, Lester and Solow (1989) conducted a survey of US manufacturing firms. They found six key similarities in firms that were doing well. They were:

- focus on continuous improvement in cost, quality and delivery
- closer links with customers
- closer relations with suppliers
- effective use of technology for strategic advantage
- less hierarchical and compartmentalised organisations for greater flexibility
- human resource policies that promote continuous learning, participation and flexibility.

This study encouraged organisations to look outside themselves for help in continuously improving. The emphasis on flexibility and less hierarchical structures were also important new findings.

Miles and Snow (1994) put together a formula for success. Based on their extensive research, teaching, study and consulting experience, but not based on a particular set of firms or study, they argued that keys to success were:

- tight fit
- responding to external change
- creating a stable network
- investing in people to achieve this.

Their study highlighted alignment, people and external focus – all key elements in our framework.

Pfeffer (1998) reviewed hundreds of studies in organisational change and human resource practice conducted over a 30-year period, and concluded that the following seven practices that 'seem to characterise' handling people well is the way to success. These practices are:

- providing secure employment
- selective hiring of new people
- self-managing teams and decentralised decision-making as the basis for organisational design
- comparatively high remuneration contingent on organisation performance
- extensive training
- reduced status distinctions and barriers
- extensive sharing of financial and performance information.

Coming from an organisational behaviour background, Pfeffer passionately argues the business case for a focus on people as the driver of business success. This highlights the 'people' element in our framework and others.

De Geus (1997) reported on Shell's 1983 study of long-surviving organisations – i.e. organisations that were older than Shell (which began in the 1890s) and relatively as important in their industries. The report found 40 companies that met the criteria, of which 27 were examined in detail. De Geus found that four factors were common across the sample. The organisations were:

- sensitive to their environment
- cohesive, with a strong sense of identity
- internally tolerant/decentralised decision-makers/able to build constructive relationships internally and externally
- conservative financially.

This is a very process-oriented list. De Geus made the interesting point that none of the organisations still operated in their core businesses, as they had to adapt to survive and often their core business simply did not exist any more. The factors identified imply an external sensitivity more than an internal focus and a conservative bent rather than an aggressive bent.

AUSTRALIAN STUDIES

In addition to the international studies, there have been several Australian pieces of research that have considered 'success' from a variety of perspectives.

Best practice studies

The Australian Manufacturing Council (1994) published a survey of 1,400 manufacturing sites which identified leading practices for manufacturers. Its findings for best practices were:

- having effective people practices: creating co-operation and trust by commitment to teamwork, training, effective communication and employee morale
- building a shared vision
- benchmarking for best practice
- having a customer focus

357

- effectively utilising technology
- having a shared responsibility for total quality.

This study highlights leadership (through shared vision), people, strategy, an external focus and continuous improvement.

Rimmer et al (1996) studied the organisations chosen to participate in the first two rounds (1991–92) of the Australian Government's 'best practice' program, to try to understand what the common practices were amongst those organisations. Some of these organisations were in fact divisions of firms rather than whole organisations and 35 of the 43 firms were manufacturers. The organisations were not necessarily high performers, but were seeking to be high performers. Rimmer et al concluded that the following elements were important:

- having a consistent and cohesive strategy that is fully resourced
- having empowered, work-based teams of trained people
- having a focus on process improvement
- having integrated and comprehensive formal measurement and control systems
- people management
- forming links and relationships with outside organisations.

The findings here are similar to the Australian Manufacturing Council findings above. Once again strategy, people, leadership (through people management), continuous improvement and external focus are important factors. This study also includes reporting systems as a key element.

Quality movement studies

In the 1990s, as discussed previously, Australian business focused on improving quality to catch up to changes that had been made overseas. The Australian Quality Council established a framework which is now called the Australian Business Excellence Framework (ABEF). Proponents of this framework believe that organisations can be measured against the criteria and a point score used to assess their level of overall quality as well as what gaps need to be addressed. The main areas of the framework (and by implication the keys to success) are:

- Leadership and innovation   (180 pts)
- People   (160 pts)
- Processes, products and services   (160 pts)
- Customer and market focus   (150 pts)
- Business results   (150 pts)
- Strategy and planning processes   (100 pts)
- Data, information and knowledge   (100 pts).

Hausner (1999) demonstrated a strong correlation between high ABEF scores and a wide-ranging definition of performance. He concluded that senior executive leadership, analysis and use of data and information, and having measures of success and planning processes were key drivers of this relationship.

Bell (2002), an ABEF assessor, published '10 principles of business excellence for increased market share'. They are:

- senior executives as role models
- focus on achievement of goals
- (focus on) customer perception of value
- to improve the outcome, improve the system
- improved decisions
- (decrease) variability
- enthusiastic people
- learning, innovation and continual improvement
- corporate citizenship
- value for all stakeholders.

While based on his experience as an ABEF evaluator, Bell does not give any specific organisation examples to illustrate these principles. Interestingly, they do not correspond clearly to

Hausner's findings. This suggests that the key differentiators for success are not the same as the set of factors that need to be managed by all organisations.

Samson and Challis (1999) published a set of principles for success 'based on a global study of the world's best organisations'. Their principles are:

- alignment
- distributed leadership
- integration
- being out front (leading the industry)
- being upfront (being honest)
- resourcing the medium term
- being time focused
- embracing change
- (having a) learning focus
- being disciplined
- (having good) measurement and reporting
- (delivering) customer value
- (focus on creating) capabilities
- (linking) micro to macro.

Unfortunately, in this work there is very limited reference to Australian organisations or particular practices, despite the Australian origins of its authors.

Finally, a series of 'most admired' surveys have begun to be collated annually by magazines such as *Business Review Weekly* and consultants. These tend to highlight only the currently perceived 'good' organisations in the short term. However, they do reflect the increasingly intense interest in this subject.

Bibliography

In addition to the annual reports of the winning organisations for the period 1980 onwards, published case studies, major press and stockbroker analysis, websites and other public information, the following sources were used:

Anonymous (undated) *The Detailed Westfield Story: The First 40 Years*, www.westfield.com.au.

Anonymous (undated) *The Qantas Story*, www.qantas.com.au.

Ashkenasy, N. & Trevor-Roberts, E., 2001, 'Leading in Australia: The Egalitarian Visionary Suits our Style', *Mt Eliza Business Review*, Summer-Autumn, pp. 33–39.

Australian Manufacturing Council 1994, *Leading the Way*, Australian Manufacturing Council.

Bell, G., 2002, *The Competitive Enterprise*, McGraw-Hill.

Carew, E., 2000, *Brambles: Working its Way Around the World*, Brambles.

Carnegie, R., Butlin, M., Barratt, P., Turnbull, A. & Webber, I., 1993, *Managing the Innovating Enterprise*, Business Council of Australia.

Collins, J., 2001, *Good to Great*, HarperBusiness.

Collins, J., 2001, 'Level 5 Leadership: The Triumph of Humility and Fierce Resolve', *Harvard Business Review*, January, pp. 67–76.

Collins, J. & Porras, J., 1994, *Built to Last: Successful Habits of Visionary Companies*, Century.

Condon, M., 2002, 'Why the genius in Harvey Norman still keeps going', *The Sunday Age*, p. 13.

De Geus, A., 1997, *The Living Company*, Harvard Business School.

Dertouzos, M., Lester, R. & Solow, R., 1989, *Made in America: Regaining the Productive Edge*, Harper.

Eisenhardt, K., 1999, 'Building Theories from Case Study Research', *Academy of Management Review*, vol. 14, no. 4, pp. 532–550.

Hausner, A., 1999, 'Australian Quality Awards for Business Excellence', *The Quality Magazine*, August, pp. 47–50.

Hubbard, G., 2000, *Strategic Management: Thinking, Analysis and Action*, Prentice Hall.

Hubbard, G., Pocknee, G. & Taylor, G., 1996, *Practical Australian Strategy*, Prentice Hall/Australian Institute of Management.

Jackson, M., 2002, 'Rapid response', *Management Today*, August, p. 5.

Jaques, E., 1989, *Requisite Organisation*, Cason Hall.

Kaplan, R. & Norton, D., 1996, *The Balanced Scorecard*, Harvard Business School.

Kavanagh, J., 2001, 'Superstar Performers', *Business Review Weekly*, November 1–7, p. 62–66.

Lewis, G., Morkel, A., Hubbard, G., Davenport, S. & Stockport, G., 1994, *Australian Strategic Management*, Prentice Hall.

Margo, J., 2000, *Frank Lowy: Pushing the Limits*, HarperCollins.

Miles, R. & Snow, C., 1994, *Fit, Failure and the Hall of Fame*, Free Press.

Murray, J., 1999, *The Woolworths Way*, Focus.

Peters, T. & Waterman, R., 1982, *In Search of Excellence: Lessons from America's Best-run Companies*, Harper & Row.

Pfeffer, J., 1998, *The Human Equation*, Harvard Business School.

Rimmer, M., Macneil, J., Chenhall, R., Langfield-Smith, K. & Walls, L., 1996, *Reinventing Competitiveness: Achieving Best Practice in Australia*, Pitman.

Samson, D. & Challis, D., 1999, *Patterns of Excellence*, Prentice Hall.

Telstra 1994, *Quality in Australia: The Telecom Archetype Study*, Telstra.

Viljoen, J., 1991, *Strategi.c Management*, Longman.

Welch, J., 2001, *Jack: What I've Learned Leading a Great Company and Great People*, Headline.

Whitford, B., 1992, *Success Through Excellence*, Beaumont.

Young, P., 1996, 'The Coaching Paradigm: Developing the Next Generation of Excellent Managers', *The Practising Manager*, October, pp. 50–52.

Index

367